A 21-day journey of seeking God's provision for your life

THE
daniel
fast
for financial
breakthrough

susan gregory

TYNDALE
MOMENTL

The Tyndale nonfiction i

D1738874

Visit Tyndale online at tyndale.com.

Visit Tyndale Momentum online at tyndalemomentum.com.

TYNDALE, Tyndale's quill logo, *Tyndale Momentum*, and the Tyndale Momentum logo are registered trademarks of Tyndale House Ministries. Tyndale Momentum is the nonfiction imprint of Tyndale House Publishers, Carol Stream, Illinois.

Published in association with the literary agency of Ann Spangler and Company, 1420 Pontiac Rd., S. E., Grand Rapids, MI 49506.

For information about special discounts for bulk purchases, please contact Tyndale House Publishers at csresponse@tyndale.com, or call 1-800-323-9400.

Library of Congress Cataloging-in-Publication Data
Names: Gregory, Susan, date- author.
Title: The Daniel fast for financial breakthrough : a 21-day journey of
   seeking God's provision for your life / Susan Gregory.
Description: Carol Stream, Illinois : Tyndale House Publishers, 2020. |
   Includes bibliographical references (pages 436-45) and index.
Identifiers: LCCN 2020021210 (print) | LCCN 2020021211 (ebook) | ISBN
   9781496427762 (trade paperback) | ISBN 9781496427779 (kindle edition) |
   ISBN 9781496427786 (epub) | ISBN 9781496427793 (epub)
Subjects: LCSH: Fasting--Religious aspects--Christianity. | Finance,
   Personal--Religious aspects--Christianity. | Daniel (Biblical figure)
Classification: LCC BV5055 .G74 2020 (print) | LCC BV5055 (ebook) | DDC
   248.4/7--dc23
LC record available at https://lccn.loc.gov/2020021210
LC ebook record available at https://lccn.loc.gov/2020021211

Printed in the United States of America

26   25   24   23   22   21   20
7   6   5   4   3   2   1

To the women, men, and couples who have felt the gut-wrenching fear of financial stress, and have chosen to search for Christ-centered solutions.

To you, I send my best hope as you discover, learn, and act to move from fear, to hope, to unwavering trust that God is your Provider and that He will show you the way out of the darkness and into His safe and secure light.

Contents

Before You Begin

THE DANIEL FAST includes a very healthy eating plan. However, please allow the Great Physician to work hand in hand with your earthly physician. Anytime you enter into a significant change to your diet and exercise routines, it's a good idea to check with your health professional for his or her input.

Fasting should never harm the body. If you have special dietary needs—if you are pregnant or nursing, if you have a chronic illness such as cancer or diabetes, if you are a young person who is still growing or an athlete who expends more than typical amounts of energy on a regular basis—contact your health professional and modify the Daniel Fast eating plan in a way that is appropriate to meet your health needs.

At this writing, the world is in the midst of the COVID-19 pandemic. Many of us are making changes in our daily lives to mitigate the spread of the virus. We know that the economy has suffered greatly, and we're unsure how this crisis will affect our personal finances. Please visit my website at Daniel-Fast.com/breakthrough to stay current on how you can pray and to read about some actions you can take regarding your money matters. Know for sure that the pandemic didn't take our God by surprise. He is with you, and now, more than any other time in your life, you may learn more about experiencing Him as your Provider.

part
one

CHAPTER ONE

A Spiritual Fast to Draw You Nearer to God

I bow my knees to the Father of our Lord Jesus Christ, . . .
that He would grant you, according to the riches of His glory,
to be strengthened with might through His Spirit in the inner man,
that Christ may dwell in your hearts through faith.

EPHESIANS 3:14, 16-17

WE'VE ALL HEARD THE SAYING "Money isn't everything." However, when you think about it, money does touch just about everything. That's most likely why it's mentioned more than eight hundred times in the Bible—and when we count references to both money and possessions, the number goes above two thousand.[1] Clearly our perspective on money is important to God. And your interest in money is probably why you picked up this book.

Money is a big deal. If you have a full-time job, you spend about one-third of your time earning money, and then you can use those valuable dollars as a means of exchange. We trade our time for money. Then we trade that money for food, clothing, transportation, entertainment, and even knowledge. And you most likely traded money for just about everything in your home, including your Bible, your Christian devotionals, and this book.

Almost every day, you interact with money in some way. You pay bills. You make purchases. You balance your bank accounts. You deposit your paychecks. And maybe you also worry about money. If that's the case, you're not alone.

A recent study conducted by the nonprofit Center for Financial Services Innovation (CFSI) reported that millions of Americans struggle with their finances—even here in what we call the land of opportunity. A mere 28 percent of Americans are considered "financially healthy," according to the study.[2] Sadly, 17 percent of Americans are considered "financially vulnerable," meaning nearly all financial aspects of their lives are challenging. The remaining 55 percent of Americans are "financially coping," meaning they have some aspects of their finances in control but grapple with others. The report says, "Many are dealing with an unhealthy amount of debt, irregular income, and sporadic savings habits."[3]

None of these statistics surprise me. In my teachings about the Daniel Fast, a twenty-one-day partial fast based on two passages from the book of Daniel, I encourage people to decide on a purpose for their fast. The defined purpose helps individuals focus their prayers, study, and meditation in God's Word as they go through the twenty-one days. Every year since 2007, when I started writing and teaching about the Daniel Fast, the number one purpose for fasting and seeking God's guidance has been finances.

Just as money touches virtually every aspect of life, the way we handle money affects us at a deep level. Worries about money can cause health problems, create tension in relationships, and distract us from what is most important. Conversely, having a handle on our finances can have powerful ramifications now and in the future. The CFSI says, "Financial health enables family stability, education, and upward mobility, not just for individuals today but across future generations."[4]

Not being financially healthy is a scary place to be. I know that from hearing from tens of thousands of women and men around the world, but I also know it from my own experience. Over my decades of living, I've had my tribulations, including eight years with a chronic disease, an unwanted divorce, heartbreaking betrayal, and a life-threatening car accident. Yet I can honestly say that the scariest time in my life was when I was flat broke and not sure how I could pay my bills. I was beyond "financially vulnerable"; I was financially desperate. I'll share more of my story in chapter 3. But if you've picked up this book because you're struggling with money matters, I want you to know that I understand at least some of what you're going through. You're not alone.

No matter what your level of financial stress, I want to assure you that you're making a wise decision to seek God and His wisdom about money. As you experience the Daniel Fast, you can lean into God and gain understanding, direction, and answers to your prayers for help.

Everyone's situation is different. Maybe your bills are paid and you feel comfortable with your financial wellness, but you have a big dream for a ministry or a project. You want to see the dream come true, but you know you don't have the money to cover the expenses. So you want to bring the dream to the One who fulfills the desires of your heart, and partner with God to bring Christ's light to people who don't yet know His love. You, too, are in the right place.

Or perhaps you're weighing financial priorities or trying to pay down your debt and plan for the future. Whatever the state of your bank account, doing the Daniel Fast with a financial focus will allow you to draw near to God, learn to rest in His provision, and understand His priorities for money. You'll be poised for a breakthrough as you grow to trust God and seek His direction for your finances.

FASTING FOR FINANCES

Back in 2007, God gave me an assignment to help His people have a successful experience on the Daniel Fast. That's what I want to do for you on these pages. I want to serve as your guide as you enter into this powerful time of extended prayer and fasting. I'll teach you about biblical fasting and how to use this twenty-one-day experience as your personal retreat with the Lord. I'll direct you on how to prepare your spirit, soul, and body for the fast. I'll provide the information you need about the practical elements of the Daniel Fast, including the food restrictions, tips for meal preparation, dealing with food cravings, and how to overcome some of the challenges your flesh is likely to present to you, especially in the first few days of your fast.

While the Daniel Fast is a plant-based eating plan, I'm going to serve you giant servings of meat. Not the kind of meat you buy at a grocery store, but instead the meat that is waiting for you in God's Word. I want to show you how you can develop your faith muscles and learn to trust God in ways you may never have trusted Him before. I want to show you how to rely on your activated faith to find wellness in your financial vulnerability. And I want to walk with you as you step away from fear, worry, and stress and move into the hope, peace, and assurance of the good news Christ proclaims.

If you've done the Daniel Fast before, some of this will be familiar. The basic building blocks of the fast remain the same no matter what goals you have for the twenty-one days, but now you'll be approaching it differently, looking through the specific lens of finances as you seek God's direction in this area.

When we do the Daniel Fast, our main goal is to seek God and grow closer to Him—and we often see additional benefits of becoming healthier, developing better eating habits, and perhaps losing weight. When we do the fast with a financial focus, we will better understand our reliance on God's provision—and then we may also experience natural benefits such as gaining a clearer financial focus or developing better spending habits. Our ultimate goal is always drawing nearer to God and listening to His direction.

My desire is that during your twenty-one-day Daniel Fast you will step into new revelations of faith as you focus on God, His truth, and His priceless love for you. I want to show you how you can co-labor with God to dig out of the hole you may feel you're in and step onto the solid ground of trusting that your Lord cares for you and for your financial well-being. And I also want to share some tools and resources you can use as you bring order into your financial matters and become the financially healthy, wise steward that your Father wants you to be.

HOW TO USE THIS BOOK FOR YOUR SUCCESSFUL EXPERIENCE

My editorial team and I have organized this guide with you at the forefront of our minds. The book is ordered so you can gain a clear understanding of your upcoming spiritual journey.

I suggest you read most of part I as your first step to prepare for your Daniel Fast. (Save chapter 10 to read when your fast is almost completed.) Not only will you begin to grasp what's ahead, you'll also start feeding your soul with encouragement, faith, and hope. We'll talk about what I mean by "financial breakthrough," and I'll help you focus your attention on what God's Word teaches His people about finances, stewardship, walking in faith, giving, and putting your trust in Him.

While you're reading, you'll find thoughts popping into your mind about your circumstances. You'll begin to discover insights about God and His ways. And you likely will begin hearing the still, small voice of your Father. Please be sure to capture these thoughts, insights, and messages on paper. I encourage you to use a journal, which can become your personal travel log for this spiritual journey.

I've also prepared action steps that appear at the end of each chapter. Plan to work through these steps as you fast, putting your knowledge into action. After all, you want results. You want change, and you want success. You can have it as you join hands with your Lord. He will do His part as you do yours. Partner with Him by taking appropriate actions. Enliven your faith with your works and enjoy the benefits that await you.

Part II of the book includes practical tools for your fast. I've included more than seventy recipes for you to use during your fast. I've also included my best tips for meal planning and preparation. You're wise to prepare some meals in advance. I promise that you'll feel much more grounded when you're equipped ahead of time rather than racing to catch up.

You'll also find a collection of twenty-one Daniel Fast daily devotions that you can use during your fast. They are specifically written to feed your soul with the truth of God's Word and to nourish your spirit with His wisdom.

Plus, I created a Frequently Asked Questions section to give quick answers for questions you may have. Skim them to find the information you may need. Also, be sure to visit the Daniel Fast website for even more information (Daniel-Fast.com/breakthrough).

Think of this book as your travel guide. Keep it with your Bible, journal, and other tools used in your daily quiet time. And as you touch these pages, know for sure that every word has been lovingly chosen to serve you as you enter into this powerful time of transformation and God's blessing on your life.

BEGIN TO BEGIN

Imagine that you are planning to go on a three-week spiritual retreat. You registered for the retreat because you want to learn some new skills, and you have questions you want answered—questions about money, about priorities, about faith. You want to experience growth, moving from where you are now toward where you want to be. You've set aside time for the retreat, and you have a lot of excitement because of the retreat Leader.

You know about Him. You've read about Him. And now you get to go away with Him for an intense time of learning, discovering, gaining understanding, and hearing from Him. You'll also be able to share your thoughts with Him.

During your retreat, you will quiet yourself so you can hear the still, small voice of the Leader. You'll set your mind in a learning mode. You'll eat differently, enjoying simple, nutritious meals so you can pay more attention to your studies and your time with the Leader. You'll reduce distractions because you want to receive the insights, lessons, and messages that He wants to share with you. You'll make sure you get enough sleep so you're well-rested and alert. And even though you may need to step away to fulfill some day-to-day tasks or meet obligations, you can still continue to think about what you're learning and what you want to receive.

Your retreat is a place of safety. You get to open your heart and share your innermost thoughts with the Leader. You've been assured that He wants to hear from you and comfort you. He wants to wipe away any tears that may fall or calm any nerves that may show up. He wants you to know that He has the answers to your questions and concerns. He is bigger than any struggle you may be experiencing. He is stronger than any circumstance that has come your way. He is more loving and more caring than any person you have ever known or even imagined. He promises to provide for you. He knows how to change your perspective on money to ease your worry and help you set wise priorities. And you get to be with Him on this personal retreat. Just the two of you. Together. Sharing. Solving problems. Learning skills. Receiving blessings.

This is your Daniel Fast for financial breakthrough, and it's waiting

for you to begin. It's waiting for you to separate yourself from your typical daily routines so you can enter into a short period of focused prayer,
study, and interaction with God. And the Daniel Fast is waiting for you
to step away from the challenges and on to victory and solutions.

SEEKING A SUCCESSFUL FUTURE

Do you remember the Old Testament story of Ruth? It's a short book—
only four chapters—so you might want to pause now and read it. While
our lives today look very different from Ruth's, if you read the story with
an eye for the theme of God's provision, you may find some similarities
between your life and hers.

Ruth, a young woman from the land of Moab, found herself in
distress when her husband, her brother-in-law, and her father-in-law
all died. Ruth made the choice to stay with her Israelite mother-in-
law, Naomi, even though it meant leaving her own home in Moab and
traveling to Judah, hoping for provision in the land of her husband's
family. Ruth was a woman who was financially vulnerable. Young and
able-bodied, she carried the responsibility of her own well-being as well
as the well-being of Naomi.

Ruth and Naomi lived in poverty, with little natural hope for relief.
Ruth scrounged for food in the best ways that she knew, working diligently and always being honest and honorable. She remained tena-
cious, doing whatever was necessary to meet Naomi's needs and her
own. During her time of focused effort, Ruth met Boaz, who owned the
land from which Ruth was gleaning grain. After a series of events, Boaz
took Ruth as his wife. Through this union, Ruth and Naomi received
financial security. Even more significant was that Ruth, who perhaps had
thought she would never marry again, had a child with Boaz. His name
was Obed, and he was the father of Jesse. Jesse was the father of David,
who features prominently in the genealogy of Christ.

I remind you of this story because it illustrates the lovely assurance
we have available to us: the assurance that God will redeem and provide.
Ruth was a seeker. She left the home where she lived in poverty and
chose a different way—a way that led to Judah, where God had blessed
the land. Ruth kept the faith and the hope, and she stayed the course.

She worked with integrity and honor. And then she met Boaz, one of the most dramatic figures in the Old Testament, who foreshadows the redeeming work of Christ in our lives.

Boaz recognized Ruth's good heart and kind nature, shown in her care for Naomi. He redeemed her from the old life of poverty, stress, and survival and gave her abundance, security, and well-being.

We also have an open invitation to experience the redeeming power of God in our lives. The Lord can turn around seemingly impossible circumstances, and He calls us to trust Him to provide what we need. Right now you can make the decision to place your hope in the Lord, your Redeemer. And you can learn more about how to do this during your time of extended prayer and fasting.

YOUR JOURNEY FROM FEAR TO TRUST

A while back, I sent a gift to a loved one: a copy of a newly released book called *The Latte Factor: Why You Don't Have to Be Rich to Live Rich* by David Bach and John David Mann. It's written specially to help millennials see the benefit of saving a little every month for a relatively short period of time to help them gain financial security in their older years. My loved one is hardworking, but he was holding down one full-time job plus a part-time job to cover his family's living expenses. I thought the book could help him out.

I had the gift shipped to him directly from Amazon. On the day the book arrived, my loved one called to thank me for the gift and said he was eager to read it. But then he told me, "When I walked up to my doorstep and saw the package from Amazon, I was so upset. I knew I hadn't ordered anything, so why were they sending me a package? Then I started a rant inside my head. 'What's this going to cost me? Did they charge it to my account? I can't afford anything right now. I need to give them a call.'"

Clearly, my loved one was coming from a place of stress, worry, and anxiety about his finances. And when he saw the package, he immediately went to the "fear place" instead of a happy place of anticipation. I could identify with his feelings since I'd been there in my own times of financial challenge. I remember how I hated to go to the mailbox because I feared what bill I might find. I was reluctant to answer the phone, worrying that a bill collector was calling me.

Maybe you are fearful about your money matters. You toss and turn in the night, feeling restless because you're not sure you can pay your mortgage or make your car payment. Or you feel like you're carrying around a fifty-pound weight on your shoulders because you don't see any way out of the survival mode of living paycheck to paycheck. You know that if the car breaks down or your electricity bill soars because of unexpected weather conditions, you won't have the money to cover the added expense.

Stress, worry, and fear grate on your soul. Many times, these emotions become our own sounds in the silence of the night. And for married couples, the stress, worry, and fear become fuel for arguments, threats, blame, and even breakups.

Financial problems can also negatively affect your relationship with God. You might be so full of fear that you don't remember what it's like to trust Him. You might be unable to think about how you can serve God or others because you have to focus so much energy on your daily needs. The financial strain can exhaust you, leaving you feeling isolated and disheartened.

But there is another way. And my hope is that within these pages you will shift from fear about your money matters and move into hope, trust, and peace. Yes, peace in your soul—no matter how impossible it seems right now—because you'll learn how to bring Christ into the center of your finances. You'll partner with Him to calm the storm and regain your sleep.

This isn't a budget book or a financial planning book. For that information, the Tools and Resources section refers you to some respected authors who specialize in teaching those important skills. Instead, this book is a guide to lead you into a spiritual experience so you can leave fear in the past and step into the rest that is yours through Christ. The breakthrough you will experience isn't going to be money raining from the sky or the discovery of a long-lost relative who left you a fortune in their will. That's not to say that God can't or won't provide in miraculous ways. I've heard story after story from my readers about ways that God stepped in to meet their needs or help them get back on track. Yet the most valuable breakthrough any of us can experience is a step forward in our faith and in our trust in God and His priceless, immeasurable care for us.

God's Word says, "Humble yourselves under the mighty hand of God, that He may exalt you in due time, casting all your care upon Him, for He cares for you" (1 Peter 5:6-7). My guess is that you can't quite imagine casting all your care upon the Lord. That's because making that shift isn't instantaneous. It's a process. It's part of your walk in faith. And using the Daniel Fast for this leg of your journey will help you progress on your faith walk.

God's Word is a treasure chest of promises for all believers. And my plan is to help you discover them and realize they are God's gifts to you. He wants you to have them, because He cares for you. And that's the truth!

THE DANIEL FAST IS A SPIRITUAL EXPERIENCE

The purpose of biblical fasting is to learn from God's truths about His ways for living. To communicate with Him and hear His instructions. To humble yourself before Him so you can receive His direction and guidance. To receive the revelations that come from His Spirit to your spirit that will point you on the way you should go. And in this Daniel Fast for financial breakthrough, you'll also learn to discern God's purposes for money and how He wants you to use it and think about it.

During your twenty-one-day fast, your daily life will be different from your typical routine. I've come to believe that God designed biblical fasting to specifically involve restricting food for a spiritual purpose. It's a way to call our whole being (spirit, soul, and body) to attention so we can experience God's presence to a greater degree during our separated time.

During your fast, you prepare to be away from some of your typical daily activities. You most likely can't take three weeks off work, school, or other responsibilities, but you can try to cut back on other obligations to give yourself more time with God. You set intentions for what you want to experience during your three weeks of personal retreat. You make plans for when you will begin and when the retreat will conclude.

You anticipate the mystery of what you will experience because you're not quite sure what the Leader will tell you or what He will ask you to do.

This particular retreat has your financial matters as the focus because that's what you've asked of the Leader. Psalm 66:19 assures us, "Certainly God has heard me; He has attended to the voice of my prayer." You can plan your retreat with expectations that the Master Leader will do His part to provide what you need.

BE FILLED WITH ALL THE FULLNESS OF GOD

The book of Ephesians is packed with powerful truths about the life we have available to us because of Christ. Paul wrote this letter to the women and men in the church at Ephesus because he saw that they didn't understand the benefits given to them through the grace of their Father. I encourage you to read all six chapters of Ephesians as if Paul were writing the letter just to you. But for now, let's look at a few verses:

> For this reason I bow my knees to the Father of our Lord Jesus Christ, from whom the whole family in heaven and earth is named, that He would grant you, according to the riches of His glory, to be strengthened with might through His Spirit in the inner man, that Christ may dwell in your hearts through faith; that you, being rooted and grounded in love, may be able to comprehend with all the saints what is the width and length and depth and height—to know the love of Christ which passes knowledge; that you may be filled with all the fullness of God.
> EPHESIANS 3:14-19

My hope is that you will pray that same prayer for yourself. During your time of extended prayer and fasting, may you be strengthened with might through the Holy Spirit. I pray that you will grasp the love and truth of Christ, which is a revelation to your spirit so you will know the fullness of God in your life.

The revelations are already there waiting for you. As a follower of Christ who is looking to God for your future, you can do your part by humbling yourself before Him, learning from Him, and then following His instructions. Hear Christ's message to you: "Let not your heart be troubled; you believe in God, believe also in Me. . . . I am the way, the truth, and the life" (John 14:1, 6). Following Him is the way to abundant life.

GOOD NEWS FOR THE INWARD MAN

Your God treasures you. He is your Father, and He wants the very best for you. He teaches and ministers to your inner self, or what some translations of the Bible call your "inward man." When Paul wrote to the Christians in Corinth, he taught about the invisible nature of our faith that, while not seen with our natural eyes, is still very real. He pointed out that while we may go through challenging experiences in our natural life, these difficulties bring priceless rewards and benefits to us that are not seen.

The apostle Paul writes this to the Corinthians:

> *Therefore we do not lose heart. Even though our outward man is perishing, yet the inward man is being renewed day by day. For our light affliction, which is but for a moment, is working for us a far more exceeding and eternal weight of glory, while we do not look at the things which are seen, but at the things which are not seen. For the things which are seen are temporary, but the things which are not seen are eternal.*
>
> 2 CORINTHIANS 4:16-18

As you humble yourself before your Lord and open your heart to His truths, He will minister to your inward man in ways you can't even see. He will reveal more about His nature, His authority, and His immeasurable love and care for you. He likely will give you instructions that you will receive by quieting yourself so you can hear His still, small voice speaking to your spirit.

As you go through your Daniel Fast, look for the breakthroughs you will gain in your understanding and direction from the Lord. Some may be tangible. Yes, many people have told me of receiving new jobs during their Daniel Fast, about selling their home that was "stuck on the market" for months, or about receiving an advancement in their work.

Star wrote and told me that she was the only believer in her household, and doing the Daniel Fast was hard for her. The fasting experience was intensified by her financial pressures. She had been out of work for months, and she and her family were barely scraping by. They had little to no money for food. She was thankful for the help she received from her church, but at the time she wrote to me, she was living on potatoes. She was also feeling very down about not being employed. She couldn't understand why it seemed like everyone around her was getting blessed, but she wasn't.

So as she started her Daniel Fast, she focused her prayers on asking God to help her get a job. During the last week of her fast, she made another call to a store that had previously not been taking any applications. This time they invited her to come for an interview that very day. The interview went well, and Star wrote to me with big capital letters, "I'M HIRED!" She was thrilled and gave God all the glory for working in her life. He opened shut doors and led her on the path to her success.

Financial breakthroughs like this are gifts from God. However, the most priceless breakthroughs are those of the heart, when we learn to trust God as our Provider, as the One who loves us and will never leave us or forsake us. That's what I received back in 2007, and that's what Becky received also. She sent me this message about her breakthrough and shared how it's not limited to the dollars and cents:

Susan—by far these have been the best 21 days of my life. When I started the Daniel Fast I thought it was about finances, but as I got honest with God, I asked Him how could I expect Him to help me with my finances when I wasn't even sure He loved me. Since I didn't have an earthly mother and father that showed they loved me, I have never been sure of love. Why would this "GOD" be any different? The revelation He gave me concerning His love for me wouldn't begin to fit in this space. But I have walked that revelation out for the last 21 days. When GOD reveals Himself to you, it is something you never forget, and it is something you know because you know, because you know. So I've decided to go further and for the next 21 days I will be doing the Daniel Fast for my finances, and you know what? My wonderful "FATHER" will be beside me. You will never know, Susan, how much your help has meant to me. All I can say is BE BLESSED and continue to be GOD'S anointed vessel. Becky.

I am so thrilled for Becky and the many others who open their hearts to God and experience His amazing love and truth. In the midst of my own financial crisis, God revealed to me truths about His nature that I didn't know—just as He revealed truths to Becky. Since then, I've learned so much more about how to live by faith and not by sight. I've learned to trust Him more deeply than I even knew was possible. And I've gained a relationship with Him that I had previously only longed for.

God has a breakthrough waiting for you with your name on it. It's already there. Your part is to open your heart, enter into the experience, and receive the blessings He designed just for you.

Faithful Servant Action Steps

These Faithful Servant Action Steps are intended to help you bring God into the center of your finances as you go through your twenty-one-day Daniel Fast. Again, I encourage you to read through the steps now, then come back to them in more detail after you've read the rest of part I and you're beginning your fast.

1. The Daniel Fast is based on the life of the Old Testament figure of Daniel, whom we'll talk more about in chapter 2. In preparation, read the Old Testament chapters of Daniel 1 and 10 and imagine the man of God in both of the situations described in the passages. Think about his deep devotion to God as well as how he must have longed for freedom after being in captivity for so many decades.

2. Think back to your childhood. What messages about finances did you receive from your parents and other people of influence? When you hear the word "money," what are three words that immediately come to mind?

3. Consider the goals you have for your finances. Where are you today regarding your money matters? Where would you like to be as God leads you on this leg of your faith journey?

CHAPTER TWO

Preparing for Your Daniel Fast

I ate no pleasant food, no meat or wine came into my mouth,
nor did I anoint myself at all, till three whole weeks were fulfilled.
DANIEL 10:3

THE DANIEL FAST is a method of fasting. It's a partial fast, which means some foods are eaten while others are restricted. It is based on the fasting experiences of the Old Testament prophet Daniel, along with typical Jewish fasting principles.

Perhaps you already have experience with the Daniel Fast and want to do it again with a financial focus. While some of this material may be review for you, read through it as a reminder of what you can expect during the twenty-one days of the fast.

If you're new to the Daniel Fast, I encourage you to get a copy of my bestselling book *The Daniel Fast: Feed Your Soul, Strengthen Your Spirit, and Renew Your Body* to give you more background and understanding of this method of fasting. The book is considered the "go-to guide" for the Daniel Fast and will help you go even deeper with your fast as you gain greater understanding of this powerful spiritual discipline.

AN ANCIENT EXPERIENCE FOR TODAY'S BELIEVERS

The foundation for the Daniel Fast comes from two specific passages from the book of Daniel. In Daniel 1 we learn about a young Hebrew man who, along with his companions, was in captivity in Babylon during the reign of King Nebuchadnezzar. What we now think of as the Middle East was undergoing great turmoil during this time in history, and Babylon had become a mighty force that was taking over many nations. Since the Babylonian territory was expanding massively, the kingdom needed more manpower. Nebuchadnezzar's forces took thousands of Hebrew men and women into captivity, including Daniel and his companions. These young men, who had been well-educated and trained while in Judah, were to be groomed for leadership positions in Babylon's swelling domain.

King Nebuchadnezzar wanted these trainees to be in tip-top shape, both physically and mentally. He instructed his leaders to bring the men into the palace quarters, where they could receive excellent care while they grew into the leaders he needed in his government. After three years of training, they would be well prepared to serve the king.

The king's plan was for them to have a daily provision of the same food delicacies he ate and the same wine he drank. Can you imagine being offered the best of the best food and the tastiest of the tasty wines? Truly, food fit for a king! Only the finest foods and the premium wines were offered to the young men being tutored for key leadership positions.

Most of the trainees were delighted with the offering. But Daniel's inner man had a different reaction—and those desires were much stronger than his fleshly appetite or cravings. Daniel maintained a deep commitment to God, and he wanted to live according to the ways of his Lord.

> *Daniel purposed in his heart that he would not defile himself with the portion of the king's delicacies, nor with the wine which he drank; therefore he requested of the chief of the eunuchs that he might not defile himself.*
> DANIEL 1:8

Daniel had been raised under the Jewish laws for food preparation, which required meat to be prepared in a specific manner. The Babylonians didn't follow these practices. Plus, biblical scholars report that it's likely King Nebuchadnezzar's food had been offered to the Babylonian gods before it was brought to the king's table. Daniel likely felt that eating the foods would make him a participant in idol worship. Daniel was committed to his faith, and he kept the Hebrew laws that had been deeply implanted in him since early childhood. He didn't want to defile, or contaminate, his body by eating the food being offered to him.

Yes, Daniel was in captivity, and on the surface it seemed that he had very little control over his circumstances—even down to the food he ate. However, God was still with him. I believe God knew of His servant's conundrum and He went ahead of His faithful man to prepare a way. Daniel 1:9 tells us, "Now God had brought Daniel into the favor and goodwill of the chief of the eunuchs." So when Daniel told the chief of the eunuchs, Ashpenaz, that he didn't want the rich food of the king and asked that he and his friends be given only "pulse" (food grown from seed; see 1:12, KJV) to eat and water to drink, he found a listening ear.

At first Ashpenaz resisted; after all, disobeying the orders of the king could result in death. However, he favored Daniel. He trusted him and his word, and so he eventually agreed to a test where Daniel and his companions would eat only food grown from seed and drink only water for ten days. The results were measurable:

> *At the end of ten days their features appeared better and fatter*
> *in flesh than all the young men who ate the portion of the king's*
> *delicacies. Thus the steward took away their portion of delicacies*
> *and the wine that they were to drink, and gave them vegetables.*
> DANIEL 1:15-16

Oh, and that's not all. The passage goes on to report God's blessing on these young men of faith:

> *As for these four young men, God gave them knowledge and skill*
> *in all literature and wisdom; and Daniel had understanding in all*
> *visions and dreams.*
> DANIEL 1:17

Take note, dear reader: These men were led by their deeply rooted beliefs about who they were in the eyes of God. They saw themselves as God's servants, and their entire beings were sanctified—separated for a holy purpose—to their Lord. Their outward behavior was ruled by their inner convictions, and God honored them and blessed them with His power.

In this historical account we find one of the primary references that establishes the guidelines for the Daniel Fast:

> *Prove thy servants, I beseech thee, ten days; and let them give us*
> *pulse to eat, and water to drink.*
> DANIEL 1:12, KJV

While many translations use the word "vegetables" here, I believe the King James Version is the best translation for this verse. The word "pulse" means foods grown from seed. Thus, during the fast, we eat only plant-based foods, including fruits, vegetables, whole grains, legumes, nuts, seeds, healthy oils, spices, and herbs. All food from animals is withheld during the fast, including fish, beef, pork, poultry, dairy products, and eggs. The only beverage on the fast is water. No tea, no coffee, and no juice—just water to comply with this Scripture.

The second passage that establishes the guidelines for the fast is Daniel 10:3, which captures Daniel's words after he had been in captivity for more than seventy years. Daniel describes coming to God for insight and direction in a time of extended prayer and fasting:

> *I ate no pleasant food, no meat or wine came into my mouth, nor*
> *did I anoint myself at all, till three whole weeks were fulfilled.*

This verse gives us a few more guidelines for the fast. First, we see that Daniel fasted for "three whole weeks." Because of this, most people practice the Daniel Fast for twenty-one consecutive days. Second, we see that Daniel ate no meat, drank no wine, and refrained from eating "pleasant foods." We use this Scripture (as translated in a variety of Bible versions) to add a few more food restrictions to the Daniel Fast guidelines. These include no sweeteners and no deep-fried foods. Typical

Jewish fasting practices, which Daniel most likely followed, also exclude leavening agents. It's possible this is intended by his noting of "no pleasant food," as some translations specify bread.

As you can see, when we merge the points from Daniel 1:12 and Daniel 10:3, along with typical Jewish fasting principles, we develop our list of foods allowed during the Daniel Fast: fruits, vegetables, whole grains, legumes, nuts, seeds, herbs, spices, and healthy oils. The only beverage allowed is water. The foods not allowed on the Daniel Fast are any that are produced from animals or that include leavening agents, solid fats, sweeteners (either natural or artificial), chemicals, food additives, preservatives, or processed ingredients. We also avoid deep-fried foods.

A more extensive list of allowed foods is included before the recipe section of this book. I also provide useful tips for preparing meals so you are not burdened by spending so much time in the kitchen. Food preparation has gotten easier over the years. When I started teaching about the Daniel Fast in 2007, finding canned or frozen foods that met the guidelines was very difficult. Consequently, most meals had to be prepared from scratch at home with fresh ingredients (which I still prefer to do). However, now that consumers are more health conscious, food producers are responding by providing more wholesome prepared foods free of chemicals and sweeteners, giving us more options.

People often ask me whether the Daniel Fast is expensive. I believe it can be quite cost-effective. While you may purchase more fresh produce, you will be eliminating some of what increases the food budget for many people: meat, dairy products, expensive prepared foods, and many meals at restaurants. The key to saving money and time is to plan ahead and prepare your meals at home. Plus, you'll most likely eat much healthier dishes. (For more information on this question, see the Frequently Asked Questions beginning on page 219.)

Keep in mind that while restricting food is at the core of the fast, it's not what the fast is really about.

THE VENUE OF YOUR CHOICE

The choices we make today affect our futures in ways we can't even imagine. I grew up in a suburb of Seattle, Washington. When I was a child, Seattle was the scene for the Century 21 Exposition—the 1962 World's Fair, which sprawled throughout downtown. That was when Seattle's famous Space Needle was erected, along with a lot of other buildings and exhibits at what is now known as the Seattle Center.

When my parents took my two sisters and me to the fair, my eyes were as big as saucers. I'd never seen anything that spectacular. So many things to learn about. So many rides to enjoy. And so much food to eat!

More than fifty vendors set up in a centrally located building that became known as the Food Circus. You could go wild, fun, and extravagant for breakfast, lunch, and dinner. It was at Century 21's Food Circus that America was introduced to Belgian waffles and puffy pancakes called Dutch babies. The world's nations were well-represented with global dining, including French cuisine, Thai, Japanese, Mongolian, Mexican, Danish, German, Creole, Native American, Korean, and many other fares.

We had so many choices! So many different foods from various cultures, including some things I had never seen before. Everything was so tempting! I could have spent the whole day in the Food Circus and still not seen, smelled, tasted, and enjoyed it all.

But do you know what? I'm glad I didn't. Because if I had stayed in the Food Circus, I never would have visited the World of Science and seen a NASA exhibit that included the Project Mercury capsule used in 1961 to take Alan Shepard and his crew into space. I would have missed all the international exhibitions, including a technology display from Great Britain that steered my vision with mind-boggling inventions and showed me a path into a future I never could have imagined. I would have missed the artisan exhibits from Mexico, Peru, and Japan that spoke to my little-girl soul about valuing and respecting people from other cultures and from other places in our world.

If I had stayed in the Food Circus so I could have a caramel-covered apple or a foot-long hot dog, I also would have missed seeing paintings by Vincent van Gogh and Georgia O'Keeffe. I would have missed the dancers from Thailand and General Motors' fully operational space age car, the Firebird III.

My parents let me eat a meal or two at the Food Circus, but I'm so glad they didn't let us stay there. They knew the Fair was about more than just food, and there was more they wanted us to experience.

Likewise, the Daniel Fast is about more than just food. Of course, the food restrictions are central to the fast, but the food restrictions are primarily a means to an end. Restricting food serves as a significant change in our everyday lives to keep us alert to the highly focused time we are experiencing. The change in our eating plan helps us remember that we are living in a different way for this period of time. When we fast, we are separating ourselves from our typical daily life. The Bible calls this change sanctifying ourselves. Changing the way we eat for the twenty-one days of the fast helps us notice the difference in a more profound way. I believe that God's intention for fasting is always about restricting food for a spiritual purpose. He knows us. He knows how we operate, and He knows what we need to be successful in this highly focused time of prayer, meditation, and study.

Consider again the spiritual retreat image from chapter 1. When you have a chance to spend time with your Leader, will you spend all your time in the kitchen? Are you going to focus on your meals or on how to manipulate recipes to satisfy your cravings? That sounds kind of counterproductive, right?

Sadly, that's the approach of so many people who use the Daniel Fast. Their focus becomes the food, and they spend hours preparing meals to satisfy their fleshly desires. They become anxious because they can't serve their sweet tooth the jamocha almond fudge ice cream it craves, or they stress because they can't have their usual multilayered caramel macchiato espresso drink. Rather than leaning into the cravings and using them as a reminder to trust God, they try to feed their cravings by looking for a substitute food that's allowed on the fast.

That mindset is for people who are willing to settle for less. Meanwhile, they miss the best of what their Daniel Fast experience has to offer.

As you consider your fasting experience, make the choice to humble yourself before the Lord and learn from Him. Keep your meals simple. (All the recipes you need are in Part II of this book.) Eating and cooking differently is an adjustment and can take time, but if you use the wise preparation practices that I've laid out for you in part II, you won't need to spend so much time preparing meals that it takes away from the precious time learning, meditating, praying, and being in the presence of your Lord.

I'll cover all of this in more detail in the coming chapters. For now, like a wise sailor, set your sails so you will travel in the direction you want to go. Decide now that you will not focus on the food or the beverages you must avoid during your spiritual experience. Instead, decide to focus on feasting on the rich, satisfying solid food from God's Word. Hear the words of Paul as he addressed the immature Christians in Corinth:

> *Brothers and sisters, I could not talk to you as to spiritual people, but [only] as to worldly people [dominated by human nature], mere infants [in the new life] in Christ! I fed you with milk, not solid food; for you were not yet able to receive it. Even now you are still not ready.*
> 1 CORINTHIANS 3:1-2, AMP

I pray that you will be ready to receive the solid food and enter more deeply into your new life in Christ.

PREPARATION IS A KEY TO YOUR SUCCESS

I have the joy of ministering to tens of thousands of women and men around the world who use the Daniel Fast as their method of extended prayer and fasting. Many of them write to me about their fasting experiences, so I hear both the highs and the lows. When people struggle with the Daniel Fast, the number one reason is because they have not adequately prepared for their twenty-one-day spiritual experience. Those who invest the time, energy, and resources and prepare their spirits, souls, and bodies for the fast usually complete the experience with great success. That's what I want for you. And so please, right now, decide to plan for your fast. Read the rest of part I, which will lay the spiritual groundwork, and then set aside the necessary time to prepare before you begin your fast. You will be so very glad you took this initiative to get ready.

As I mentioned in the previous chapter, think of your fast as a personal retreat that you will attend. Before you go, you need to think through what you'll need, what you'll do, and how you can get the most out of this experience.

In 1 Thessalonians 5:23, God's Word lets us know that our being is made of three parts: "Now may the God of peace Himself sanctify you completely; and may your whole spirit, soul, and body be preserved blameless at the coming of our Lord Jesus Christ." You are a spirit (made in the likeness of God, who is a Spirit). You have a soul, which includes your intellect, your will, and your emotions. And you live in a body, the flesh-and-blood "earth suit" that you can touch and feel.[1]

Read the verse again, noticing Paul's prayer for us. He prayed that we will be sanctified completely, which means to be fully separated for the purpose of God—set apart for a holy purpose. His prayer is that we will lean into the invitation God gave us when He said, "Be holy, for I am holy" (1 Peter 1:16).

During your Daniel Fast, you will separate yourself in a magnified way in spirit, soul, and body. You will focus more time on your spiritual life. You will focus your attention on learning new truths and discovering how to trust God more fully. And you'll adhere to the Daniel Fast guidelines by eating different foods to nourish your body. While you may not realize it now, your focus on knowing the Father more deeply gives Him the opportunity to reveal more of Himself to you—loving truths and insights that you don't yet have. He's eager to share them with you as you enter into the powerful spiritual discipline of extended prayer and fasting. Prepare your whole being for the challenges ahead.

PREPARE YOUR SPIRIT

Your spirit is that part of you that was once dead because of the sin of Adam. When you accepted Jesus as your Lord, your spirit was born again.

Adam and Eve brought brokenness into their lives because of their disobedience and disloyalty to God. Their spirits, which had been in perfect union with God's Spirit, suffered death (see Romans 5). Because of their sin, every human being from that time to now has been inflicted with brokenness in their spiritual connection to our Creator. If you have invited Jesus into your heart, praise God! At that very moment your spirit was redeemed and reborn because of Christ. Romans 5:19 says, "For as by one man's disobedience many were made sinners, so also by one Man's obedience many will be made righteous." You are made righteous in Him, and now you can be in God's presence. Connecting with Him is what the fast is all about.

You can prepare your spirit for your Daniel Fast by spending some quiet time seeking your Father's wisdom. Open yourself to Him. Humbly share with Him whatever is on your heart about your finances, your challenges, or anything else. Declare to Him that you are opening yourself to His counsel, direction, wisdom, and guidance. Sit quietly with Him. Sense His presence. Remember, when you gave your life to Jesus, your body became the dwelling place of God's Holy Spirit. You are reunited with your Creator:

> *Do you not know that your body is the temple of the Holy Spirit who is in you, whom you have from God, and you are not your own? For you were bought at a price; therefore glorify God in your body and in your spirit, which are God's.*
> 1 CORINTHIANS 6:19-20

Make a promise to your Lord that you will take His hand during your Daniel Fast. Commit to this time of spiritual discipline where you will look to Him for answers regarding your money matters, your priorities, and your faith.

PREPARE YOUR SOUL

I mentioned earlier that the soul incorporates our minds, emotions, and wills. Because our souls encompass so much of our conscious thought, it's vitally important that we prepare them for the fast. If we don't, we'll struggle to stay the course.

You'll be more likely to succeed on the Daniel Fast if you know why you're doing it. That's one reason I recommend that people decide their purpose for the fast before they begin. Take some time to pray and think about what your specific financial focus should be. Here are a few ideas:

- Developing a God-honoring attitude toward money
- Dealing with debt
- Changing a pattern of living paycheck to paycheck
- Setting priorities for giving and spending
- Growing in wisdom for making financial decisions
- Considering what kind of legacy you hope to leave

Ask God to guide you as you decide on the focus for your fast and consider how to implement it.

Preparing your soul also involves some very practical considerations, including the timing of your fast. The three weeks on your Daniel Fast will be different from your typical days. While you can continue to fulfill your responsibilities to your vocation and your family, you will find more success if you can forgo other activities as much as possible.

Calendar: Decide when you will begin your Daniel Fast. I'll cover more about how to enter into your fast in later chapters; however, now is a good time to review your schedule and reserve twenty-one consecutive days for your spiritual retreat with your Lord. Target your beginning date (starting at sunrise) and your completion date (ending at sunset). Are there activities that you can reschedule or pause to give yourself more time for prayer, study, focus, and hands-on attention with your financial business? Are there commitments that you can plan ahead for, such as celebrations or events that involve food? Decide ahead of time how you're going to handle them, whether by altering your plans, making special arrangements to bring your own food, or eating before or after the event.

You may want to schedule time to work on your financial records and systems, unless this is already part of your routine. If your bills and spending records are not in order, plan a few hours during your fast to prayerfully focus on getting everything organized—or at least getting a start on reviewing your financial situation.

In addition, plan when you will pray, study, and be with your Father each day. I suggest a minimum of thirty minutes daily. I've also found that first thing in the morning is the best time. If we wait until later in the day, too often distractions and interruptions keep us from fulfilling our plans.

Think about other times when you can incorporate prayer and Scripture into your daily routine. You might plan to listen to Christian music while you prepare food, listen to Scripture or a faith-related pod-cast in the car, memorize Scripture while you get ready for the day, or pray as you're getting ready for bed. Let these twenty-one days be set apart, different from your usual routines and saturated with times of connection with God.

Study Materials: Before you begin the fast, assemble resources that will be helpful. I encourage you to immerse yourself in biblical studies about home finances, stewardship, and a Christian's approach to money management. Let your twenty-one-day Daniel Fast be your God-centered financial study immersion program, where you can learn valuable lessons in a short period of time. That's what happened when my teenage son was struggling with learning Spanish in high school. During the sum-mer months before his senior year, he and I traveled to Antigua, a small town in Guatemala. We stayed there for six weeks so my son could learn Spanish in an intensive study program. Six days a week, for six hours each day, he studied the language. His teacher spoke no English to him. My son was immersed, surrounded, soaked in the Spanish language. And after just six weeks of intensive learning, he emerged with a good com-mand of the language.

You can have a similar experience as you become highly focused on learning about how to bring God into the center of your money matters. Learn about stewardship and money management. Develop new skills and habits. Become proficient at managing the resources God provides for you.

While we'll touch on several of these topics over the next few chap-ters, I've also supplied a list of focused resources on page 223. Plan to use the daily devotionals included in part II of this book, which will help you turn to the Lord each day. I also suggest that you use a journal dur-ing your fast. Write about your feelings, the messages you may receive from the Lord, plans you want to make, changes you hope to impose, and whatever is on your heart. Your fast will be a rich time of discovery, so you'll want to capture your thoughts and ideas.

Home Office Supplies: Because you'll be focusing your attention on money matters during your fast, this will be a perfect time for you to get your financial house in order. A set of file folders and ledger paper are all that is essential. You can gather other supplies as you develop your systems and decide what approach works for you.

Also, think about a business space you can use at least twice a month where you'll have everything you need to pay your bills, review your progress, and plan your future. Your "space" can be as simple as a cardboard box containing your records and supplies that you use on your kitchen counter or table. Or it could be a home office or a desk where you can work on your finances in an organized, consistent, and peaceful manner. (See chapter 9 for more information.)

PREPARE YOUR BODY

You want to make sure you prepare your physical body for the Daniel Fast. During your fast, you will not use any caffeine or sweeteners. Your body may not like this change and may rebel with physical symptoms that can be quite painful and debilitating.

If you drink coffee, tea, or other caffeinated beverages, you'll want to wean your body from them before you begin your fast. Plan at least seven days (ten days is better) to taper off using caffeine. Gradually replace what you typically drink with decaffeinated beverages. For example, for two days, mix half caffeinated coffee with half decaf coffee. Continue to add more decaf until that's all you're drinking a day or two before your fasting start date. Also, increase the amount of water you drink, which will help flush your body.

The same goes for sugar. Cut back on sweetened foods, including candy, desserts, and sugary beverages. Slowly reduce the consumption of any sugar so that when you begin the fast, you are free of cravings. Again, drinking more water will help flush your system and reduce your desire for sugar.

By the way, a special benefit of the Daniel Fast is that it abolishes sugar cravings. Rarely does a well-nourished body crave sugar. During your fast, you will eat lots of fruits, vegetables, and whole grains, which are the nourishing foods that your body desires. When your body is happy, it won't send out craving signals.

ENTERING THE FAST

Your fast isn't an obligation. It's not a diet. It's not something you'll pile on top of your already too-busy schedule. Your Daniel Fast is a spiritual experience where you will draw closer to God. You'll gain clarity, peace, and understanding. You'll hear from your Father and learn more about how you can live in His peace and rest, trusting Him as Provider as you seek to understand the way He wants you to think about money.

I hope you're excited. I receive messages from women and men all over the world about the glorious experiences they've had on their Daniel Fast. Most are surprised by how they were able to hear from God like never before in their lives. Many are stunned by the answers to their prayers. And everyone who enters into this lovely spiritual discipline is thankful for the rich blessings of the Lord. They experience His love, His care, and His presence as they turn away from the rush of the world and focus their hearts on their Father.

Without faith it is impossible to please Him, for he who comes to God must believe that He is, and that He is a rewarder of those who diligently seek Him.
HEBREWS 11:6

God promises you unexpected benefits when you focus on Him with your heart and soul. You are His precious child. Imagine yourself as a little one standing before your Father. He's looking down at your face with a tender, loving smile as He gazes into your eyes. His hands are behind His back, hiding the pleasant surprises He has just for you. Your heart is filled with expectation and hope. You know He gives you only what is good and what is best for you. You can count on Him.

That is your Father. Prepare to enter the fast and receive the many blessings He has for you. You can receive them from Him, follow His ways, practice them in your everyday life of faith, and gain the confidence, peace, and joy that only He can provide.

Faithful Servant Action Steps

1. Plan your fast by scheduling twenty-one consecutive days to focus on the Lord. Plan to study, pray, and be in His presence for at least thirty minutes each morning, if possible. Reduce activities so your time is more open with fewer distractions, making it easier for you to be with Him.

2. Gather the resources you will use to support your learning during your fast. (See the list of tools and resources on page 223.)

3. Gather the home office supplies that will help you organize your financial business. Plan a workspace where you can attend to your bills and financial records at least two times each month.

CHAPTER THREE

Your Personal Fast for Financial Breakthrough

It was the best of times, it was the worst of times.
CHARLES DICKENS, *A TALE OF TWO CITIES*

BREAKTHROUGH!

The very word implies a before and an after. Being on one side of a problem and then reaching the other side.

That was my experience when I went through my financial crisis. And just like Charles Dickens wrote, it was for me the best of times and the worst of times. Let me share my breakthrough story with you.

COMING THROUGH A CRISIS

In 2007, I was living on a little farm in a small college town in central Washington. I was single, upper middle age, and the owner of a real estate investment company that bought both residential and commercial properties. Often we would buy broken-down houses that needed a lot of work, and then my crew of carpenters, plumbers, and electricians would transform them into sparkling homes to be sold to new buyers. Most of our buyers were young couples or first-time homeowners.

I loved the business of transformation. Taking a broken-down property and turning it into a lovely new residence for a couple or family was very satisfying. Plus, the profits paid my crew and my office staff, and contributed to my own personal income. I wasn't rolling in money, but I was doing okay. Life was good!

That was, until the summer of 2007. I'll never forget the day I was talking on the phone to Kim, the broker who handled all my mortgages at the firm that provided short-term loans for real estate investors. I was calling about securing another loan when Kim said, "Susan, I've got to call you back in a couple of days. We don't know what's going on, but all of a sudden, mortgage money is freezing up. I'll get back to you as soon as I know more."

What was happening was that the wheels were beginning to come off the economy—and it all centered on the subprime mortgage industry. Looking back now, we know that the money business for many mortgages was like a house of cards. And when one card got wobbly, the entire weak structure collapsed. Those of us in the real estate investment business, especially those like me who sold homes to first-time home buyers, felt the collapse first.

Money froze up within days.

Meanwhile, I still owned several homes in various stages of rehab. That meant I had mortgage payments on each property. I had work crews who needed payment. I had supplies to purchase. Plus I had an office staff and overhead expenses to pay.

At that time, none of the financial experts were calling the situation a recession. Instead, they deemed it a correction or a blip in the economic markets. I figured it would pass, so here in my little college town, I shifted into tighten-the-belt mode. I couldn't just give up. As the business owner with my name on all the contracts and people looking to me for their livelihood, I had to keep things moving forward. I tapped into my business reserves. But as the economic fall continued month after month, they were eventually tapped out.

Bold moves were necessary. I laid off my office staff, closed my downtown center of operations, and moved everything home. I figured I could manage my construction crews from my home office, keep everything moving forward, and get through this hard time. I kept paying the bills, but now I was using my personal savings.

Month after month I kept going. And while the economy and the housing market screeched to a halt, my anxiety and stress soared. The future outlook kept getting darker and darker. Even though I had been through several really hard times before, nothing had prepared me for the level of fear that I was going through in this financial crisis.

Winter entered the scene fast and hard that year. As the days grew shorter, I spent longer hours in prayer. I had been a Christian since my early twenties, but never had I prayed longer or more desperately. I also cried more tears than I thought could ever come from my five-foot, four-inch body.

The experts still weren't calling the downturn a recession because the numbers didn't fit the formula that had been established by the money authorities. Meanwhile, it felt like a recession. Tens of thousands of families lost their homes to foreclosure as interest rates rose and unemployment increased. This was just the beginning of the more than seven million homes that eventually went into foreclosure.[1]

I watched my savings dwindle, with no change in sight. With no potential buyers for the properties I owned, I had to keep paying the mortgages. I had to keep paying my work crews. I had to keep buying the supplies needed to rehab the properties. That is, unless I chose to let them fall into foreclosure, which I didn't want to do.

I kept tightening my spending as much as possible. I continued to pray. And finally all the work was completed on the properties. No more wages for the work crews. No more expenses for the supplies. Now I just had to cover the mortgages, taxes, insurance, and utilities for the properties until I could finally sell them. That was some relief, but those expenses were still thousands of dollars each month. And the savings account would soon come to an end.

I pretty much kept to myself, partly because I didn't want to spend money on gas to drive the ten miles into town, but also because I didn't want people to know about the challenges I was experiencing. I knew family and friends would offer to loan me money, but I didn't need any more loans. Plus, the amount of money I needed each month was way more than I would ever want to borrow from loved ones, and I had no idea when the financial hemorrhaging would end.

December was around the corner. The snow was beginning to fall, along with the temperatures. I cooked and heated my little cottage with propane gas that came from a tank near my house. When the tank was nearly empty, I shut off the heating unit and started using my woodstove and fireplace. To conserve energy and heat, I closed off as many rooms as possible, including my bedroom. That meant I slept on the couch. Every other day I would scrounge around on my property to find wood to burn. I set my alarm for 3:00 a.m. to stoke the fires so the house would stay warm.

Every morning I spent hours in prayer and study, combing God's Word for answers. Never before had I been more desperate. I felt as if I were standing on the edge of hopelessness. But I never crossed over, because while I felt so alone, I still had a glimmer of hope because of my faith.

I clearly remember the morning when the hope seemed to flicker as if it were about to expire. Even now, tears fill my eyes as I recall the feelings of despair. Never before had I felt so desolate. So consumed with fear. With tears falling from my face, I cried out to God, "Are you going to let me go down even further? Are you going to let me fall even more?"

That was the moment when I came to the end of myself. Any strength that I could muster from my own will was gone. Any solution I could create for myself was out of sight. I was at the bottom. I still got out of bed and followed my usual routine of stoking the fires, studying God's Word, and living my simple life. I could still breathe. I still had food to eat. I still had a roof over my head. I kept moving on, day by day, but I felt hope dwindling from my soul.

A couple of days later, I was in my living room sitting on my couch. I wasn't praying at the time, or even thinking about God. Instead, I was just being quiet and getting ready to start my day. That's when it happened. That's when God spoke to me.

I didn't hear an audible voice. Instead, I heard Him speaking to my spirit loud and clear. He gave me a one-sentence instruction: "Write about the Daniel Fast."

I felt the jar of the unexpected message. A shift was about to happen. A new direction entered my life that cold December morning.

I had used the Daniel Fast before. And since the New Year was approaching, I had planned to begin 2008 with extended prayer and fasting. I also had experience writing, which I had done professionally for many years before I started my real estate investing business. However, I had never created a website, and I knew the internet was the only way to get information out about the fast in time for the New Year.

That flicker of hope turned into a blazing flame, getting stronger and brighter each day. I started working at six o'clock in the morning and continued almost nonstop until eleven o'clock at night. I researched as much as I could about the Daniel Fast.

I also learned how to create a free website so I could teach people about the Daniel Fast. Every day I posted messages, food lists, and instructions, and soon people started to visit the site. I responded to every post and answered every question. If I didn't know the answer, I researched it until I could give the visitor a good response. Soon many people started asking for more information, and they asked where they could buy a book about the Daniel Fast. I also connected with a man in Texas who had previously written about his wife's healing experience using the Daniel Fast. He was so overwhelmed with all the online visitors that he started sending everyone to my simple little Daniel Fast website.

I decided to use my skills as a writer to create an e-book about the Daniel Fast. I spent long days writing the document I titled (drumroll) *Everything You Want to Know about the Daniel Fast.*

By now it was mid-December. My bank accounts were all emptying as I tried to keep paying my bills and covering my business expenses. I held on to hope, but I have to admit that worry and fear remained. I continued to pray and spend time with the Lord and His Word.

On December 18 I checked my bank balances in all the accounts I had anywhere. Each one was empty except for my personal checking account, which had a balance of twenty dollars. That was all the money I had in the world. The sinking feeling in my stomach was intense, yet I didn't feel like giving up. Hope kept me going.

That's when I got even busier learning and planning and executing. I continued writing my e-book and figured out how to sell it online. This was before Kindle and Nook became standard, so e-books were created in a word processing program, converted to a PDF file that could be read from multiple types of computers, and sent through the World Wide Web.

I continued to write articles on my website, and I responded to every post left by visitors. The work helped me get through the tough days. I worked hard each and every day, and the activity fed my soul, even though I had only twenty dollars to my name.

Almost all of this work was new to me. I was a sojourner approaching a new land, yet I felt a closeness to God and a sense of His presence like I had not experienced before. Even as the days marched on toward the beginning of January when more bills were due, I felt calmer and not as scared. And I kept working.

I continued interacting with women and men who visited the website. And then, when I had finished writing and formatting my manuscript and all was in order, I added a link so anyone who wanted more information packaged in one document could purchase my new little e-book for a whopping $4.95.

Christmas came. I celebrated with my church family, and then I spent the holiday with my adult children and my grandchildren. Simple gifts were exchanged. And my heart's celebration of Christ's birth held a special intensity as I felt closer to Him than ever before. He was my light in the darkness. My hope in the time of despair.

On December 26 I started my day as usual, stoking the fires and then sipping hot coffee as I read God's Word and prayed. After getting dressed, I continued my morning routine and went to my computer to check my email. That's when I saw it: the sprout from the seeds of hope that I had planted and watered with faith. My first sale!

An unknowing onlooker would have thought I'd won the Mega Millions lottery by the way I screamed and danced and praised God. Yes, it was just one sale, and just $4.95 (actually less, with the selling cost deducted). But this one sale represented so much more to me.

Over the next couple of days, sales poured in! More and more people came to my website, which by now was the first site that popped up on Google when people searched for the Daniel Fast. The questions and requests for more information also increased, including many requests for Daniel Fast recipes. So I got busy and created *The Daniel Fast Cookbook*, which included dozens of recipes for breakfasts, lunches, and dinners. I priced this e-book at $8.95.

Over the next several weeks, hundreds of people purchased the two e-books. And by the time sales slowed, my bank account had filled with enough money to cover my bills for the next two months. I had my financial breakthrough. I was out of the darkness and in the light of relief. The weight had lifted, and a new level of faith had entered my soul.

The following months included some ups and downs. However, now my faith was stronger and the hole of despair wasn't as deep. My e-books continued to sell, but more slowly, since the New Year had passed and that's when most people use the Daniel Fast as their method for extended prayer and fasting. I still lived very frugally and figured out how to make ends meet by selling some antiques I had collected. As time passed, eventually I found buyers for the properties I had prepared for sale. I had to reduce the prices and didn't make a lot of money on them, but they were off my books and I had funds to cover my living expenses for the remainder of the year.

THE PRICELESS GIFT

God blessed me with His love and grace by taking me out of what could have been an even darker experience for me. I never had any foreclosures on the properties I owned, and I didn't have to declare bankruptcy, although my financial advisors told me I qualified and it would be a good strategy. I am forever thankful that God spoke to me on that cold winter morning and gave me a new calling for my life.

As you can imagine, the financial blessing was an enormous relief. However, the even more valuable gift the Lord led me to receive was my increased faith and spiritual growth. As hard as it was, I look back on the end of 2007 with gratitude because of all I learned. My breakthrough was a financial blessing, but it was so much more. I grew in my understanding of God, His Word, and my relationship with Him as my Provider.

I also grew in my vocation. What I thought then was a onetime writing assignment, He knew was much more. He had a much bigger dream for me than I could have had for myself. Today, I have sold hundreds of thousands of books about the Daniel Fast. I've had the honor of ministering to hundreds of thousands of women and men around the world. And even greater than that, I have an ever-growing faith and trust in God that I never thought possible.

I now realize that before, even though I had been a Christian for decades, I had walked around being held up by a set of invisible crutches. I looked like a strong woman of faith, but one of the crutches that held me up was a thriving US economy. The other crutch was reliance on my own skills, education, creativity, and intelligence. When both of those crutches were knocked out from under me, I fell. My faith was weak, and I needed Him and His truth to bring me up so I could stand.

Today, I stand in faith. Now when I encounter troubles, I know what to do: I cast my cares on Him. I lean into His Word. I depend on His promises. And I walk by faith, not by sight.

That's the true breakthrough. Yes, it happened in the midst of a financial crisis. But the most valuable part of it all was stepping into a deeper and more profound faith that I know will never fail and is not subject to worldly circumstances.

My hope for you is that you will move more deeply into an abiding faith in the Lord during your Daniel Fast. You have so much you can learn and encounter with your God. As you focus on your finances, I pray that you will grow in your understanding of money and stewardship, grow in your willingness to give, and grow in your trust in God as your Provider.

YOUR FINANCIAL BREAKTHROUGH

You're reading this book because some things are keeping you from getting where you want to go. You may have a pile of bills that seem more like a mountain. You're standing at the bottom while the bill collectors are shouting at you to hurry up and reach the top in one or two steps. You can't do it. You need a solution. You need a breakthrough.

Maybe you're peering into the coming seasons. Your kids need soccer shoes. Your car needs new tires. Your dentist just recommended significant work on your teeth. Plus, your mother will celebrate a milestone birthday, and you really want to fly across the country to be with her. *Ka-ching. Ka-ching. Ka-ching.* The sound of expenses piling up faster than you can keep up builds stress and feelings of anxiety and dread. You need a breakthrough.

Perhaps you're worried about your future. You're not at all financially prepared for your older years, but you know you can't work forever. Time keeps marching on. You know you should have a retirement plan, and yet you're barely keeping up on your monthly bills. You need a breakthrough.

On your own, you don't see a way over the obstacles. You see only impossibilities. You feel defeated before you start. You need a breakthrough from God.

Is the breakthrough going into your front yard, digging into the ground, and discovering gold, diamonds, or oil? Or do you open the mail each day hoping to find that you have a long-lost aunt who recently passed and left you millions in her will? Perhaps you imagine that God is going to open the heavens and the clouds above will rain hundred-dollar bills for you to collect off the ground.

We can fantasize. We can dream of striking it rich and becoming a modern-day member of the Beverly Hillbillies. However, let's step back and get in touch with what a fantasy really is: an improbable, unrealistic story we create in our minds—something that makes us feel good inside. Walt Disney knew that very well. Mickey Mouse. Tinker Bell. Jiminy Cricket. Cinderella. Ariel. They are all fantasies. They are unreal.

Fantasies make for good entertainment. But they can distort our thinking, making us believe that the unseen realities of God are also fantasies with no hope of coming true. As a result, that which is real, possible, and available to all who follow Christ is regarded as impossible and unreal—and therefore not believed.

Jesus instructs those who believe in Him, "Do not fear; only believe" (Luke 8:50, esv). Believe in Him. Believe in God's Word. Believe that God has a breakthrough for you.

After years of helping people through their fasting experiences, I am convinced that God works in our lives in a special way when we dedicate time to Him. When we set aside time for the fast, restricting our food as a reminder to spend time in prayer and Scripture, we are able to listen more carefully to what God is saying to us. We become more attuned to His leading and the way He wants us to live. And that's when breakthroughs happen.

God's financial breakthroughs come in various forms. Sometimes it's an idea for a new business or an invention. That's what happened to George Washington Carver, the most prominent black scientist of the early twentieth century. Carver gave the credit for his success to God alone, saying, "There is literally nothing that I ever asked to do, that I asked the blessed Creator to help me to do, that I have not been able to accomplish."[2]

Breakthroughs from God can come when He intervenes and puts His loved one in the right place at the right time. That's what happened to Ron, who had been unemployed for seven months. His wife dedicated her Daniel Fast to seeking God's help for their finances. During that time Ron applied for a new employment position opening up in his town. The human resources manager deemed Ron as the perfect fit and offered him the job within hours of his interview.

God's breakthroughs can also come as an instruction heard by listening ears. That's what happened to me back in December of 2007. God told me to do something I had never done before. Praise God I didn't think of His directive as a fantasy. Instead, I considered it as a possibility. I took action. And my life was changed forever. Now when I face a trial, I know where to turn.

Let me share another challenge that I experienced more recently as I was preparing for the Daniel Fast to start in January of 2019. I really needed help from the Lord. My finances were hemorrhaging due to a gigantic financial pressure centered on the last rental property I owned. The renters, a couple with a young child, had been in the property for more than five years and were usually on time with their rent payments. Then things started to fall apart. The rent was late. They wouldn't answer my phone calls or knocks on the door. Months passed, and finally I had to use the legal system to evict them from the home. The attorney fees and court costs amounted to nearly $7,000, plus I was covering the costs of the property, including the mortgage and insurance, out of my personal funds.

When I finally gained access to the property, to my horror I found that the husband had retaliated against me and the eviction by ravaging the home. He flooded the master bedroom, ruining the carpet and underflooring. He broke windows, smashed huge holes in the walls, stole doors, and damaged the plumbing and heating system. Everything totaled about $25,000 in damages.

My heart sank. Thankfully, I had insurance, and I was so relieved when my agent told me everything would be covered. I just needed to meet with the insurance adjuster.

The company's insurance adjuster was shocked by the damage. I'll never forget the look on his face as we stood in the midst of the mess in the home's living room. His eyes were filled with grief, and then chilling words came from his mouth: "Susan, your insurance policy doesn't cover this damage. This is all considered tenant vandalism, and you don't have that rider on your policy. If someone had broken in and done all this, you would be covered. But because it was your tenant, you're not entitled to any money."

My knees nearly buckled. Even though I had owned multiple rental properties in the past, I had never been informed about "tenant vandalism riders" for an insurance policy. Plus, I was still in my financial recovery from the 2007 down-to-$20 experience. I knew no bank would loan me the money to cover the damages, and I had no idea how I could get out of what looked like a deep, dark hole that someone had pushed me into.

I didn't have answers for this crisis, but I believe what God's Word says about challenges we face: "For we do not wrestle against flesh and blood, but against principalities, against powers, against the rulers of the darkness of this age, against spiritual hosts of wickedness in the heavenly places" (Ephesians 6:12). So I stood on God's promise in Malachi 3:11: "'I will rebuke the devourer for your sakes, so that he will not destroy the fruit of your ground, nor shall the vine fail to bear fruit for you in the field,' says the LORD of hosts."

In December 2018 I began praying diligently about this need. I really had no idea how God would solve this problem, but I knew He would. So I asked. I believed. And I waited.

Then one day an idea popped into my head. I had a contractor friend who had come into a lot of money. Maybe he would be open to investing enough to cover the materials needed for the repairs and then work with me to restore the property so I could sell it. His payment would be to split the equity. I called him, and bingo! His time was open. And after I sent him some photos and we discussed terms, he said yes!

There were a few setbacks along the way, but within six months the property was sold, my friend collected a generous payment, my savings account received an infusion of cash, and the financial hemorrhage was totally healed. That's a financial breakthrough, dear one. And I promise that if it can happen for me, it can happen for you! We don't always know how God will work. Our part is to believe without a doubt that He will. Why? Because He says He will.

Financial breakthrough doesn't mean God is going to make you a multimillionaire. It doesn't mean He's going to give you the winning numbers for the lottery or change all your circumstances. It does mean He's going to give you peace. He's going to increase your wisdom and put you on the path toward knowing His will and finding solutions. He's going to show you how to overcome those barriers that now hold you back. He's going to break through the walls, the roadblocks, and the obstacles and provide what you need. He's going to transform your thinking and your faith.

What must you do to receive a breakthrough from God? Train yourself to fulfill the command of Jesus: "Do not fear; only believe."

OVERCOMING OBSTACLES AND CHALLENGES

During your Daniel Fast, you will diligently seek God in a more focused way, asking for His direction for your finances. And because of that, it's likely that the enemy of your soul will fight any growth you experience. Jesus teaches us, "The thief does not come except to steal, and to kill, and to destroy. I have come that they may have life, and that they may have it more abundantly" (John 10:10).

Don't be surprised if challenges arise during your fast. Greet the battles as a great opportunity to grow in your faith. John 10:10 makes it clear that there is an enemy, the thief, working against you. But greater than the enemy is Jesus! The enemy wants to take from you, but Jesus has come to give you abundant life. And Jesus has already defeated the enemy we now stand firm against. The apostle Paul instructs us how to resist him:

Finally, my brethren, be strong in the Lord and in the power of His might. Put on the whole armor of God, that you may be able to stand against the wiles of the devil. For we do not wrestle against flesh and blood, but against principalities, against powers, against the rulers of the darkness of this age, against spiritual hosts of wickedness in the heavenly places. Therefore take up the whole armor of God, that you may be able to withstand in the evil day, and having done all, to stand.
EPHESIANS 6:10-13

In Colossians 2:15 we learn that Jesus conquered the enemy so that he has no power over you: "Having disarmed principalities and powers, He made a public spectacle of them, triumphing over them in it." You don't need to battle against an enemy that is already defeated. However, you do need to put your faith and trust in the Lord when this enemy tries to cause problems in your life. Recognize what is happening. Focus your thoughts, emotions, and behaviors on the Lord, and keep moving forward, walking in the way of faith.

Another opponent may challenge you during your fast, and that's your own natural mind, or what the Bible calls your flesh. Your flesh may try to sabotage your fast through cravings or sheer rebelliousness. Again, one of the best ways to prevent the flesh from winning is to prepare for the fast by weaning yourself off caffeine and sugar. Planning your meals ahead each morning will also set the course for what you will eat for that day to keep your body nourished and satisfied.

If you're still experiencing cravings, sometimes you may have to do what I do, and that's to have a little talk with my flesh. I take on the wiser-self role and tell my flesh to sit down. I remind it that it has no control over me, that it needs to be quiet and submit to the plans for the remaining days of the fast. I remind my flesh that I am dead to its desires and alive to the ways of God. Take the authority and remind yourself that these little cravings or whims are brief impulses that will pass when you don't feed them, but instead feed your faith!

It may also be helpful for you to find accountability with wise members of the faith as you adhere to the fasting guidelines.

ENTER YOUR HOPEFUL JOURNEY

Use your imagination to again picture yourself getting ready to attend a retreat. Imagine that you will be leaving your typical everyday life so you can enter into a new experience. During the days away, you will behave differently. You will use your time in a different way, eat differently, and, most important, have a specific purpose for what you want to receive while you're there.

The great news is that the retreat Leader is a Master! He knows you and what you need better than you do, which means you can have confidence in Him and the experience you are about to undergo.

We're talking about an unseen spiritual retreat. However, I encourage you to treat your fast as a very tangible affair. Prepare for it as you would for a physical retreat. Clear your calendar of appointments. Plan your time "away." Prepare for the event. Get ready for the deep encounter you can have with the most awesome Leader at your fast.

Imagine stepping into this new experience. As you begin, you want to leave some things behind, including worry, fear, distractions, and anxiety. Heed the instructions for your retreat found in Philippians 4:6-7:

> Be anxious for nothing, but in everything by prayer and supplication, with thanksgiving, let your requests be made known to God; and the peace of God, which surpasses all understanding, will guard your hearts and minds through Christ Jesus.

And here is another instruction to help you prepare for your time with the Lord:

Humble yourselves under the mighty hand of God, that He may exalt you in due time, casting all your care upon Him, for He cares for you.
1 PETER 5:6-7

Set your eyes on the bright and hopeful future your Lord has for you. You're going to share a time with Him so you can receive what He has for you. You will learn from Him, gaining understanding, revelations, and insights that only the Lord can give you.

When I was so low in money, I couldn't envision any way out of the dark existence of my life. I couldn't see the solution with my natural eyes or with my natural mind. However, my loving Father knew all along the answer He had for me, even though it took me a while before I could hear Him. I had some inner work that needed to be done first.

I can relate a bit to Paul on the road to Damascus. Paul's mind was filled with untruths about Jesus, to the point that he was on a mission to murder and destroy followers of Christ. That's when Jesus met Paul (who was called Saul then) on the road and said, "Saul, Saul, why are you persecuting Me?" (Acts 9:4).

Paul was stuck in one way of thinking. He was following a set of beliefs that had been deeply implanted in his mind for decades. But our Lord had a different plan for Paul. When Jesus met him on the road, Paul was struck blind by the encounter, and for three days he was without sight and ate nothing. Then God instructed one of His servants to go to the place where Paul was staying and deliver a message to him:

Ananias went his way and entered the house; and laying his hands on him he said, "Brother Saul, the Lord Jesus, who appeared to you on the road as you came, has sent me that you may receive your sight and be filled with the Holy Spirit." Immediately there fell from his eyes something like scales, and he received his sight at once; and he arose and was baptized.
ACTS 9:17-18

My encounter wasn't nearly as dramatic, nor did the outcome have such a profound impact. However, over the many stressful weeks in the winter of 2007, some scales of doubt, worry, and lack of faith needed to fall from my eyes. They needed to disappear so I could see a different way of living . . . a different future. I started learning how to walk by faith and not by my natural sight. I began my journey into the Kingdom-of-God way of thinking, believing, and behaving.

Even when God said, "Write about the Daniel Fast," I had no idea what He had in mind for me. His plan was much bigger than mine. The thief's plans were to steal, kill, and destroy any goodness in my life, but Jesus had a different plan. His rescue was as if He was saying to me, "I have come that you may have life, and that you may have it more abundantly."

God knew. I didn't. And the lesson for me? Trust in Him. He wants the best for us. He will see us through. Our part is to believe.

BELIEVING GOD FOR THE PROMISED LAND

While you and I, as followers of Jesus Christ, are under a new covenant, we can learn so much from those who have gone before us. The lives of the Israelites—coming out of bondage in Egypt, living in the wilderness under the authority of Moses, and eventually journeying into the Promised Land—hold many lessons for us.

Let's take a look at a few major points as recorded in the Scriptures. In the passage below, we see that Moses had been on Mount Sinai with God, who established the Ten Commandments and wrote them on the stone tablets. Moses was instructing the leaders about what was to come. He was forecasting the future for God's chosen people:

> *This day the LORD your God commands you to observe these statutes and judgments; therefore you shall be careful to observe them with all your heart and with all your soul. Today you have proclaimed the LORD to be your God, and that you will walk in His ways and keep His statutes, His commandments, and His judgments, and that you will obey His voice. Also today the LORD has proclaimed you to be His special people, just as He promised*

you, that you should keep all His commandments, and that He
will set you high above all nations which He has made, in praise,
in name, and in honor, and that you may be a holy people to the
LORD your God, just as He has spoken.
DEUTERONOMY 26:16-19

These are not idle words. They are declarations of the way God looks upon His people: "The LORD has proclaimed you to be His special people, just as He promised you." And as God's special people, His chosen people, the Israelites were called to follow His commandments with their thoughts, beliefs, and actions. God was establishing His people and their unique identity.

Keep in mind, about six hundred thousand men, not counting women and children, were living in the wilderness at this time (see Exodus 12:37, AMP). Daily life was challenging. God provided for their basic daily needs, and He also gave them a promise for their future. We learn about it again when Moses met with the leaders and expounded on what was to come:

Now Moses, with the elders of Israel, commanded the people,
saying: "Keep all the commandments which I command you today.
And it shall be, on the day when you cross over the Jordan to the
land which the LORD your God is giving you, that you shall set
up for yourselves large stones, and whitewash them with lime.
You shall write on them all the words of this law, when you have
crossed over, that you may enter the land which the LORD your
God is giving you, 'a land flowing with milk and honey,' just as the
LORD God of your fathers promised you."
DEUTERONOMY 27:1-3

Almighty God gave clear instructions. He created a sure path for the people to follow. The commandments were their marching orders and their guidelines for maintaining a safe and thriving community of people. And He pointed them to a land of relief, redemption, and prosperous living that He had promised them.

Later, God gave Moses an instruction about Canaan, the Promised
Land:

> The LORD spoke to Moses, saying, "Send men to spy out the land
> of Canaan, which I am giving to the children of Israel; from each
> tribe of their fathers you shall send a man, every one a leader
> among them."
>   So Moses sent them from the Wilderness of Paran according to
> the command of the LORD, all of them men who were heads of the
> children of Israel.
> NUMBERS 13:1-3

The twelve men spent forty days in the new land. They traveled
far and wide observing this new place, and most likely imagining their
future there and how life would be for them. Then they returned to the
Wilderness of Paran and gave their report to Moses:

> Then they told him, and said: "We went to the land where you
> sent us. It truly flows with milk and honey, and this is its fruit.
> Nevertheless the people who dwell in the land are strong; the cities
> are fortified and very large; moreover we saw the descendants of
> Anak there. The Amalekites dwell in the land of the South; the
> Hittites, the Jebusites, and the Amorites dwell in the mountains;
> and the Canaanites dwell by the sea and along the banks of the
> Jordan."
>   Then Caleb quieted the people before Moses, and said, "Let
> us go up at once and take possession, for we are well able to
> overcome it."
>   But the men who had gone up with him said, "We are not
> able to go up against the people, for they are stronger than we."
> And they gave the children of Israel a bad report of the land
> which they had spied out, saying, "The land through which we
> have gone as spies is a land that devours its inhabitants, and all
> the people whom we saw in it are men of great stature. There we
> saw the giants (the descendants of Anak came from the giants);

and we were like grasshoppers in our own sight, and so we were
in their sight."
NUMBERS 13:27-33

The story reveals much about the men's attitudes and thoughts. Even though God had promised them the land, they put their trust in what they saw rather than in what God swore to them by His word. They chose to walk by sight rather than by faith. As a result, they gave their bad report to the people, who followed their advice.

All the congregation lifted up their voices and cried, and the people
wept that night. And all the children of Israel complained against
Moses and Aaron, and the whole congregation said to them, "If
only we had died in the land of Egypt! Or if only we had died in
this wilderness! Why has the LORD brought us to this land to fall
by the sword, that our wives and children should become victims?
Would it not be better for us to return to Egypt?" So they said to
one another, "Let us select a leader and return to Egypt."
NUMBERS 14:1-4

Ten of the men saw themselves like grasshoppers. Weak. Helpless. Victims. Forsaken. They adopted that identity rather than the identity God had declared for them. They chose to live in fear rather than believe what God had promised.

Today, as you prepare for your spiritual encounter with God, the One who is the same today, yesterday, and forever, you will also make a choice. Will you choose to walk by faith, or will you choose to walk by sight? Will you follow the direction of your thoughts, or will you put your trust in God and the promises He has given to you by His Word? Will you believe the words of other people who see themselves as weak, helpless, and forsaken victims, or will you see yourself as the redeemed, the overcomer, the conqueror? When you begin your Daniel Fast, will you choose to enter your time of fasting in faith, knowing with certainty that God hears you and is working in your life?

There's still more we can learn from this account that will help you with your choice. Two of the twelve leaders, Caleb and Joshua, chose to walk by faith.

> *Joshua the son of Nun and Caleb the son of Jephunneh, who were among those who had spied out the land, tore their clothes; and they spoke to all the congregation of the children of Israel, saying: "The land we passed through to spy out is an exceedingly good land. If the LORD delights in us, then He will bring us into this land and give it to us, 'a land which flows with milk and honey.' Only do not rebel against the LORD, nor fear the people of the land, for they are our bread; their protection has departed from them, and the LORD is with us. Do not fear them."*
> NUMBERS 14:6-9

Joshua and Caleb remained faithful to their God. They kept the faith. They believed God and continued to follow His ways and live by His commandments. Their choice led them to the blessing. They alone of the tribal leaders were allowed to enter the Promised Land.

These men didn't depend on their own know-how or their own insights. Instead, Caleb and Joshua depended on God for direction, guidance, and strength. By the way, Daniel, whose example of spiritual fasting we follow, also put God before all else that he encountered. We want to follow these examples as we enter into our fast with faith.

YOUR BRIGHT FUTURE AWAITS YOU

Imagine having the weight of the world placed on your shoulders. A heavy, heavy load, right? A burden too big to carry. Who could take on such a task?

That's likely what Joshua felt when Moses died. Joshua had served Moses, the leader of the Israelites, but now Moses was gone and the baton of leadership and responsibility had passed on to Joshua.

God established an assignment for Joshua: He was to lead the people out of the wilderness to the other side of the Jordan River. God knew this was a big task. After all, the Israelites had proven to be an unruly bunch, often turning to their own ways rather than the ways of the Lord. God knew the plight—and He also knew the solution and how to equip Joshua with all he needed for success. God gave clear and specific instructions:

No man shall be able to stand before you all the days of your life; as I was with Moses, so I will be with you. I will not leave you nor forsake you. Be strong and of good courage, for to this people you shall divide as an inheritance the land which I swore to their fathers to give them. Only be strong and very courageous, that you may observe to do according to all the law which Moses My servant commanded you; do not turn from it to the right hand or to the left, that you may prosper wherever you go. This Book of the Law shall not depart from your mouth, but you shall meditate in it day and night, that you may observe to do according to all that is written in it. For then you will make your way prosperous, and then you will have good success. Have I not commanded you? Be strong and of good courage; do not be afraid, nor be dismayed, for the LORD your God is with you wherever you go.
JOSHUA 1:5-9

Dear reader, the Lord your God has the same message for you today. You may feel as if you're in the dark and lonely wilderness, afraid because of bad financial circumstances or uncertainties that seem too big to be resolved. I get that. That's how I felt during my darkest hours. But we don't have to stay in the wilderness.

The truth is, God has a promised land for you. It may take you a while to get there, but He has a good plan for your life. The essential part of the equation for your success is to follow the Lord's instructions. Believe in Him. Declare His Word. Don't look away. Keep your eyes on your Father and His promises for you. And you can start learning and practicing these disciplines of your faith during your Daniel Fast.

God rewards those who follow His ways and who put their trust in Him. He treated Caleb and Joshua according to their faith: "My servant Caleb, because he has a different spirit in him and has followed Me fully, I will bring into the land where he went, and his descendants shall inherit it. . . . Except for Caleb the son of Jephunneh and Joshua the son of Nun, you shall by no means enter the land which I swore I would make you dwell in" (Numbers 14:24, 30).

I have experienced with my own life and from the testimonies of others that following God fully is the way to the promises He has for you. He asks one thing of you, and that is to put your trust in Him and His Word. God promised the land across the Jordan to all the people He had saved from a lifetime of slavery in Egypt. Their assignment was to trust in the Lord, to believe what He told them, and to obey His instructions. All except Caleb and Joshua chose to walk by their own wits rather than trust in the Lord.

For forty years the unfaithful Israelites remained in the wilderness. Those whom God had delivered from slavery never entered the land He had promised them but died in the wilderness, never knowing the land of milk and honey. All except Caleb and Joshua. They believed God. They crossed over. They lived the rest of their days in the land of God's blessing.

You, too, can experience the blessings and breakthrough God has for you. Trust in the Lord's faithfulness as you seek His wisdom and guidance on your fast.

Faithful Servant Action Steps

1. Sit quietly with your eyes closed for about five minutes. Imagine yourself getting ready to meet with a highly esteemed expert who is going to share insights, strategies, and plans that will help you for the rest of your life. What are you hoping he or she might teach you?

2. After your quiet time, write down how you will prepare to be away on your personal retreat, and then write down what you hope to receive from this time.

3. Cut or tear a blank sheet of paper into eight pieces. Write on each piece a fear that's in your mind about your own money situation. Tuck all the pieces together in your Bible, and as you do, say a short prayer to your Lord about what you want to receive from Him during your Daniel Fast.

CHAPTER FOUR

Follow God's Word about Money

Your word is a lamp to my feet and a light to my path.
PSALM 119:105

AFTER I RECEIVED MY BREAKTHROUGH IN FAITH, which started in 2007 with God rescuing me from the dark and desperate place I was in because of my financial calamity, I was convinced that God's way was the best way. So I pounded a stake in the ground of my heart. A stake that marked a commitment to believe God's Word.

That didn't mean I suddenly understood everything in the Scriptures, but the decision served as a road map for my life. From that moment forward, God's Word would point me in the way I should go. If I had a question about something, I would go to His Word for the answers. If I needed direction, I would search His Word to discover the next steps. If I needed guidance, I would comb His Word for the path I should follow.

I've since come to depend on His Word to shape how I want to think, understand, believe, and behave. His Word, His Book, is the defining source and the dependable user's guide for my life. I believe this is what Christians are called to do. And so as we prepare for the Daniel Fast and begin to think about money—what it means in our lives, how we can reduce the struggles we face because of it, and how we should use it—we need to start with a commitment to God's Word and His Kingdom.

A THREEFOLD CORD

God created our minds to see in pictures. When you hear the word *dog*, you don't see the letters *d-o-g*. Instead, you see an image of a dog with your mind's eye. If you hear adjectives—"big dog" or "big black dog"— the picture in your mind changes to that description.

I believe God created this powerful tool of imagination to help us gain understanding in a deeper and more useful way. He teaches us His truths by painting word pictures for us in Scripture. For example, consider this one: "A threefold cord is not quickly broken" (Ecclesiastes 4:12). When I read that truth, I picture a rope made up of three tightly wound strands. The rope is strong, durable, useful, and effective for the purpose for which it's to be used.

I like the picture of the threefold cord, and I use it to think about how to make good and useful decisions for my life.

The first strand of the cord is God. I want to make sure He is at the very center of all I do.

When we think about what we need for our lives, Jesus gives us very clear instructions: "Seek first the kingdom of God and His righteousness, and all these things shall be added to you" (Matthew 6:33). We need to prioritize God and His Kingdom above all else.

Jesus also instructs us to build our lives on God's Word: "Whoever hears these sayings of Mine, and does them, I will liken him to a wise man who built his house on the rock: and the rain descended, the floods came, and the winds blew and beat on that house; and it did not fall, for it was founded on the rock" (Matthew 7:24-25).

So the first strand in the threefold cord is God and His Word. He is always faithful and always wants the very best for us, and His Word is always sure, communicating with us the way we should follow Him.

The second strand of the cord is made of good, sound, and proven principles that are consistent with the Word of God. As we think about our financial matters, we want to make sure our systems, plans, and perspectives are aligned with God's ways. We choose to spend and invest in things that are in harmony with His truths, and we learn to think about and manage money in a way that pleases Him. For example, we wouldn't want to engage in a "get rich quick" scheme or invest our money in companies that bring harm to people or any other part of God's creation.

Your second strand may be the advice you follow from an esteemed financial planner. You may choose to follow a money management system developed by an expert or develop an investment strategy designed for you by a godly adviser. You want to make sure that any practices you use for stewardship and management of your finances are sound and can stand with the first strand: God.

The third strand that helps us make good decisions is us. God calls us to put our trust in Him and to work according to His ways. He also calls us to perform faithfully—to do what we know we should do. When we operate in this way, we can be assured that "a threefold cord is not quickly broken." We want to make sure we're not an inactive strand. We need all three to work in harmony to realize the results we want.

Imagine this: You have God on your side wanting the best for you. You select a great money management plan and system that's in line with godly principles. And then you rarely use the tools! You continue to overspend. Your stack of unopened bills remains in a pile, and your stress continues to soar. That's being the weak strand.

Develop your third strand by setting up a consistent practice to plan your work and work your plan. Be a strong member of the threefold strand that is not quickly broken.

During your Daniel Fast, you'll want to use your threefold strand as you strive to make wise decisions about money. Learn from God's Word. Use good tools and systems. And then make sure you actively shift from taking a worldly approach to your finances to depending on God and His truths.

MONEY VS. FAITH

You don't need to read much of the Bible to know that the Scriptures teach a lot about finances, going all the way back to Genesis and stretching all the way to Revelation. Money is a means of exchange. It's a blessing from the Lord. And our relationship with money is a measure of our faith.

One of the many references to this fact is found in Mark 10:17-22, when Jesus meets with a man we call "the rich young ruler."

Now as He was going out on the road, one came running, knelt before Him, and asked Him, "Good Teacher, what shall I do that I may inherit eternal life?"

So Jesus said to him, "Why do you call Me good? No one is good but One, that is, God. You know the commandments: 'Do not commit adultery,' 'Do not murder,' 'Do not steal,' 'Do not bear false witness,' 'Do not defraud,' 'Honor your father and your mother.'"

And he answered and said to Him, "Teacher, all these things I have kept from my youth."

Then Jesus, looking at him, loved him, and said to him, "One thing you lack: Go your way, sell whatever you have and give to the poor, and you will have treasure in heaven; and come, take up the cross, and follow Me."

But he was sad at this word, and went away sorrowful, for he had great possessions.

This story is packed with valuable truths you and I can learn for our own lives. The obvious point is that the rich young ruler chose his great possessions over the inheritance of eternal life. Jesus could see into the young man's heart, and He pointed out that the man lacked one thing. It all centered on his relationship with money.

So often, we read this passage and don't relate because we don't consider ourselves rich. Consequently, the valuable lesson goes unlearned. However, we can go deeper as we see into the heart of what Jesus was trying to reveal.

For now, let's consider a stark question: *Do you trust God to take care of you?*

If you're feeling a little squeamish right now, don't worry. First, you're like most people—particularly in our society. So much emphasis is placed on what we own. What we drive. What we wear. What kind of house we live in. In our culture, people are valued by what they have and how they look rather than by who they are. And when that's what we value, we start to trust in those things instead of in God. My hope is that you will gain a new perspective about this kind of thinking as you explore God's truth during your Daniel Fast.

Second, your nervousness about this issue is also what Jesus' disciples felt when they witnessed the encounter. They saw the rich young ruler walk away from Jesus because he had more trust in money than he did in God. And when Jesus spoke to His followers, He was clear about what was at the heart of the young man's lack of faith.

> *Then Jesus looked around and said to His disciples, "How hard it is for those who have riches to enter the kingdom of God!" And the disciples were astonished at His words. But Jesus answered again and said to them, "Children, how hard it is for those who trust in riches to enter the kingdom of God! It is easier for a camel to go through the eye of a needle than for a rich man to enter the kingdom of God."*
>
> *And they were greatly astonished, saying among themselves, "Who then can be saved?"*
>
> MARK 10:23-26

If you are now wrestling with this issue, please don't think that you are not saved. Let's be clear: Your salvation doesn't depend on your relationship with money. Scripture says that our salvation rests on our relationship with Christ. But in your heart of hearts, you may know that right now, in your present state of mind, you depend more on money and financial security than you do on God.

I know. I've been there, and I had to confront this issue for myself. However, I was still God's child. I still had eternal life. What I didn't have was the kind of understanding or faith that allowed me to live fully in the Kingdom of God. I didn't know that heaven and the Kingdom of God are two different things. Let me share more.

THE KINGDOM OF GOD

Do you remember what Jesus taught about the Kingdom of God? Ponder what our Lord told the Pharisees:

> *Now when He was asked by the Pharisees when the kingdom of God would come, He answered them and said, "The kingdom of*

God does not come with observation; nor will they say, 'See here!' or 'See there!' For indeed, the kingdom of God is within you."
LUKE 17:20-21

The Kingdom of God is within you. It's a new way of thinking. A new way of believing. The Kingdom of God is different from the worldly kingdom that is under the authority of Satan.

Even if our gospel is veiled, it is veiled to those who are perishing, whose minds the god of this age has blinded, who do not believe, lest the light of the gospel of the glory of Christ, who is the image of God, should shine on them.
2 CORINTHIANS 4:3-4

When you have trusted in Christ, the Kingdom of God is in your heart. It serves as an inner influence. It is your faith and your trust. But the rich young ruler put his trust in money and therefore didn't trust in the Kingdom of God. He chose the values of the world over the values of an entirely different way of thinking and believing. Let's learn more about the Kingdom of God.

Early in Jesus' ministry, He traveled to Galilee. Carefully read the words used in this passage:

Jesus came to Galilee, preaching the gospel of the kingdom of God, and saying, "The time is fulfilled, and the kingdom of God is at hand. Repent, and believe in the gospel."
MARK 1:14-15

Let's examine the phrase that Jesus came "preaching the gospel of the kingdom of God." The word "gospel" literally means "good spell" or "good story." We often think of the gospel as being the Good News that Jesus brought to the world. When we think about the millennia from the time Adam sinned to when Jesus began His ministry on the earth, we can better understand the magnitude of the Good News that He shared with the Jews.

Because of Adam, all humans were made sinners, meaning that we all entered into this world with a "dead" spirit that had previously been connected with the Spirit of God in an intimate way. Adam ate of the forbidden fruit, and on that day his spirit died (see Genesis 2:16-17). Then Jesus came to the earth and paid the price for anyone who believes to be restored into a right relationship with God:

For as by one man's disobedience many were made sinners, so also by one Man's obedience many will be made righteous.
ROMANS 5:19

That truly is good news! The way this world thinks and acts no longer has to determine the way we think and act. We are not under Satan's authority, and we are not part of his worldly system or restrictions. We are different! Profoundly different when we understand more fully that we're now members of God's Kingdom. Jesus is the King. We are citizens in His Kingdom. And He wants God's "on earth as it is in heaven" reality for every one of His residents. This is where we want to gain greater understanding of our lives as Christians. And this is where a deep and intense change can happen in you as you meditate and even wrestle with these truths.

Jesus said, "The time is fulfilled, and the kingdom of God is at hand. Repent, and believe in the gospel." He calls us to repent. Most Christians hear that word and think, *Regret all that I've done wrong before God. Admit that I'm a sinner. Ask for forgiveness so I can be redeemed.* I don't want to toss that response out. Surely, confession and forgiveness are a vital part of our faith. This is the truth, but there's more to it.

The New Testament was written in Greek and then translated into many languages. When we go back to the original text, we find that for "repent," the Greek word used is *metanoeō*, which essentially means "to think differently." It is built from the word *noeō*, which means "to exercise the mind, to comprehend, to consider, perceive, and understand."[1]

If we understand the word this way, we might hear Jesus' message like this: "Think differently. Use your mind to gain a new understanding. The Kingdom of God is available to you right now. Believe in this good news, and it will lead to a new way of living your everyday life."

Jesus invites us to believe differently than the world does—because His Kingdom is different. It is not of this world. In John 17 Jesus underscores this point as he prays to the Father before His betrayal by Judas and arrest in Gethsemane.

> *I have given them Your word; and the world has hated them because they are not of the world, just as I am not of the world. I do not pray that You should take them out of the world, but that You should keep them from the evil one. They are not of the world, just as I am not of the world.*
> JOHN 17:14-16

I'll share more about this truth later, but for now as we focus on the Kingdom of God, take a look at what Jesus told a crowd of people who wanted Him to remain with them so they could learn more from Him:

> *I must preach the kingdom of God to the other cities also, because for this purpose I have been sent.*
> LUKE 4:43

Jesus' purpose was to preach the Kingdom of God, to teach a different way of thinking. Another realm exists beyond what we see and hear, and it's called the Kingdom of God.

Look at this exchange between Pontius Pilate, governor of the Roman province of Judea, and Jesus when our Lord was on trial in the Praetorium, which was the court of Pilate.

> *Jesus answered, "My kingdom is not of this world. If My kingdom were of this world, My servants would fight, so that I should not be delivered to the Jews; but now My kingdom is not from here."*
> *Pilate therefore said to Him, "Are You a king then?"*
> *Jesus answered, "You say rightly that I am a king. For this cause I was born, and for this cause I have come into the world,*

that I should bear witness to the truth. Everyone who is of the
truth hears My voice."

JOHN 18:36-37

Can you hear His voice? The ways of the Kingdom of God don't make sense to the world. And if we're part of the Kingdom, we have an open invitation to embrace its ways and access the benefits of our citizenship.

Can you receive the truths about the Kingdom of God? Can you perceive the mystery of our faith? Look at Jesus' explanation for why He taught some lessons in parables:

> *And the disciples came and said to Him, "Why do You speak to*
> *them in parables?"*
> *He answered and said to them, "Because it has been given to*
> *you to know the mysteries of the kingdom of heaven, but to them*
> *it has not been given. For whoever has, to him more will be given,*
> *and he will have abundance; but whoever does not have, even*
> *what he has will be taken away from him. Therefore I speak to*
> *them in parables, because seeing they do not see, and hearing they*
> *do not hear, nor do they understand. And in them the prophecy of*
> *Isaiah is fulfilled, which says:*
>
> > *'Hearing you will hear and shall not understand,*
> > *And seeing you will see and not perceive;*
> > *For the hearts of this people have grown dull.*
> > *Their ears are hard of hearing,*
> > *And their eyes they have closed,*
> > *Lest they should see with their eyes and hear with their ears,*
> > *Lest they should understand with their hearts and turn,*
> > *So that I should heal them.'*
>
> *"But blessed are your eyes for they see, and your ears for they*
> *hear; for assuredly, I say to you that many prophets and righteous*
> *men desired to see what you see, and did not see it, and to hear*
> *what you hear, and did not hear it."*

MATTHEW 13:10-17

The Kingdom of God is within. It is a mystery to those who don't have the spiritual eyes to see or ears to hear. The Kingdom of God's unseen reality for us is the way of life that followers of Christ can have when they are liberated from the bondage of the world.

When you accepted Jesus Christ into your heart, your spirit was born again. Notice the powerful truths Jesus taught Nicodemus about this in John 3:1-8.

> *There was a man of the Pharisees named Nicodemus, a ruler of the Jews. This man came to Jesus by night and said to Him, "Rabbi, we know that You are a teacher come from God; for no one can do these signs that You do unless God is with him."*
>
> *Jesus answered and said to him, "Most assuredly, I say to you, unless one is born again, he cannot see the kingdom of God."*
>
> *Nicodemus said to Him, "How can a man be born when he is old? Can he enter a second time into his mother's womb and be born?"*
>
> *Jesus answered, "Most assuredly, I say to you, unless one is born of water and the Spirit, he cannot enter the kingdom of God. That which is born of the flesh is flesh, and that which is born of the Spirit is spirit. Do not marvel that I said to you, 'You must be born again.' The wind blows where it wishes, and you hear the sound of it, but cannot tell where it comes from and where it goes. So is everyone who is born of the Spirit."*

Great is our faith. We who have been born again can see the Kingdom of God, and we believe differently from those who don't yet know Jesus and are blind to His truths and His ways. We live according to the ways of God by what Paul calls a mystery:

> *And without controversy great is the mystery of godliness:*
>
> > *God was manifested in the flesh,*
> > *Justified in the Spirit,*
> > *Seen by angels,*

Preached among the Gentiles,
Believed on in the world,
Received up in glory.
1 TIMOTHY 3:16

Our new understanding from our born-again spirit allows us to see and hear the mystery of our faith. Over and over again, Jesus taught lessons and then said, "Those who have ears to hear, let them hear." He wasn't talking about the ears you have on your head. He wasn't talking about hearing audible sounds. He was talking about the ears of your spirit understanding His words and taking them to heart. You have eyes to see and ears to hear the mystery of God's Kingdom and its truths that we can access for our daily lives.

We can hear the truths from God's Word. We can hear from the Lord. We can hear Kingdom-of-God truths from the King of kings and the Lord of lords. Our part is to learn, listen, gain understanding, and grow in our faith.

This brings us back around to the story of the rich young ruler and the questions we must ask of ourselves about the relationship we have with money. Jesus said to His disciples, "Children, how hard it is for those who trust in riches to enter the kingdom of God! It is easier for a camel to go through the eye of a needle than for a rich man to enter the kingdom of God" (Mark 10:24-25). When we have money or possessions, our instinct will be to trust in them—and Jesus is clear that doing that makes it hard for us to trust what is really trustworthy: Him.

We can place our trust in money or we can place our trust in God. The choice is ours, and it's a choice each one of us makes. Where do we find our security—in God or in our bank balance? Where do we find our hope—in God or in our retirement plan? Where do we place our trust—in God or in money? Hear again Jesus' words to Nicodemus in John 3:3, "Most assuredly, I say to you, unless one is born again, he cannot see the kingdom of God." God is calling us into His Kingdom. There we have free access to an entirely different way of life that's rich in promises for our lives now and forever.

It's so important to seek what God's Word says about trusting money, and to embrace the truths of His Kingdom instead of the deceptions of the world. This is foundational as you prepare for your Daniel Fast for financial breakthrough. Over the following chapters, I'm going to open more of the Word so you can understand what it means to trust the Lord with and for your finances. For now, examine your heart. Think about how you feel about money. Ask yourself where you want to place your trust, for that is the destination you will travel to. Remember what happened to the rich young ruler: "But he was sad at this word, and went away sorrowful, for he had great possessions" (Mark 10:22). He chose to put his trust in his possessions, which led him away from Jesus. Choose instead to follow Jesus!

Faithful Servant Action Steps

1. Do you acknowledge God and His Word as your final authority for your life? Take as much time as you need to consider your response. Unpack some of the doubts you may have. Ask the Holy Spirit to lead, direct, and teach you.

2. Where do you place your trust—in money or in God? Don't shake off a response that you wish you didn't have. Instead, recognize it so you know where you are and so you can begin building trust in God.

3. Have you made Christ the Lord of your life? If you answered yes, then you are His child and you're going to heaven. Your next experience in faith is to begin to think differently so you can live today in the Kingdom of God that Jesus came to proclaim. What are your thoughts about living in the Kingdom of God?

CHAPTER FIVE

God's Blessing and Your Stewardship

Beloved, I pray that you may prosper in all things
and be in health, just as your soul prospers.

3 JOHN 1:2

A GUIDING SCRIPTURE FOR ME IS PROVERBS 4:7: "Wisdom is the principal thing; therefore get wisdom. And in all your getting, get understanding." Our God is the author of wisdom. He is all truth. We can count on Him and His Word to be our guiding light in all we do. Psalm 119:105 reminds us, "Your word is a lamp to my feet and a light to my path."

So as we focus on finances, we need to let Scripture be our highest authority and inform our attitudes and perspectives. In this chapter we'll take a look at what God teaches us from His Word about prosperity, a hot topic in today's Christian circles.

Before we begin, try to erase from your mind your current ideas about what prosperity means. Let's learn the truth from God's Word.

The word *prosperity*, or its derivatives, appears in the Bible as a whole more than one hundred times. We find it both in the Old Testament (originally written in Hebrew) and the New Testament (originally written in Greek). The Bible is clear that prosperity is a positive condition and a blessing of the Lord, and it encompasses so much more than money. The Hebrew word most often used for "prosper" is *tsalach*, which means "to push forward, to break out, to come mightily, go over, be good, to be meet (secure), and to be profitable."[1] Another word that is sometimes translated "prosper" is the Hebrew word *sakal*, which means "to be intelligent, to be prudent, to have good success, to teach and give wisdom, to behave wisely and guide wittingly."[2] The related word *shalah*, which means "to be tranquil (secure or successful), to be happy, or to be in safety," is also sometimes used for "prosper."[3]

One of the Hebrew words rendered "prosperity" is *tob*, which means "good or a good thing, well, beautiful, best, bountiful, cheerful, at ease, favor, fine, graciously, joyful, kindly, loving, merry, most, pleasant, ready, sweet, wealth, to be well favored."[4] Another Hebrew word sometimes translated "prosperity" is *shalom*, meaning "safe, well, good health, prosperous, peace, all is well."[5]

We can clearly see from these definitions that prosperity encompassed many different aspects of life, from wisdom to safety to character to health and peace. We read in the Old Testament that God wanted His people to prosper—to have all parts of their lives good and strong and at peace. He wanted them to be secure financially, but also to have good ways of thinking and behaving. He wanted His people to be aligned with His ways and to put their trust in Him as their God, the one above all else.

When the Lord prepared Joshua to assume leadership over the Israelites before they entered the Promised Land, He gave him this instruction:

> *This Book of the Law shall not depart from your mouth, but you shall meditate in it day and night, that you may observe to do according to all that is written in it. For then you will make your way prosperous, and then you will have good success.*
> JOSHUA 1:8

The same Hebrew word is used here for both "prosperous" and "success." The Lord was telling the people to live according to His ways in all areas of life, and the result would be good, peaceful, joyful, secure, and happy lives.

God wants you to be prosperous in the fullness of what we learn in

His Word. He is first. And anytime we start thinking about prosperity in a prideful way, believing that it's about us and having more possessions, we're moving away from God and into worldly thinking. Multiple Scripture verses use variants of the word *prosper*. You can go to Daniel-Fast.com/breakthrough to find a more exhaustive list. Here are a few to consider now:

Therefore keep the words of this covenant, and do them, that you may prosper in all that you do.
DEUTERONOMY 29:9

Then the LORD your God will bring you to the land which your fathers possessed, and you shall possess it. He will prosper you and multiply you more than your fathers.
DEUTERONOMY 30:5

Keep the charge of the LORD your God: to walk in His ways, to keep His statutes, His commandments, His judgments, and His testimonies, as it is written in the Law of Moses, that you may prosper in all that you do and wherever you turn.
1 KINGS 2:3

If they obey and serve Him, they shall spend their days in prosperity, and their years in pleasures.
JOB 36:11

Who is the man that fears the LORD? Him shall He teach in the way He chooses. He himself shall dwell in prosperity, and his descendants shall inherit the earth. The secret of the LORD is with those who fear Him, and He will show them His covenant.
PSALM 25:12-14

The Greek word meaning "prosper" used in New Testament writings is *euodoō*, which is a compound word meaning "to succeed in reaching, as in business affairs or on one's journey."[6]

> *Beloved, I pray that you may prosper in all things and be in health, just as your soul prospers.*
> 3 JOHN 1:2

Prosperity from the Lord is a blessing. He wants you to prosper. He established a good life for humankind in the beginning when He gave Adam and Eve all they needed for wholeness, health, and well-being, and that's what He wants for you now, under the new covenant with Jesus as your King.

However, the prosperity and success that God wants for you are not like those of the world. Today, people's value is often measured by how much money they have or by their fame or their looks. Those are the world's measurements of success. Our God measures success through the heart, as we see in these Scriptures:

> *The LORD said to Samuel, "Do not look at his appearance or at his physical stature, because I have refused him. For the LORD does not see as man sees; for man looks at the outward appearance, but the LORD looks at the heart."*
> 1 SAMUEL 16:7

> *Examine me, O LORD, and prove me; try my mind and my heart.*
> PSALM 26:2

During your Daniel Fast, I encourage you to examine your heart. You can identify attitudes, desires, and beliefs that are not consistent with the way of the Lord—and then change them. Allow new understanding to permeate your thoughts. Let your attitudes about possessions, wealth, success, and health be renewed by truths from God's Word.

Those who examine their thoughts become the best thinkers, which may be why God's Word calls us to test every thought against the truths of Christ. Scripture tells us, "For the weapons of our warfare are not carnal but mighty in God for pulling down strongholds, casting down arguments and every high thing that exalts itself against the knowledge of God, bringing every thought into captivity to the obedience of Christ, and being ready to punish all disobedience when your obedience is ful-filled" (2 Corinthians 10:4-6).

Because God is most concerned with our hearts and minds—our inward thoughts and attitudes—it's clear that his view of prosperity involves so much more than finances. Prosperity is living a Kingdom-of-God lifestyle. It's putting God first in your life and seeing Him as your Provider. It's loving Him, serving Him, and inviting Him to be the Master over every part of your life. It's the life in Christ that each of us can live as we enter the Kingdom of God and accept the invitation of our Lord Jesus to change the way we think.

YOU ARE GOD'S STEWARD

Are you ready for an additional transformation of your thoughts? I'm inviting you to make a shift in your thinking about all that you have now and all that you want for your future.

The Bible teaches us that everything is God's. We read in Psalm 24:1, "The earth is the LORD's, and all its fullness, the world and those who dwell therein." And the Word also teaches us that God gave humankind, including you and me, possession of the earth: "The heaven, even the heavens, are the LORD's; but the earth He has given to the children of men" (Psalm 115:16).

Everything is God's through His creation. After He created, He gave the earth to Adam and all humankind that would follow:

Then God said, "Let Us make man in Our image, according to Our likeness; let them have dominion over the fish of the sea, over the birds of the air, and over the cattle, over all the earth and over every creeping thing that creeps on the earth. . . . Then God blessed them, and God said to them, "Be fruitful and multiply; fill the earth and subdue it; have dominion over the fish of the sea, over the birds of the air, and over every living thing that moves on the earth."
GENESIS 1:26, 28

To help understand this concept of stewardship and our role with God, we can consider a human example. You've most likely heard of Bill Gates, the cofounder of Microsoft and one of the richest men in the world, whose net worth is more than $100 billion. He and his wife lead a nonprofit called the Bill and Melinda Gates Foundation. At this writing, they have donated more than $27 billion through their acts of philanthropy and give about $5 billion each year focusing on global health, education, and poverty.

Bill and Melinda Gates fund the foundation. They set the mission and the direction for the work that will be conducted through the foundation. But they don't run the day-to-day operations. It's their money. It's their foundation. It's based on their hopes and dreams. But the administration of the charity is the responsibility of their CEO (Chief Executive Officer). He is the steward, or the caretaker. And he has been given the task of making sure everything functions in the manner that Bill and Melinda Gates desire.

The same is true for you and me and everyone to whom God has given the goods of the earth. It's all His as the Creator and as almighty God. He shares it with us and gives us the responsibility to wisely care for all that He's placed in our possession.

Take a minute right now to look around at the things you consider yours. If you're reading this book in your home, you might see furniture, books, a vehicle, clothes, food, a roof over your head, and much more. Everything you have is from God through His creation. He's put you in position as the steward, or the caretaker, for what He's placed in your care.

King David talked about the things that come from God:

Both riches and honor come from You, and You reign over all. In Your hand is power and might; in Your hand it is to make great and to give strength to all.
1 CHRONICLES 29:12

We're not only stewards of money and physical things but of spiritual gifts and skills as well:

As each one has received a gift, minister it to one another, as good stewards of the manifold grace of God.
1 PETER 4:10

Imagine that your life purpose is to fulfill the mission of your Lord. He is the leader. He is the one who set the mission, He is the one who provides the resources, and He is the one who places you in the position of responsibility to fulfill His desires. You are a caretaker. You are the CEO of your life.

When we adopt the role and the mindset of being God's stewards, we behave differently. We come under His authority in a more profound way. We realize that we are vital members of God's purpose on the earth, and we want to align our lives and actions with His ways. We are His and He is ours! Hebrews 8:10 underscores our identity: "I will put My laws in their mind and write them on their hearts; and I will be their God, and they shall be My people."

Here is the simple yet profound truth about God, you, and your life.

1. God created you in His image in the exact way He wanted you to be.

2. When you accepted Christ as your Lord, you became a child of God and a dwelling place of God's Holy Spirit.

3. As you love the Lord your God with all your heart, all your soul, and all your mind, His laws are written on your heart.

4. You have become a citizen of the Kingdom of God through your faith. You are in this world but not of it. You are a member of the holy family, separated for His purposes on the earth.

5. God gives you everything you need to live for Him, safe and secure in His love, finding happiness and success in His will. You are a steward of all that He has placed in your hands.

6. You are a vital player in His work.

As you gain understanding of God's ways for your life as a steward, see yourself in the parable of the talents:

> *For the kingdom of heaven is like a man traveling to a far country, who called his own servants and delivered his goods to them. And to one he gave five talents, to another two, and to another one, to each according to his own ability; and immediately he went on a journey. Then he who had received the five talents went and traded with them, and made another five talents. And likewise he who had received two gained two more also. But he who had received one went and dug in the ground, and hid his lord's money. After a long time the lord of those servants came and settled accounts with them.*
> MATTHEW 25:14-19

Do you see the similarity between this parable and the story about Bill and Melinda Gates? In the parable, the master placed his money into the hands of three different men. He gave them the responsibility of managing the resources and acting in his best interests. Then he came back to see how the men had served him.

> *He who had received five talents came and brought five other talents, saying, "Lord, you delivered to me five talents; look, I have gained five more talents besides them." His lord said to him, "Well done, good and faithful servant; you were faithful over a few things, I will make you ruler over many things. Enter into the joy of your lord." He also who had received two talents came and said, "Lord, you delivered to me two talents; look, I have gained two more talents besides them." His lord said to him, "Well done, good and faithful servant; you have been faithful over a few things, I will make you ruler over many things. Enter into the joy of your lord."*
> MATTHEW 25:20-23

There are a few valuable lessons for us in this passage. First, the master expected the men to use his resources wisely and act on his behalf as a prosperous businessman. He expected them to be wise stewards, as careful with his money as they would be with their own. Second, while the two men were given different amounts, one more and one less, they were both expected to do their best with what they had for the sake of their master. And in fact, they both doubled the investment and they both gained the same reward.

The reality is that some people do have more than others. However, no matter what our income level, we are each called to use the resources put into our care wisely and for the purpose of our Master. What does He want us to do with the money, possessions, and abilities He has given us?

Now let's look at the third man who received money from the master:

Then he who had received the one talent came and said, "Lord, I knew you to be a hard man, reaping where you have not sown, and gathering where you have not scattered seed. And I was afraid, and went and hid your talent in the ground. Look, there you have what is yours."

MATTHEW 25:24-25

What can we learn from this part of the story? First, the third man perceived the master in a way that didn't match who he really was. Don't we do the same at times? We need to make sure we know the truth about God so we respond to Him the right way. We get to know Him by developing a relationship with Him, studying Scripture, and learning His true character.

Second, the man acted in fear. His motivation for hiding the money was to be safe. He didn't serve his master; he served himself, which is the opposite of being a good steward. His master was not pleased.

Third, the man focused on what he *didn't* want—the negative response from the master—rather than what he *did* want, which was success for himself and the master.

His lord answered and said to him, "You wicked and lazy servant, you knew that I reap where I have not sown, and gather where I have not scattered seed. So you ought to have deposited my money

*with the bankers, and at my coming I would have received back
my own with interest. So take the talent from him, and give it to
him who has ten talents.*

*"For to everyone who has, more will be given, and he will have
abundance; but from him who does not have, even what he has
will be taken away."*
MATTHEW 25:26-29

The consequences of poor stewardship in this parable are fierce. Yet
the rewards for responsible stewardship are better than we can ever create
for ourselves. The master said to his faithful servants, "Well done, good
and faithful servant; you have been faithful over a few things, I will make
you ruler over many things. Enter into the joy of your lord."

Faithful servants are rewarded. Our faithfulness and our abilities are
expected to grow and get better. And as they do, we are given more.
More for ourselves? No, more to be of service to the Lord.

GROWING IN ABUNDANCE

As you prepare for your Daniel Fast and consider yourself as the steward of all that God gives you, take hold of the truths about financial
resources in this passage from His Word:

*God will generously provide all you need. Then you will always
have everything you need and plenty left over to share with others.*
2 CORINTHIANS 9:8, NLT

Our God is so amazing, and His Word is powerful and awesome.
Look at what He's showing us in this passage.

First, God puts His grace into action so that you will have what you
need for your livelihood—and "plenty left over" so you can be generous
with others. Some translations use the word "abundance." I believe that
means bills paid. Food in the cupboard. Clothes on your back. A roof
over your head. And more to share . . . that's abundance.

And it all comes from Him. We'll talk more about seeing the Lord
as your Provider in the next chapter, but start to get this truth into your

thinking. Bill and Melinda Gates are the ones who fund the good works of the Gates Foundation. The master in the parable of the talents was the one who funded the work of his servants. And here we see that God is the one who, through His grace, serves as our Provider. Yes, we work for wages. We are part of the equation. But He is the force behind it all. Deuteronomy 8:18 says, "You shall remember the LORD your God, for it is He who gives you power to get wealth, that He may establish His covenant which He swore to your fathers, as it is this day."

God is the funder! He is your Source. He is your Jehovah Jireh, God the Provider. He is the one who is able to make all grace abound toward you so you will have everything you need for your life.

He provides more than enough for you because it's part of His economic plan! He wants you to have a good life. He wants you to serve Him by ministering for Him on the earth, so He gives you more than you need so you can do His work as His steward. When you do, you're beginning to fulfill your purpose.

Faithful Servant Action Steps

1. What are three things you've learned about God's vision of prosperity that you want to embrace and experience in your life? List them in your journal.

2. What do you believe to be God's purpose for giving you money?

3. Pause and think about where you get your attitudes and beliefs about money and finances. Do your beliefs come from your parents? From the world? From the teachings of friends or associates? Or do they come from God and His Word?

CHAPTER SIX

God Is Your Provider

Seek first the kingdom of God and His righteousness,
and all these things shall be added to you.

MATTHEW 6:33

MY BREAKTHROUGH BACK IN DECEMBER 2007 changed both my mind
and my life. Scales of misunderstanding fell from my spiritual eyes, and
I saw God in an entirely different way. He became more real to me.
More present. More significant in my everyday life. My spiritual growth
soared, yet I still had so much to learn and to experience.

What I now realize is that even though I had been a Christian for
more than thirty years by that time, I was still a baby Christian. A carnal
Christian. That's what Paul called the immature believers in the church
in Corinth.

> *I, brethren, could not speak to you as to spiritual people but as to*
> *carnal, as to babes in Christ. I fed you with milk and not with*
> *solid food; for until now you were not able to receive it, and even*
> *now you are still not able; for you are still carnal.*
>
> 1 CORINTHIANS 3:1-3

The Greek word translated "carnal" is *sarkikos*, which means "pertain-
ing to the flesh," "fleshly," or "unregenerate."[1] The word is derived from
sarx, which means "flesh" or "of the body" as opposed to "of the spirit or

the soul."[2] These words can also reflect the notion of "from the human nature," a nature which has a desire to follow the passions of the flesh and has a mind set on the natural way of thinking rather than on the spiritual way of thinking and believing.

Yes, I believed in God. I believed in Christ. I was saved and I was assured of eternal life. But I was still living too much from my "natural man" rather than my born-again spirit. I still depended too much on myself and not enough on God. I was still ignorant of much about living a spirit-led life. Galatians 5:25 gives us an important instruction: "If we live in the Spirit, let us also walk in the Spirit." My spirit was born again. I had the Holy Spirit of God living in me. But I wasn't walking in the Spirit the way Romans 8 tells us to do.

There is therefore now no condemnation to those who are in Christ Jesus, who do not walk according to the flesh, but according to the Spirit.
ROMANS 8:1

I'm not talking about living a sinful life. I lived an upstanding life and I had a good reputation. I studied the Bible and even taught Bible study classes to children and adults. But I was still spiritually immature. I just didn't know it—that is, until I began my journey in December 2007.

We grow in our faith over the years. And while we have periods of stability or even stagnation, where nothing much changes, we also have times when we make major shifts as God reveals more of Himself and His wisdom to us. Sometimes it takes a life challenge for us to be open enough—shocked enough—to receive the new and life-changing information and act on it.

It's similar to people who haven't taken their health seriously. They eat whatever they want whenever they want. They don't worry about the ingredients in foods or if a meal has too much fat, salt, or sugar. If it's satisfying to the taste buds, they eat it . . . and oftentimes they want more satisfaction, so they overeat. But then they have a health crisis. Their bodies can't keep up with their poor eating habits, so their bodies go on strike. Type 2 diabetes. High blood pressure. High cholesterol. Heart attack. Stroke. Obesity. The health crisis serves as the catalyst that sets these individuals on a new course of discovery and change. They bring what was out of order into order. They take better care of their bodies, which then respond in a positive way with more energy, weight loss, and safe levels for their blood sugar, cholesterol, and blood pressure.

In the same way, my financial crisis ignited my spiritual growth. I started to see God differently. I entered into a Kingdom-of-God understanding of Him. And one of the most notable shifts occurred when I stopped depending on myself and started seeing God as my Provider.

GOD THE PROVIDER

We've talked about the Bible being our ultimate authority for life, so we want to go to the Scriptures to see the truth about God and His provision for us. In Matthew 6, Jesus teaches about two types of dependency. He's talking about money issues, stress, worry, and where we invest our trust and reliance.

> No one can serve two masters; for either he will hate the one and love the other, or else he will be loyal to the one and despise the other. You cannot serve God and mammon.
>
> Therefore I say to you, do not worry about your life, what you will eat or what you will drink; nor about your body, what you will put on. Is not life more than food and the body more than clothing? Look at the birds of the air, for they neither sow nor reap nor gather into barns; yet your heavenly Father feeds them. Are you not of more value than they? Which of you by worrying can add one cubit to his stature?
>
> So why do you worry about clothing? Consider the lilies of the field, how they grow: they neither toil nor spin; and yet I say to you that even Solomon in all his glory was not arrayed like one of these. Now if God so clothes the grass of the field, which today is, and tomorrow is thrown into the oven, will He not much more clothe you, O you of little faith?
>
> Therefore do not worry, saying, "What shall we eat?" or "What shall we drink?" or "What shall we wear?" For after all these

things the Gentiles seek. For your heavenly Father knows that you
need all these things. But seek first the kingdom of God and His
righteousness, and all these things shall be added to you. Therefore
do not worry about tomorrow, for tomorrow will worry about its
own things. Sufficient for the day is its own trouble.
MATTHEW 6:24-34

Jesus is teaching some deep, profound truths here. Let's take a close look at His words so we can hear Him with our spiritual ears, update our thinking, and then respond from our renewed minds.

First, Jesus says there are two places where we will place our love, loyalty, and service: either in God or in mammon, which is wealth personified with the characteristics of greed and covetousness. Most people think only the wealthy put their trust in money, but it's clear from this passage that this isn't the case.

Jesus is pointing out that when people worry about their livelihood, food, and clothing, they are placing their trust in money. Wealthy people don't often need to worry about such trivial matters, but people of lesser means do. I did—and so I found myself in this passage. I don't think I was greedy; in fact, I've always liked giving money to worthy causes and volunteering my time and talents. But I was crazy worried about my business, my money, my bills, my mortgage, and my future. I wasn't trusting God to meet my needs, and I didn't see God as my Provider. Instead, I focused on my bank balance. On the upcoming invoices. On the dark picture of my future that I painted in my mind.

Jesus tells his listeners not to worry, but instead to trust in God as their Provider. He gave the comparison of the Gentiles worrying about what they will eat or drink or wear. Gentiles in this case meant those who didn't believe in the God of Abraham, Isaac, and Jacob. Then, by contrast, in verse 34 Jesus made this powerful statement about how you and I, as believers, are to think and trust:

Your heavenly Father knows that you need all these things. But
seek first the kingdom of God and His righteousness, and all
these things shall be added to you. Therefore do not worry about

tomorrow, for tomorrow will worry about its own things. Sufficient for the day is its own trouble.
MATTHEW 6:32-34

Don't worry. Trust God as your Provider. That is our instruction from Jesus Christ, whether we are rich or poor or anywhere in between.

As harsh as this may sound, our worry and stress about money is a measure of our faith. Do we put our trust and confidence in God? Or do we put our trust and confidence in money?

This is a big deal. And as I've mentioned earlier, this shift requires some deep thinking, praying, and transforming regarding how we believe. Your Daniel Fast is the perfect runway for you to enter into this deep spiritual transformation.

Let's back up for a minute. My assumption is that you are reading this book because you want to know how God can help, lead, and direct you concerning your finances. Right? Maybe you're in crisis and you're not sure what to do. Or perhaps you're exhausted from carrying the weight of your money issues for so long, and you want relief and answers. Maybe you want to take a step in your faith and bring Christ into the center of your financial business. Whatever the reason, you're reading this book to see what God has to show you about Him and your money.

Here is a fact that you need to accept: The truths that the Bible teaches about finances won't operate in your life until you first recognize God as your Source. And I don't mean in a platitudinal kind of way, where you say it but don't really believe it. I mean in a stark, unqualified, deep-in-your-heart kind of way. God alone is the source of everything we have.

That's the way Abraham thought about God. He recognized Him and honored Him as his Source for all he owned.

ABRAHAM BELIEVED GOD TO BE HIS SOURCE

The life of our patriarch Abraham, his coming to faith, and his long journey as our father of faith work together to give us a powerful model to follow. Genesis 17:5 shows God renaming Abraham as part of the covenant:

*No longer shall your name be called Abram, but your name
shall be Abraham; for I have made you a father of many
nations.*

In the book of Romans, Paul holds up Abraham as our father in
faith:

*Therefore it is of faith that it might be according to grace, so that
the promise might be sure to all the seed, not only to those who are
of the law, but also to those who are of the faith of Abraham, who
is the father of us all (as it is written, "I have made you a father of
many nations") in the presence of Him whom he believed—God,
who gives life to the dead and calls those things which do not exist
as though they did.*
ROMANS 4:16-17

Let's look at Abraham and his journey in faith as God introduces
Himself to the man and shows Himself to be the source of all.

When his father died, Abram (whose name God later changed to
Abraham) was married to Sarai (later called Sarah) and living in Haran,
now in present-day Turkey. That's when almighty God spoke to him
and instructed him to leave all he had known and move to another
place.

Now the LORD had said to Abram:

    "Get out of your country,
    From your family
    And from your father's house,
    To a land that I will show you.
    I will make you a great nation;
    I will bless you
    And make your name great;
    And you shall be a blessing.
    I will bless those who bless you,

And I will curse him who curses you;
And in you all the families of the earth shall be blessed."
GENESIS 12:1-3

The number of promises in this short passage is amazing. The Lord told Abram He would:

- show him a new land,
- make him a great nation,
- bless him,
- make his name great,
- bless those who blessed him, and
- curse those who cursed him.

God established Himself as the Source of everything for Abram and the Source of everything to all his descendants (of whom you are one—see Romans 4:13). The great I AM instituted Himself as the all-in-all "I will." Every good thing that would come into Abraham's life was from the hand of God.

When you study the entire story of Abraham (Genesis 12–25), you'll see that God gave him a whole-life blessing. A complete blessing. God blessed Abram in every area of his life, even when Abram made serious mistakes. And Abram received the blessing of God through faith, not because of his own effort.

God blessed Abram with a position as the father of many nations and more people than he could count.

Therefore from one man, and him as good as dead, were born as
many as the stars of the sky in multitude—innumerable as the
sand which is by the seashore.
HEBREWS 11:12

He also blessed Abram with possessions and wealth. Abram became rich in livestock, silver, and gold. His riches weren't due to his business prowess; he was rich because of God. We see proof of that when Abram gave up the best land to his nephew, Lot. Lot had traveled long distances with Abram. And both men, after leaving their homeland, had become very rich, and their herds had multiplied:

> *Lot also, who went with Abram, had flocks and herds and tents. Now the land was not able to support them, that they might dwell together, for their possessions were so great that they could not dwell together. And there was strife between the herdsmen of Abram's livestock and the herdsmen of Lot's livestock. The Canaanites and the Perizzites then dwelt in the land.*
>
> *So Abram said to Lot, "Please let there be no strife between you and me, and between my herdsmen and your herdsmen; for we are brethren. Is not the whole land before you? Please separate from me. If you take the left, then I will go to the right; or, if you go to the right, then I will go to the left."*
> GENESIS 13:5-9

Imagine that scene. Abram had huge herds, a wife, and many people who looked to him for their support. The choice about which land he would dwell in was a choice for his future. Yet he let Lot make the choice because Abram saw God as his Source. He trusted God with his future.

> *Lot lifted his eyes and saw all the plain of Jordan, that it was well watered everywhere (before the LORD destroyed Sodom and Gomorrah) like the garden of the LORD, like the land of Egypt as you go toward Zoar. Then Lot chose for himself all the plain of Jordan, and Lot journeyed east. And they separated from each other. Abram dwelt in the land of Canaan, and Lot dwelt in the cities of the plain and pitched his tent even as far as Sodom. But the men of Sodom were exceedingly wicked and sinful against the LORD.*
> GENESIS 13:10-13

At first glance, we see that Lot chose the best land—land that was "well watered everywhere." It appears that he would have the best future. But then we also see that there's more happening here, as there often is in our own lives. Proverbs 21:2 shows us that what seems right to us may not always be so: "Every way of a man is right in his own eyes, but the LORD weighs the hearts." Lot chose the best land from what seems to have been a heart of greed and selfishness. He could have chosen the best land for his elder uncle, Abram, but he didn't. And an unseen challenge awaited him in his new home. Meanwhile, Abram put his trust in God.

> *The LORD said to Abram, after Lot had separated from him: "Lift your eyes now and look from the place where you are—northward, southward, eastward, and westward; for all the land which you see I give to you and your descendants forever. And I will make your descendants as the dust of the earth; so that if a man could number the dust of the earth, then your descendants also could be numbered. Arise, walk in the land through its length and its width, for I give it to you."*
>
> *Then Abram moved his tent, and went and dwelt by the terebinth trees of Mamre, which are in Hebron, and built an altar there to the LORD.*
>
> GENESIS 13:14-18

God gave Abram more than he could ever gain, inherit, or even imagine for himself. God gave the land along with the blessing for what was to come. God was Abram's Source.

Meanwhile, Lot had gone a different way, to a land full of evil and warring men. He chose to go one direction, which brought him into a region where four kings warred against five other kings. The four kings and their armies were overpowered. Some fled the region. Others died. Meanwhile, the five kings gathered all the goods and some captives— and one of them was Lot, Abram's nephew.

Word of Lot's capture reached Abram, and his loyalty immediately kicked in. He gathered all his available forces and arranged a plan to rescue his nephew.

Now when Abram heard that [Lot] was taken captive, he armed his three hundred and eighteen trained servants who were born in his own house, and went in pursuit as far as Dan. He divided his forces against them by night, and he and his servants attacked them and pursued them as far as Hobah, which is north of Damascus. So he brought back all the goods, and also brought back his brother Lot and his goods, as well as the women and the people.

And the king of Sodom went out to meet him at the Valley of Shaveh (that is, the King's Valley), after his return from the defeat of Chedorlaomer and the kings who were with him.

GENESIS 14:14-17

Abram to the rescue! He not only liberated Lot, but he also salvaged all his goods, as well as all the goods of the kings and their women and children. He was the hero and clearly deserved honor. Then something unusual happened.

Then Melchizedek king of Salem brought out bread and wine; he was the priest of God Most High. And he blessed him and said:

"Blessed be Abram of God Most High,
Possessor of heaven and earth;
And blessed be God Most High,
Who has delivered your enemies into your hand."

And [Abram] gave him a tithe of all.

GENESIS 14:18-20

This passage is packed with truths and foretelling, which we'll talk about more in chapter 7. For now, let's look at a couple of key points. First, Melchizedek was the king of Salem and the priest of God. Hundreds of years later, the psalmist wrote, "In Salem also is His tabernacle, and His dwelling place in Zion" (Psalm 76:2). Mount Zion is the easternmost of the two hills of ancient Jerusalem. So Melchizedek was not only a priest but also the king of the area that would come to be known as Jerusalem.

Second, Melchizedek declared that God had delivered Abram's enemies into his hands. This was a fulfillment of God's promise to Abraham: "I will curse him who curses you."

And third, while Abram was being blessed for his heroism, he honored Melchizedek with a tithe (one-tenth) of all the goods he had gained in the battle. This is the first recorded tithe, given to the king of Salem and the priest of the Most High God.

Abram had defeated the enemy and taken all the goods they had stolen. He freed the women and children from captivity, and he freed his nephew Lot and regained all his stolen goods. Now the king of Sodom wanted to reward Abram:

> Now the king of Sodom said to Abram, "Give me the persons, and take the goods for yourself."
> But Abram said to the king of Sodom, "I have raised my hand to the LORD, God Most High, the Possessor of heaven and earth, that I will take nothing, from a thread to a sandal strap, and that I will not take anything that is yours, lest you should say, 'I have made Abram rich'—except only what the young men have eaten, and the portion of the men who went with me: Aner, Eshcol, and Mamre; let them take their portion."
> GENESIS 14:21-24

Abram said he had made an oath to God and he didn't want anyone to think that they had made him rich, so he took none of the goods for himself. He looked out for the needs of his troops, but he personally took nothing. None of the goods were ever his; he had only served and recovered what had been lost. And throughout this situation, he saw God as his Source.

ENTERING INTO A COVENANT

> After these things the word of the LORD came to Abram in a vision, saying, "Do not be afraid, Abram. I am your shield, your exceedingly great reward."

> *But Abram said, "Lord GOD, what will You give me, seeing*
> *I go childless, and the heir of my house is Eliezer of Damascus?"*
> *Then Abram said, "Look, You have given me no offspring; indeed*
> *one born in my house is my heir!"*
> *And behold, the word of the LORD came to him, saying,*
> *"This one shall not be your heir, but one who will come from*
> *your own body shall be your heir." Then He brought him outside*
> *and said, "Look now toward heaven, and count the stars if you*
> *are able to number them." And He said to him, "So shall your*
> *descendants be."*
> *And he believed in the LORD, and He accounted it to him for*
> *righteousness.*
> *Then He said to him, "I am the LORD, who brought you out*
> *of Ur of the Chaldeans, to give you this land to inherit it."*
> *And he said, "Lord GOD, how shall I know that I will*
> *inherit it?"*
> GENESIS 15:1-8

Please keep in mind that God, over and over again, was establishing that He is the source of all that is good. He is the source of the blessing. And now He was showing Abram that he would be the forefather of more people than he could ever count.

Abram was an older man by now. And Sarai, his wife, was past her childbearing years. Yet Abram heard God's promise to him, and he believed. But now he was asking the Lord for a sign. "How will I know, Lord?"

This leads us to a stunning display of God's goodness that was for Abram's benefit then and remains for our benefit today: God instituted an everlasting covenant with Abram. This wasn't like a handshake agreement; this was a deeply committed promise.

In ancient Hebrew culture, a covenant was established between the two parties of the agreement, and a ritual was practiced to mark the solemn occasion. The men would take one or more fattened animals, usually the best of the flock, and cut them into two pieces. They would then lay the pieces in two rows, leaving a path through the center. The blood of the animals would flow onto the path, and the two individuals making the covenant with each other would walk on the path between the pieces, symbolizing their commitment to the promise. By their actions they were saying, "If I do not hold to the agreements of this covenant, you can do to me what we did to these animals."[3]

This practice of establishing a covenant is recorded clearly in Jeremiah 34:18-20:

> *I will give the men who have transgressed My covenant, who have not performed the words of the covenant which they made before Me, when they cut the calf in two and passed between the parts of it—the princes of Judah, the princes of Jerusalem, the eunuchs, the priests, and all the people of the land who passed between the parts of the calf—I will give them into the hand of their enemies and into the hand of those who seek their life. Their dead bodies shall be for meat for the birds of the heaven and the beasts of the earth.*

This type of covenant is called a "cutting covenant" or a "blood covenant." A covenant was not a light notion; instead, it was a promise that would never be broken. When Abram asked God how he would know that the promises about his having countless descendants would come to pass, God's response was to instruct Abram to arrange the blood covenant.

Carefully read what took place during this covenant between these two parties, God and Abram:

> *He said to him, "Bring Me a three-year-old heifer, a three-year-old female goat, a three-year-old ram, a turtledove, and a young pigeon." Then he brought all these to Him and cut them in two, down the middle, and placed each piece opposite the other; but he did not cut the birds in two. And when the vultures came down on the carcasses, Abram drove them away.*

Now when the sun was going down, a deep sleep fell upon Abram; and behold, horror and great darkness fell upon him. Then He said to Abram: "Know certainly that your descendants will be strangers in a land that is not theirs, and will serve them, and they will afflict them four hundred years. And also the nation whom they serve I will judge; afterward they shall come out with great possessions. Now as for you, you shall go to your fathers in peace; you shall be buried at a good old age. But in the fourth generation they shall return here, for the iniquity of the Amorites is not yet complete."

And it came to pass, when the sun went down and it was dark, that behold, there appeared a smoking oven and a burning torch that passed between those pieces. On the same day the LORD made a covenant with Abram, saying:

"To your descendants I have given this land, from the river of Egypt to the great river, the River Euphrates—the Kenites, the Kenezzites, the Kadmonites, the Hittites, the Perizzites, the Rephaim, the Amorites, the Canaanites, the Girgashites, and the Jebusites."

GENESIS 15:9-21

Did you see the amazing act of love that your God displayed when He made the everlasting blood covenant with Abram? Abram readied everything, but then he went into a deep sleep. And while he slept, God, in the form of a flame, walked between the pieces making the covenant with Himself.[4] Nothing Abram would do in the future could break the covenant, because the promise that God made to Abram then, and to all the descendants to come, was to Himself. No person could ever void this promise.

When God made a promise to Abraham, because He could swear by no one greater, He swore by Himself, saying, "Surely blessing I will bless you, and multiplying I will multiply you."

HEBREWS 6:13-14

The same promise God made to Abram is yours today. As a follower of Jesus Christ, you are a descendant of Abraham and under the same covenant of blessing, as we read in both Romans and Galatians.

Therefore it is of faith that it might be according to grace, so that the promise might be sure to all the seed, not only to those who are of the law, but also to those who are of the faith of Abraham, who is the father of us all.
ROMANS 4:16

If you are Christ's, then you are Abraham's seed, and heirs according to the promise.
GALATIANS 3:29

God is your Source, just as He was Abraham's Source. Abraham had unshakable confidence that His God was the source for all he needed in his life. God continued to bless Abraham, and Abraham continued to prosper.

Now it's time for us today to make the shift from seeing ourselves as the source of what we have to recognizing God as our Source for all we need. This brings us back to believing that God is who He says He is and that His Word is true. And Jesus gives us very clear instructions about where to place our trust in all things, including our financial matters: "Seek first the kingdom of God and His righteousness, and all these things shall be added to you" (Matthew 6:33).

This is a foundational point as you begin your Daniel Fast focusing on your finances. Before you can deal with debt, or budgets, or financial stressors, you first want to step back and consider what it means for God to be the source of all you have and all you need. Your resources may be limited, but His are not. Can you trust that He is enough?

Making this shift is all part of maturing in our faith. It's about choosing the ways of the Kingdom rather than the ways of the world. It's about seeing God as our Source and the provider of all we need, and seeing our role as stewards of His blessing.

Faithful Servant Action Steps

1. One of your action steps for chapter 3 was to write down on eight pieces of paper your fears about money and then place those papers in your Bible. Take them out now and read each one. Do you sense any shift in your thinking since you wrote these down? Are hope and faith replacing those fears? How can you encourage that process? (When you're finished, return the papers to your Bible; we'll use them again later.)

2. Make a list of at least ten things that you value. In your mind and heart, recognize each one as a blessing from your God. Thank Him for providing all of these to you and then rest in His presence as you experience your grateful heart.

3. Think about where you are today concerning your finances. Do you trust God with your future? Spend time with your loving Father and ask Him to help you see Him as your Source. Lay your future at His feet and begin believing that He will provide the very best for you.

CHAPTER SEVEN

Giving from a Grateful Heart

Let each one give as he purposes in his heart,
not grudgingly or of necessity; for God loves a cheerful giver.
2 CORINTHIANS 9:7

PAUL'S SECOND LETTER TO THE CORINTHIANS includes a phrase that has become well known: "God loves a cheerful giver." But for many, "cheerful" and "giving" don't go together. If that's an issue for you, how can you change your thinking about giving? And as Christians, how should we approach giving?

I hear from many people who are doing the Daniel Fast with an emphasis on finances. Many want to reassess their giving and figure out how they can give more, but they're confused about the idea of the tithe. Because this is such a stumbling block for some people, I'd like to talk through some of our misconceptions about tithing and consider a better way to approach giving.

RETHINKING THE TITHE

Do you shudder when you hear the word "tithe"? Do you immediately feel guilt or shame? If you haven't been a faithful tither, is there a sprinkling of fear as you worry that God will punish you? Let me set your mind at ease. If you haven't been tithing, God isn't mad at you. He's not punishing you. In fact, while this may come as a shock to you, I believe that as a born-again follower of Jesus Christ, you aren't required to tithe.

Let me show you why as I put together some puzzle pieces about our faith and our giving.

I won't go into the Mosaic law in a lot of detail; however, it's important to understand its place in the history of God's chosen people and what it means for you today. What is called the law of Moses was established after God freed the Israelites from slavery in Egypt. Moses, under God's direction, led the people to the desert wilderness. The desert was not the final destination, but rather part of the journey toward the Promised Land that God would give them.

Before the people entered the Promised Land, God gave them the law, with rules and guidelines that showed the right way to live and defined their sin. The law served as the "rule" for how the Israelites were to live. It also served as a measuring tool to reveal where each individual placed their obedience, loyalty, and trust.

God knew He was the source of all that the people needed. When they were in the wilderness, they needed food, and God told them He would supply it. Each day for six days He would make bread (manna) fall from heaven. The sixth day there would be a double portion of bread for the people to gather so they could rest on the seventh day, the Sabbath.

> Then the LORD said to Moses, "Behold, I will rain bread from heaven for you. And the people shall go out and gather a certain quota every day, that I may test them, whether they will walk in My law or not." . . .
>
> Now it happened that some of the people went out on the seventh day to gather, but they found none. And the LORD said to Moses, "How long do you refuse to keep My commandments and My laws? See! For the LORD has given you the Sabbath; therefore He gives you on the sixth day bread for two days. Let every man remain in his place; let no man go out of his place on the seventh day."
> EXODUS 16:4, 27-29

The Law served as the dos and don'ts for the people. They didn't have God's Holy Spirit in their hearts, so the written law provided the guiding principles that would form and fashion God's elect. And there were many rules that the people were to follow. The law showed them if they were following God or if they were putting their trust and loyalty in themselves or in human authority.

The law was a covenant that God made with His people, and there were consequences for not following it. Unlike the covenant God made with Abraham, this Mosaic covenant was more of an if-then agreement. If the people followed God's ways, then they would be blessed in the land. If they didn't follow them, then things would not go well. In Deuteronomy 28 we can see the benefits of following the law, which is the blessing:

> *Now it shall come to pass, if you diligently obey the voice of the LORD your God, to observe carefully all His commandments which I command you today, that the LORD your God will set you high above all nations of the earth. And all these blessings shall come upon you and overtake you, because you obey the voice of the LORD your God.*
> DEUTERONOMY 28:1-2

The curse, or consequence, is invoked for not following the law.

> *But it shall come to pass, if you do not obey the voice of the LORD your God, to observe carefully all His commandments and His statutes which I command you today, that all these curses will come upon you and overtake you.*
> DEUTERONOMY 28:15

The priests, from the tribe of Levi, were appointed by God to be overseers of the law. God also established that all people would work their own assigned portions of land except the Levites, as they were the servants of God and the people. The people were to provide tithes and offerings to support the Levites and fund the holy holidays and rites. So the tithe, which means ten percent, functioned like a tax. The people were to pay ten percent of all their earnings to the works of God

(Leviticus 27:30). They were also required to give offerings for various life events, like the birth of a child, and at certain festivals.

The tithes and offerings were required by the law. If the people didn't abide by the law, there would be consequences. That leads us to a passage frequently used in some churches and by some television preachers to promote giving:

> "Will a man rob God? Yet you have robbed Me! But you say, 'In what way have we robbed You?' In tithes and offerings. You are cursed with a curse, for you have robbed Me, even this whole nation. Bring all the tithes into the storehouse, that there may be food in My house, and try Me now in this," says the LORD of hosts, "if I will not open for you the windows of heaven and pour out for you such blessing that there will not be room enough to receive it.
>
> "And I will rebuke the devourer for your sakes, so that he will not destroy the fruit of your ground, nor shall the vine fail to bear fruit for you in the field," says the LORD of hosts; "and all nations will call you blessed, for you will be a delightful land," says the LORD of hosts.
>
> MALACHI 3:8-12

What we have to keep in mind is that this was part of the Mosaic covenant. God's people were required to live by these laws to be in right standing with God. But later He sent His Son to earth to offer new commandments and a new covenant.

When you accepted Jesus as your Savior, the spirit in you that was dead immediately came to life. You are "born again." When Nicodemus asked Jesus how he could be reborn into a new Kingdom, our Lord responded:

> Most assuredly, I say to you, unless one is born of water and the Spirit, he cannot enter the kingdom of God. That which is born of the flesh is flesh, and that which is born of the Spirit is spirit. Do not marvel that I said to you, "You must be born again."
>
> JOHN 3:5-7

When you're born again, God's Holy Spirit then comes and lives in you. We read evidence of this in 1 Corinthians 6:19: "Do you not know that your body is the temple of the Holy Spirit who is in you, whom you have from God, and you are not your own?" Your spirit came alive because of Jesus, and you were made righteous. Perfect. Without a mark or a blemish of sin. Romans 5:19 says: "For as by one man's disobedience many were made sinners, so also by one Man's obedience many will be made righteous." You are perfect in the sight of God because Jesus took your sin. He paid your debt. He redeemed you from the curse, and now you are in right standing with almighty God.

The apostle Paul writes:

For as many as are of the works of the law are under the curse; for it is written, "Cursed is everyone who does not continue in all things which are written in the book of the law, to do them." But that no one is justified by the law in the sight of God is evident, for "the just shall live by faith." Yet the law is not of faith, but "the man who does them shall live by them."

Christ has redeemed us from the curse of the law, having become a curse for us (for it is written, "Cursed is everyone who hangs on a tree"), that the blessing of Abraham might come upon the Gentiles in Christ Jesus, that we might receive the promise of the Spirit through faith.
GALATIANS 3:10-14

You are no longer required to live by the Mosaic covenant or the law. You are transformed. You have the Spirit of God living inside of you. You have been reborn, and you have a new heart. Hebrews 10:16 says, "This is the covenant that I will make with them after those days, says the LORD: I will put My laws into their hearts, and in their minds I will write them."

No longer are you required by the law to tithe or give specific offerings, and I don't believe God is angry at you or punishing you if you don't tithe. Under the new covenant, Jesus still calls us to give—but now with a new motivation.

THE LAW OF LOVE

Jesus was considered a radical in the religious circles of his day. He brought a new message and preached about a new way of living. One day He was challenged by the Pharisees, Jewish religious leaders who practiced the Mosaic law:

> *Then one of them, a lawyer, asked Him a question, testing Him, and saying, "Teacher, which is the great commandment in the law?"*
>
> *Jesus said to him, "'You shall love the LORD your God with all your heart, with all your soul, and with all your mind.' This is the first and great commandment. And the second is like it: 'You shall love your neighbor as yourself.' On these two commandments hang all the Law and the Prophets."*
>
> MATTHEW 22:35-40

Jesus told us to love God with every part of who we are, and to love others and ourselves in that same way! Love is the last word. Loving God with all of who we are fulfills all the law and all the teachings of the prophets. That idea was revolutionary.

We want love to inform our giving, as well. If we are not required by the law to tithe, we will not be cursed if we don't tithe, so we don't need to give out of fear. Instead, God has a new way for us to obey. It's all about loving Him, loving ourselves, and loving others.

Am I telling anyone not to tithe? Absolutely not! What I am saying is that this new teaching transforms our motivations for giving. We want to give out of love. Out of thanksgiving. Out of a desire to care for others.

And how can we give cheerfully out of love? By knowing God as our Source and understanding that everything we have comes from Him.

This glorious freedom we can have is all part of God's economy. It's all part of being His chosen people who live by a new covenant that's in our hearts and minds. We think differently than the world around us because we live by a different standard and our trust is in the Lord.

God uses His children to fulfill His desires on the earth. And we do that out of love. He is our Source, just as He was Abraham's Source and the Israelites'. He calls us to be love in the world as He is love in the world, and one way we show our love is by cheerfully and generously giving of our resources. Here is God's economic plan in a nutshell:

He who sows sparingly will also reap sparingly, and he who sows bountifully will also reap bountifully. So let each one give as he purposes in his heart, not grudgingly or of necessity; for God loves a cheerful giver. And God is able to make all grace abound toward you, that you, always having all sufficiency in all things, may have an abundance for every good work.
2 CORINTHIANS 9:6-8

God knows He is our provider. Now we are invited and encouraged to see Him in that same way, and to let that transform the way we think about giving money away.

RELIGIOUS TITHING

God is all about love. He *is* love. And He wants us to grow into the abiding love He has for us and for others so it informs every area of our lives, even our giving. He wants us to give because there are needs in this world that He wants us to meet. Our generosity can help establish His love in the earth.

If we aren't giving with a loving heart, the Bible teaches that our gifts bring no pleasure to God. They are meaningless and missing the mark:

Though I speak with the tongues of men and of angels, but have not love, I have become sounding brass or a clanging cymbal. And though I have the gift of prophecy, and understand all mysteries and all knowledge, and though I have all faith, so that I could remove mountains, but have not love, I am nothing. And though I bestow all my goods to feed the poor, and though I give my body to be burned, but have not love, it profits me nothing.
1 CORINTHIANS 13:1-3

Note that the passage doesn't say giving out of poor motives profits no one. When we give with a resentful attitude, others are still helped and God's will can be done. But we're not pleasing God with that negative approach. God's desire for us is to be transformed into love. To be so driven by love that we receive pleasure in giving, just as our Lord receives pleasure by our giving.

Jesus saw that the legalistic giving of the Pharisees missed the mark. They were so focused on fulfilling the law rather than on loving God and others that Jesus rebuked them:

> *Woe to you, scribes and Pharisees, hypocrites! For you pay tithe of mint and anise and cummin, and have neglected the weightier matters of the law: justice and mercy and faith. These you ought to have done, without leaving the others undone.*
> MATTHEW 23:23

ACCORDING TO THE ORDER OF MELCHIZEDEK

An Old Testament verse that's often referenced in the New Testament comes when Abram gave the first recorded tithe. As we discussed in the last chapter, Abram had defeated the unruly kings who had stolen goods and captured women and children. Abram had also rescued his nephew, Lot, and recovered all of Lot's possessions.

Abram, in honor of his God, gave a tenth of all the spoils to Melchizedek, the High Priest of Salem.

> *Then Melchizedek king of Salem brought out bread and wine; he was the priest of God Most High.*
> GENESIS 14:18

Fast-forward to the New Testament and the book of Hebrews, chapters 5 through 7. The author teaches the Hebrew believers about the qualifications of the High Priest for God's chosen people. He confirms that Jesus is the High Priest forever, and that He is of the order of Melchizedek.

When Abram gave the tithe to Melchizedek, it was a gift of honor.

He saw the High Priest as the one representing almighty God. He gave, not out of requirement or to fulfill the law, which was established hundreds of years later. Instead, Abram gave from a heart of love and respect for his God.

You and I are blessed under the new covenant. We give to our High Priest according to the order of Melchizedek. We give, not because of a requirement that lives outside of us, but by the love that resides inside, the love in our hearts and minds.

Abram gave a tithe to the priest of the God Most High from a grateful heart. We get to do the same. Praise be to God and to our forever High Priest, Jesus Christ.

YOUR GIVING

When we want to change our hearts toward giving, we can start by increasing our gratitude. During your Daniel Fast, set a purpose to be grateful for the many blessings in your life. And I don't mean just for your life as it is today, but for your entire life. Think back to your childhood and consider the things that were paid for your benefit. Be grateful and give thanks to God for caring for you then through the efforts of others. Did you have a bike to ride? Did you attend school? Did you have toys or books? Did you go to the doctor and the dentist? Take a few minutes now to think of a few things in your childhood that you received, and be thankful.

As you fast and pray, intentionally consider all the many blessings, big and small, that you've received. Extend your gratitude and thank your loving Father for His love and care toward you. That sense of thanksgiving can permeate your days and prepare your heart to share more of what you have with others.

How do we decide where and how much to give? My guess is that there are some needs in your immediate community, your country, and the world that touch your heart. You're sensitive to specific problems you see or learn about. Even now, as you're reading these pages, pause for a moment and think about the needs that pull at your heartstrings.

Let's look again at the work of the Bill and Melinda Gates Foundation and their choices for where to give. You can imagine, because of Bill's background with Microsoft, that they first started to focus on education and getting computers into the hands of underprivileged children. That seems logical, right? But one day Melinda, who was then a young mother, read a newspaper article about the thousands of children who die each year because of diarrhea, primarily due to poor sanitation. Her mother-heart was shocked by the statistics. She shared the details with Bill, who also was struck with this new-to-him information. The compassion that stirred in their hearts that day shifted their giving priorities.

Their compassion drove their focus. Since that point, their foundation has donated billions of dollars to improve sanitation in developing countries so children don't get sick as often. Parents don't bury so many young children, and the children grow up to be the people God created them to be.

I realize you can't give at that billion-dollar level. Neither can I. But we can still do something.

I'll introduce you to an adage I like to use: "I can't do it all, but what *can* I do?" I use it about giving and also for many other situations in my life. For example, "I can't clean my whole house today, but what *can* I do?" Or "I can't write the whole book today, but what *can* I do?" The question keeps me moving forward to the success I want to experience. It keeps me taking small steps toward the goal I want to reach.

I learned recently that Bill Gates uses a similar approach when he has a big challenge before him: "Before you get all the way there, you have to get part of the way there."[1] That perspective helps him break down huge challenges into bite-size pieces.

Our Lord uses the same principle. Do you remember the parable of the talents from Matthew 25 that we talked about in chapter 5? When the master returned after having given his servants money to invest, he didn't focus on the amount he gave each of the servants to manage. Instead, he looked at their behavior. The first two were both faithful, and they both received the same reward. Jesus asks us to be faithful in giving no matter how much we can afford to give. He asks us to give out of love, even if we don't have much at all to share.

We can also learn from Jesus' reaction to the poor woman who gave her last pennies.

Now Jesus sat opposite the treasury and saw how the people put money into the treasury. And many who were rich put in much. Then one poor widow came and threw in two mites, which make a quadrans. So He called His disciples to Himself and said to them, "Assuredly, I say to you that this poor widow has put in more than all those who have given to the treasury; for they all put in out of their abundance, but she out of her poverty put in all that she had, her whole livelihood."

MARK 12:41-44

When we give, our Lord looks at our hearts. He looks at our motives. Our giving isn't about how much money, but instead how much service and how much love. How much trust do we have in the Lord to meet our needs so we can give from compassionate and loving hearts?

As you prepare for your Daniel Fast, ask God to open your heart to greater gratitude, greater generosity, and greater love for those around you.

Faithful Servant Action Steps

1. You are a valued child of the Most High God. He is your provider and He gives you everything you need and more. Make a list in your journal of things you can thank God for.

2. God loves you and your cheerful giving. He understands that you may be in a place of transition as you get your finances in order. So for now, what can you give with a grateful heart, and to what cause? Right now, give that gift and thank God for the mighty work He is doing in your heart.

3. If you are changing from giving out of requirement to giving out of love, take a few minutes and shake off the old. Step into the way of love, kindness, generosity, and godly charity. See yourself as a cheerful giver.

4. The Lord has placed compassion in your heart for some causes. What do you feel called to do? How will you use the resources the Lord entrusts to you as His steward so you can bless those in need or invest in a worthy cause? You might consider categories such as your local church, international or domestic humanitarian aid, disaster relief, evangelism, Bibles, or education.

CHAPTER EIGHT

God's Promise for Your Desires

Delight yourself also in the LORD,
and He shall give you the desires of your heart.

PSALM 37:4

I HOPE THAT AS YOU HAVE READ in these past chapters about steward-ship, God as our Source, and giving out of love, you are beginning to understand how closely connected your finances are with your relation-ship with God. Your faith can transform your attitudes toward money and possessions. I also hope you see that your relationship with God, together with all that you do with and for Him, is centered on love. Love for God. Love for others. Love for yourself.

You are a highly valued child of God. He treasures you. He wants the very best for you and wants you to have success in all you do. That, my dear reader, is the truth. Your God loves you more than you can ever imagine, and He wants you to love Him.

Your God wants you to love Him with all you have because that's part of His very best plan for your life. It's what He had in mind from the beginning, when He created humans in His image and His like-ness. He is love. You are loved. In a loving, caring, sharing relation-ship, He wants you to walk in His ways because they're the best ways. And He wants you to successfully fulfill His purpose for your life, which is to present Him to those who don't yet know His love. As the psalmist says:

> *Let them shout for joy and be glad,*
> *Who favor my righteous cause;*
> *And let them say continually,*
> *"Let the LORD be magnified,*
> *Who has pleasure in the prosperity of His servant."*
> PSALM 35:27

Your purpose, your success, your joy, and your happiness—it all boils down to some very simple truths: Love God. Be with God. Ground your life in Him. Submit to Him so that He truly is your Alpha and Omega—your first and last, your beginning and end.

God will always be faithful to you, and you receive all blessings as you are faithful to Him. He made a lasting covenant to you and wrote it on your heart and mind:

> *This is the covenant that I will make with the house of Israel after those days, says the LORD: I will put My law in their minds, and write it on their hearts; and I will be their God, and they shall be My people.*
> JEREMIAH 31:33

Your loving Father wants you to live life with Him. Because He loved you so much, He sent His Son to the earth to fulfill the demand for a once-and-for-all sacrifice, and now with Jesus you can have an "out of this world," blessed-by-God life. Jesus said,

> *Come to Me, all you who labor and are heavy laden, and I will give you rest. Take My yoke upon you and learn from Me, for I am gentle and lowly in heart, and you will find rest for your souls. For My yoke is easy and My burden is light.*
> MATTHEW 11:28-30

Enter the rest offered by Christ. Love God. Recognize Him as your Source. Fulfill your position as His child. As you begin your Daniel Fast, think about how you can "re-present" God to the world through your acts of love—your words, your compassion for others, and even your choices about money.

RECEIVE THE DESIRES OF YOUR HEART

One of my hopes for you during your Daniel Fast is that you will embrace more fully the fact that God is your Father. He treasures you and He wants the very best for you. As established in His Word, He wants you to live an abundant life, blessed in every respect.

Imagine yourself, even though you're a full-grown adult, as a child coming to your loving and caring Father. You love Him and He loves you. And then He asks you, "What do you want, my precious child?" And here is His promise for you in Psalm 37:4,

Delight yourself also in the LORD,
And He shall give you the desires of your heart.
PSALM 37:4

When you delight yourself in your Father, your heart is full of love for Him and a desire to bring Him pleasure. Because you love Him, you want to serve Him. Because you love Him, you want to be your very best. Because you love Him, you want to live a successful life that reflects God's love and power.

Now think to the heart of your loving Father. What does He want for you? What kind of life does He want you to have? What kind of home does He want for you? What kind of experiences does He want you to have? As you spend time with your Father, you will find that the desires you have in your heart are the desires He has for you too.

So what do you want? What are the desires of your heart? Have you spent time thinking about what you really want out of life? If not, you're not alone; many people haven't. But you can now.

Your desires don't need to be "spiritual," although many will come under that category. They can also be physical things, experiences, or insights. And they can also encompass your finances.

What do you really want? What do you really need? You have a promise from your Father to give you the desires of your heart when you delight yourself in Him and pattern your desires after His desires for you.

When we ask, we want to prepare to receive. Remember what the apostle Paul wrote about being a cheerful giver? I believe God also wants you to be a cheerful receiver. When you think about the things you want, don't shift into "religious thinking." By that, I mean a mindset that is influenced by a set of rules from a church or denomination. For example, many churches used to teach that a Christian shouldn't go to movies, dance, or listen to rock and roll. Yet, none of those "religious rules" are supported by Scripture or commanded by God.

Religious thinking can also influence your desires. You may say to yourself, "Oh, God wouldn't want me to have that car. It's far too fancy." Or "I shouldn't even want nice things when so many others are going without." These thoughts aren't directly informed by Scripture. They come from distorted ideas we have about who God is and what He wants for us.

Instead, with a heart full of love for God and the full knowledge that He loves you, ask Him to shape your desires. Yes, we are called to care for the poor and use our money wisely. That's all part of being a good steward. But that doesn't mean you can't buy a new couch for your living room while also generously and cheerfully supporting your local homeless shelter with your financial gifts. God has more than enough to meet all our needs.

Our motives are important here, and checking them is a way to make sure we're on the right track. Be sure your desires are aligned with the ways of God. If you want that new car so you can show it off to people and get their respect, then you're wanting with an ungodly motive: pride. But if you want a new car because it will give you safe and secure travel conditions, then go for it! Share your desire for a car with God.

The same goes for wanting enough money in your bank account to pay your bills, or an increase in your salary so you can fund your retirement account or pay for your child's or grandchild's education. Consider your motivation. Do these things honor God? Are you asking out of pride, or out of love for Him or others?

Doing the Daniel Fast provides us an ongoing opportunity to discern the difference between needs and wants—and to evaluate our desires. For example, if you crave chocolate or potato chips or any of the foods you're avoiding on the fast, you can take a moment to acknowledge the desire but recognize that it's your flesh speaking. You might want sugar or deep-fried foods, but you don't need them and you won't suffer if you pass them up. You can say no to selfish desires and instead turn your mind toward something else that is more in line with what God wants for you during the twenty-one days of prayer and fasting.

Use the experience of the fast to test your desires against your motives. If all is aligned with your desire to give love and receive in His love, then seek the Lord and ask Him for what you desire.

Keep in mind that God works in our lives in a variety of ways. Sometimes he answers prayers in a seemingly miraculous way—the car that someone in your church felt moved to donate to you, the surprisingly large holiday bonus, the full-price offer on your house that seemed to come out of nowhere. Other times, He might answer by guiding you toward wise choices—so in the car example, He might help you figure out where you can cut expenses so you can save money for a newer car. Both results involve God at work, and both are answers to prayer.

How do you obtain the desires of your heart? Jesus gave an easy and concise answer to that question:

Therefore I say to you, whatever things you ask when you pray, believe that you receive them, and you will have them.
MARK 11:24

Jesus tells us first to ask in prayer, and then to believe we receive it. Then, He says, we will have it. Ask. Believe. Have. That's totally different from the world's approach, which is "I'll believe it when I see it." That's akin to the mindset of doubting Thomas after the Lord appeared in the upper room after His crucifixion.

Now Thomas, called the Twin, one of the twelve, was not with them when Jesus came. The other disciples therefore said to him, "We have seen the Lord."

> *So he said to them, "Unless I see in His hands the print of the*
> *nails, and put my finger into the print of the nails, and put my*
> *hand into His side, I will not believe."*
> JOHN 20:24-25

For Thomas, seeing was believing. And that's a mistake we, too, can so easily make. By contrast, believing without seeing is an act of faith and trust. We trust God, and so we believe before we see. But that's not what Thomas did.

> *After eight days His disciples were again inside, and Thomas with*
> *them. Jesus came, the doors being shut, and stood in the midst, and*
> *said, "Peace to you!" Then He said to Thomas, "Reach your finger*
> *here, and look at My hands; and reach your hand here, and put it*
> *into My side. Do not be unbelieving, but believing."*
> *And Thomas answered and said to Him, "My Lord and my*
> *God!"*
> *Jesus said to him, "Thomas, because you have seen Me, you*
> *have believed. Blessed are those who have not seen and yet have*
> *believed."*
> JOHN 20:26-29

You will be blessed when you believe in your heart before you see with your natural eyes. It's the way of faith. We can believe that God is our Provider even before we see evidence of it in our own lives. We believe the truth of who God is as we're asking Him for what we need.

God's Word also gives us a clear pattern to live by. We're called to submit our hearts to the Lord, trusting Him to provide all we need and being about His work on the earth:

> *Rejoice in the Lord always. Again I will say, rejoice!*
> *Let your gentleness be known to all men. The Lord is at hand.*
> *Be anxious for nothing, but in everything by prayer and*
> *supplication, with thanksgiving, let your requests be made known*

to God; and the peace of God, which surpasses all understanding,
will guard your hearts and minds through Christ Jesus.
PHILIPPIANS 4:4-7

God is always faithful. His Word is always true. Our part is to believe. We want to see through the lens of faith, not the lens of the natural or unrenewed mind. We are to believe. James tells us,

Let him ask in faith, with no doubting, for he who doubts is like a
wave of the sea driven and tossed by the wind.
JAMES 1:6

Again, our faith and security come down to a very simple equation: Believe in God and believe He is our Source. Love Him. Walk in His ways and seek to honor Him. His promise to us is that when we live this way, we can count on Him and the instructions He gives us in His Word.

ANYTHING AND EVERYTHING

The heart that delights in the Lord can ask God for anything and everything. His Word says that when we do that in faith, we will have what we ask for.

Now I know the mind immediately goes to "Yeah, but what about . . . ?" We can all think of experiences we've had where this didn't seem to be true. But here is a valuable insight: Base God's truth on His Word and not on your experiences—unless they agree with His Word.

During the first decades of my Christian life, I underestimated the ability for God to work in my life. It wasn't done purposely or out of rebellion. Frankly, it was out of ignorance. I believed in God. I had committed my life to Christ. I was saved and knew without a doubt that I had eternal life with Him in heaven. But I didn't know about the very different everyday life I could have here on earth as a citizen in God's Kingdom. Yes, I believed in Christ, but I didn't believe *like* Christ. Consequently, I didn't pray with the absolute belief that Jesus would answer my prayer.

So often, Christians are not aware of this radically different way of living. God's promises and His truths are watered down. People discount some of God's promises because they haven't seemed to work for them. Often folks don't see answers right away, so they think they must not be coming at all and give up. Or they don't see the exact answer they're looking for, so they disbelieve God's work. So many Christians who spend time in prayer haven't been taught how to "only believe," and so their faith is often weak. The hope-brimming good news is that as we experience God and believe that He will do what He says He will do, our faith grows. Our faith muscles get stronger. We gain understanding. We get to know God better, and He reveals more of His truths to us. And praise God, our Lord is always faithful.

I can promise you that your Daniel Fast is a perfect opportunity to develop your faith. To learn more about this different kind of living. And to grow stronger in your trust in God and His promises for what you desire for your life.

I encourage you to think about what's on your heart. What do you really want? Are you asking for it with a Kingdom-of-God motive? Here's one reason why our prayers are sometimes unanswered:

> *Even when you do pray, your prayers are not answered, because you pray just for selfish reasons.*
> JAMES 4:3, CEV

We never want to be self-serving or prideful. Yet God wants to give you things that bring joy, peace, and happiness to your life. He's your Father, and He wants to bless you. Jesus' words in the Gospel of Luke show God's heart for us:

> *I say to you, ask, and it will be given to you; seek, and you will find; knock, and it will be opened to you. For everyone who asks receives, and he who seeks finds, and to him who knocks it will be opened. If a son asks for bread from any father among you, will he give him a stone? Or if he asks for a fish, will he give him a serpent instead of a fish? Or if he asks for an egg, will he offer him a scorpion? If you then, being evil, know how to give good gifts to*

your children, how much more will your heavenly Father give the
Holy Spirit to those who ask Him!
LUKE 11:9-13

MY PRAYER BOARD

Believing before we see is a strength that we develop. We can use a practical method to keep our desires in front of us so we can stay strong in our faith. This is what the Lord told the Old Testament prophet Habakkuk to do:

Write the vision and make it plain on tablets, that he may run
who reads it. For the vision is yet for an appointed time; but at the
end it will speak, and it will not lie. Though it tarries, wait for it;
because it will surely come, it will not tarry.
    Behold the proud, his soul is not upright in him; but the just
shall live by his faith.
HABAKKUK 2:2-4

Using your journal is an important practice to adopt as you seek solutions from the Lord. As you prepare for your Daniel Fast and during it, anytime something comes into your mind about what you desire, be sure to capture the thought in your journal. You can use these notes to make decisions about the requests you will make to God.

You can also create another tool fashioned after the Lord's instruction to "Write the vision and make it plain on tablets." A while back, I created what I now call my prayer board. It's a simple, framed 24″ x 18″ corkboard that I got on Amazon for less than ten dollars. I also purchased some colored pushpins. My board isn't a work of art; it's a work of prayer. Here's what I do:

First, I think specifically about what I want or need. Sometimes it's a material need or a financial request, but other times I'm asking for a breakthrough in a work challenge or a relationship. Whatever it is, I then make sure that this desire of my heart is aligned with the truth of God. Does it reflect God's Kingdom values or the fruit of the Spirit? Is it rooted in love? I find promises in the Bible that relate to the desire, and then I build my faith by reminding myself that God is faithful to perform His Word (see Jeremiah 1:12).

Second, I find an image that will remind me of the request. It's usually a picture or words I cut from a magazine. Sometimes I just write words on a card.

Third, I post the image (or words) on the board with pushpins, and I ask the Lord to provide what I have requested. I thank Him for giving it to me. Next, I wait patiently for God to provide.

This third step used to be my place of failure. I was more like doubting Thomas; I didn't have the fully convinced faith that I needed. I doubted. But now I have trained myself to believe before I receive. That's how we grow in our faith. Patience is a teacher and helps us learn about ourselves and how we can become more mature:

> My brethren, count it all joy when you fall into various trials,
> knowing that the testing of your faith produces patience. But
> let patience have its perfect work, that you may be perfect and
> complete, lacking nothing. If any of you lacks wisdom, let him ask
> of God, who gives to all liberally and without reproach, and it will
> be given to him.
> JAMES 1:2-5

Not long ago, I had several situations rise up in my life that I needed God's help to overcome. On the surface, this was an invitation for me to worry, fret, and feel frustrated. Instead, I presented everything to the Lord in prayer, using my prayer board as a tool.

Let me share a few of the prayer postings on my board. First, I needed a new place to live! I spend hours teaching Christians how to increase their faith and bring Christ into the center of every area of their lives. Because I do that through online courses and live teachings, I need a strong internet connection to do my work well. I won't go through all the tech issues, but the internet service at my rural home where I have my office was crazy slow and inhibiting my work to the point that it was becoming almost impossible. I needed to find a new place to live in town where I could get strong, fast internet service, so I followed Christ's instructions and asked Him. I posted "New Home" on my prayer board. This addition joined another post I had placed on the board, asking for an inspirational workspace.

A couple of weeks later, I attended an outdoor event in our little town and ran into my friend Chris, who is a remarkable wood artist and also a real estate investor. He told me he was preparing one of his properties for a new renter. *Click!* I told Chris I was looking for a new place to live in town, and I'd be very interested in viewing his property.

When I arrived at the house, my heart melted. I felt like a hand that was slipping into a perfectly fitting kid glove. Every room was artfully adorned with Chris's wood touches, including smoothed and oiled pine logs that serve as molding on room corners and beautiful open shelves and cupboards created from various kinds of wood. The molding along the wood floors is handmade with special touches.

The space for my office has huge windows looking into the backyard, which has many tall pine trees to provide shade for our hot summer days. And here's the kicker: Even though this little house is in town, it's bordered on the north and the east with a lovely year-round stream!

The rent was very reasonable, plus the timing was also perfect for me. And now I wake up every morning in a home that I love. I work in an office with inspiring views and screaming-fast internet. My Father gave me more than I could ever have given myself. Like Jesus teaches us, God knows what we need before we ask (see Matthew 6:8). He works on our behalf before we even know what we need. He is so very good to His children.

Another desire I had was for a new friend in my life who would share some of my interests and like deep conversations and personal growth. So again, I asked the Lord and then posted the desire on my prayer board. Within a few weeks, I was invited to a small gathering and met Rhoda, a woman about my age. We had a lot in common. I learned that she and her husband live on a small farm in the country, she loves to garden, she's interested in many of the intellectual matters I like to learn about, and she's a strong Christian.

Bingo! God once again answered that prayer with such a sweet blessing. Rhoda and I are now close friends with a deep connection to one another. We get together often for events in our little town and pray for each other regularly.

Even though my trust in the Lord is a billion times stronger than it was before, I still get a bit giddy when He fulfills my requests. And every time, His answer is better than anything I could ever do for myself. His blessings have taught me to not settle for things that aren't His best for me. He's shown me to stand strong in my faith. To not give up or give in. Oh, He's so very good, and His faithfulness brings us closer to Him and helps our faith to strengthen.

YOUR DESIRES INFORM YOUR ACTIONS

When you get serious about believing God and you act intentionally to operate according to His Kingdom principles, you'll find a shift taking place in your thinking, in your believing, in your choices, in your decisions, and in your actions.

Your desires will also guide your spending. You'll become more consistent, and you'll soon be using your dollars as "soldiers" working to bring about the intentions that you and the Lord have established. Your spending plan will take on a different purpose. And when it comes to giving, you'll never again say from your renewed mind the words, "I can't afford it." God will provide the resources you need to give to the causes He has set on your heart.

It's similar to the way our desires guide our eating. When we spend twenty-one days on the Daniel Fast eating only healthy foods, our cravings lessen and our desires begin to change. The healthy food shapes what we want, and we begin to make better choices. When we let God shape our desires, we'll begin to make better choices about how we spend money and what we really want.

When you decide what you want, you're also deciding what you don't want. My cousin sent me a quote the other day that is fitting: "Instead of working so hard to make ends meet, why not work to have fewer ends?" Clever, right? And also packed with truth. When you decide what you really want, your spending will reflect your goals and your desired destination. Invest time and energy in yourself, your life, and your future.

Decide what you really want and how you will use the resources God provides.

For example, one of my favorite experiences each year is going to Mexico for a work-cation. I started going to the same intimate beachside resort in the mid-1980s. I spend two to four weeks there, and over the years I've become friends with about fifty other visitors who all choose the same time of year to visit, along with members of the staff. We've become close. We have fun in the sun, but we have also stood by one another to celebrate marriages, overcome sicknesses, and support those who have lost loved ones.

I treasure this time each year. And because it's something I want to experience, I plan my spending, my time, and my activities to make it happen. This desire informs my choices.

I also have a goal to be 100 percent debt-free. So I make extra payments on the mortgage principal for my farm property, I don't take on any new debt, and I save up to pay for items rather than charge them or take out a loan.

Do you see how deciding what you want helps you with your spending plan? Knowing what you want also guides your use of other resources, including time and energy. If you have a desire for a promotion, present it to the Lord—and then allow Him to guide you in ways you can become more valuable at your place of work.

Bring all your needs to God. Remember, the great I AM is also your I WILL. He will act on your behalf.

PRAYERFULLY CHOOSE THE DESIRES OF YOUR HEART

As you prepare to start the Daniel Fast, consider what desires you have for your finances. Are there debts you want to pay off? What do you want to save money for? What do you want to give to? What attitudes about money do you want to change?

Think about desires you have for other parts of your life. What do you want for your health? How about your relationships? Do you have hopes for your home? How do you want to grow spiritually? What impact do you want to have where you live and work? Whose lives would you like to bless?

God has placed you in the driver's seat of your life. He allows you to choose how you want to lead it. In Deuteronomy, He lays out a decision for us:

I call heaven and earth as witnesses today against you, that I have set before you life and death, blessing and cursing; therefore choose life, that both you and your descendants may live.
DEUTERONOMY 30:19

What do you want?

- Evaluate your desire based on the promises from God's Word.
- Make your request.
- Believe you will receive.
- Thank God in advance for fulfilling your request.
- Patiently wait for it.
- Praise God for His faithfulness and testify to His goodness.

Faithful Servant Action Steps

1. If you are planning to fast for a financial breakthrough, you probably have some immediate needs. What are those needs? Write them in your journal. Link them to promises of God. Present them to the Lord.

2. Consider creating your own prayer board. Use it as a reminder of those things the Lord has provided for you and those that you are patiently waiting to receive.

3. Begin making a list of the desires of your heart. Check your motives for wanting each item and test them against God's promises. Then begin the process of making your requests known to God.

CHAPTER NINE

Order in the House!

The plans of the diligent lead surely to plenty,
but those of everyone who is hasty, surely to poverty.

PROVERBS 21:5

IN CHAPTER 4 I TOLD YOU of the threefold cord that can be such a useful tool for us. God is the first strand. Good principles and techniques that are aligned with God's Word make up the second strand. Each of us is the third strand.

In this chapter, we're going to focus on the second strand: the tools, systems, and patterns we can create to manage our financial matters so we can be the faithful stewards we are called to be. As you prepare to begin your Daniel Fast, now is the time to decide what your specific financial focus will be. In chapter 2 I listed a few possibilities, such as dealing with debt, setting priorities for giving and spending, changing poor financial patterns, or considering your legacy. Think about how you will pray about this goal throughout the fast, what resources might help you grow in wisdom, and how you will begin to implement changes.

In addition, take the opportunity to start some new routines and habits during these twenty-one days that can kick-start your new approach to money.

All of God's creation is grounded in order. Think of the seasons, or natural laws like gravity or acceleration. God knows the number of hairs on your head, the number of stars in the sky, and the day when Jesus will return. And it's all determined according to His order.

Living with order is a good practice. And when our financial matters are in order and managed consistently, we feel better. Order helps us stay on track. It tells us where we are and helps us develop plans for where we want to go.

This book is not intended to help you develop a holistic financial plan. Some excellent Christian authors have written volumes about this, and you can get solid advice from their work. (See Tools and Resources, page 223.) However, I do want to offer some basic suggestions for getting started tracking your financial information if you haven't been doing this and don't know where to begin. Find a plan that works for you. Getting your financial matters in order is the first step to managing your money in a way that honors God.

ORGANIZING YOUR MATERIALS

Let's begin with a fundamental question: When I talk about financial papers or information, what am I referring to? Statements for all your accounts (checking, savings, any investment accounts, any retirement accounts). Receipts for significant purchases or charitable donations. Tax returns and other tax documents. Bills. All of these papers need a home.

Create a Workspace

You want to have a place where you can work on finances on a regular basis. This can be a desk in your home office, or it can be as simple as a file box that you take out and use at your kitchen table or counter. The main goal is to have a place where you keep all your bills, records, and supplies so you can easily pull them out when you're ready to work on them.

In today's electronic environment, you most likely will need to have a digital workspace as well as a physical workspace. Create a finance folder and relevant subfolders on your computer. You could also create a Money Matters folder in your inbox where you can store invoices and receipts that are emailed to you.

Keep Like Things Together

I use this principle for bills and financial records, as well as for things in my home. Imagine your kitchen: You most likely keep all your spices in one rack and store your knives together. Your dishes are in one cupboard. This plan to keep like things together helps you to be organized. You know where to get an item when you need it, and you can tell someone else where to find an item because you know exactly where it's stored. There's a sense of security when you keep things in order because you don't have to look all over the place to find something.

This same principle is very helpful for your financial records. Keep all your unpaid bills in one box or file folder. Create files for your account statements, tax returns, and other records so you can easily sort them, store them, and retrieve the information if you need it. Your record storage should be simple and easy to use.

DEVELOP A ROUTINE

Consider taking ten minutes each day to manage your money matters. This may sound like too much, but it doesn't have to be a separate task to remember. You can make it part of your morning routine, or perhaps do it just after you get home and you have the day's mail. Sort everything. If a bill needs to be paid, pay it online or write a check and get it ready to mail. Review any online transactions to make sure they were recorded correctly.

The advantage of a daily routine is that you'll stay on top of your money matters, and you won't need to decide when to do the work. The routine will soon be like clockwork. And if you miss one day, it's easy to make up the next day.

If you don't choose a daily routine, you'll want to attend to your financial matters at least once each week. Choose a regular time— perhaps on a Saturday when you're also seeing to other household tasks like laundry or waiting for a meal to cook. Pick something that works for you and that you're sure you can follow consistently.

Let me pop in a little tip here that can make a big difference in your life. Every time you pay a bill, give thanks for the service or goods you've received. For example, "Thank You, Lord, for the electricity and fresh water I have in my home. Bless the people who work to provide these utilities for me. And thank You for the money You've provided for me so I can pay for this valued service." Try it. You'll be surprised at how giving thanks improves your attitude about paying bills.

CHOOSE A SYSTEM

You need a physical or online system to help you track your income and expenses. Pick a system that you will use regularly and that makes sense for your needs. You want it to be simple and easy to use. There are many models from which to choose; you can find lots of ideas on YouTube or from experienced home finance managers. Here are a few:

Ledger Book

This may be the simplest way to track your finances, as it contains pages for income and pages for expenses. Using a ledger book allows you to categorize your spending to track where your dollars are going. You can also use it to plan when you will pay a specific bill at a time that will work with your cash flow.

Calendar Pages

I know of a woman who reins in her out-of-control spending by using a monthly calendar to track her income, her bills, and the money she has available for discretionary spending. Here is how she does it:

1. She logs each of her bills on the calendar on its due date.

2. She is paid twice a month, so she logs her two paychecks and color-codes them with a felt-tip marker; the first is blue and the second is pink.

3. She links each bill to one of the paychecks. For example, if her car payment is due on the tenth of the month, it's linked to the first paycheck and she color-codes it blue.

4. She then uses a ledger sheet to list the bills in each category and color-codes them.

5. The final step is to plan for discretionary spending. After all her bills are logged in her ledger, she totals each group of bills and subtracts that amount from her paycheck amount. The balance, or money left over, is what can be used for groceries, gifts, clothing, beauty care, and other discretionary spending.

   This visual approach can help you get in touch with your money and cash flow. My friend has paid off thousands of dollars of debt and now can easily and joyfully live within her means.

Envelopes

I've never budgeted with envelopes, but a lot of folks swear by this method, saying it helps them use cash to stay within limits for discretionary spending.

First, make a set of envelopes. Each one will be designated for a specific category, such as groceries, fun, gas, eating out, gifts, personal care, clothing, children's activities, and so forth. Look at a month or two of past spending to figure out what categories you should include.

Plan the amount you will spend in each of the categories. For example, let's say you have budgeted $500 a month for groceries. At the beginning of the month, withdraw $250 from your bank account and place the cash in the envelope marked Groceries. Then commit to paying cash for all your groceries and spending only that much for the first half of the month! If you're at the store and you realize your bill is going to be more than your allotted amount, put items back on the shelf rather than taking money from another category. This isn't your time to rob Peter to pay Paul. Using this method will help you control your spending and stay within your limits.

Repeat the process at the mid-month point, replenishing your envelopes. As you get used to this method, you may make some adjustments and decide to allocate different amounts to different categories. That's part of managing your money and living within your limits.

Computer Software or Smartphone Apps

Quicken is a popular home-budgeting and money-tracking software that is affordable and very useful. A great benefit of Quicken is that most banks will download all your transactions into the program. Quicken recognizes the category for each transaction, which allows you to track your spending easily, quickly, and efficiently. Quicken also can transfer your records into a companion software, TurboTax, so you can do your own taxes or easily give the information to your tax preparer. In addition to desktop software, Quicken has a mobile app that can help you track spending and manage finances on the go.

Online programs and apps are becoming more popular and can help you track spending, pay bills, access accounts, and get an overview of your financial picture. Two low-cost options are Mint and Acorns, but there are many options. Read reviews and find one that works for you.

BANK AND CREDIT ACCOUNTS

Many money management experts suggest having multiple bank accounts to keep your funds well organized and designated for the purposes you choose. Consider establishing these accounts if you don't already have them:

- **Savings account:** This is a place to deposit the money you've designated for your long-term savings. After you've accumulated a certain amount, you may want to use the funds to purchase growth instruments such as mutual funds or stocks. Your savings account is your "goose that lays the golden eggs." Don't kill the goose by using the funds for consumables! Let the account grow and produce over time. IRAs and other retirement accounts are a subset of this category.

- **Account for fixed expenses:** Each month you can deposit the exact amount necessary to pay your recurring bills, including your mortgage or rent, car payment and insurance, utilities, or monthly subscriptions. You can also deposit proportionate amounts to cover bills you pay quarterly or annually. For example, I have a time-share and pay dues three times each year. Each month I deposit a twelfth of the total amount so the funds are there when the dues are scheduled.

- **Account for discretionary spending:** You can also have a separate account for discretionary spending, such as groceries, dry cleaning, gas, personal care, and entertainment. Tracking your spending using these accounts provides order so you can control your expenditures more precisely.

- **Account for giving:** I have a friend who keeps a separate bank account for his charitable giving. He told me that since he started using this practice, he's given much more, and the joy of depositing and sharing these funds blesses his life.

CREDIT AND DEBIT CARDS

Many money experts also suggest using debit cards as much as possible, as this helps you track spending. Of course, if you're on a tight budget, this requires good record-keeping so you don't overspend. Checking your account balance daily helps prevent unpleasant surprises.

You can also benefit from credit cards if you are sure to pay the balance each month. While most businesses accept debit cards in place of credit cards, some don't, such as hotels and other businesses that provide service before a payment is made. Also, many credit cards allow you to accumulate travel miles, cash back, or other benefits.

ADDITIONAL TIPS

Be Consistent

In an era when most folks feel like they have too much to do, it's essential to be intentional about developing routines. I have to work on this regularly because I have a lot of interests, plus my work is demanding. Setting up simple routines is the answer to putting off until tomorrow what you should do today! The more frequently you work on finances, the easier it is to catch up if you miss a day.

Consider a Weekly Meeting

A couple I know goes out for coffee or breakfast once a week for a family "business meeting." They talk about their finances along with other topics about family life. This isn't a time to discuss emotional issues; it's strictly business. The communication helps them both stay on track, set goals, and make sure they are working off the same page as they plan their future together. (Of course, if you're on the Daniel Fast, you may need to adapt this meeting to take place in your home and involve hot water with lemon and Daniel Fast oatmeal!)

Conflict about money is one of the most common reasons marriages break up. This weekly meeting strategy can help you keep the lines of communication clear and make sure both parties are working together for the common good.

Study, Grow, Learn, Get Better

Keeping money management and financial stewardship at the forefront of your mind is a good plan for your success. I'm not saying you should make money your focus or let it become the most important thing in your life. Instead, make sure you're staying on top of your household business by learning ways to cut expenses, invest wisely, spend smartly, and oversee the possessions God has placed in your care as His steward.

Check out the Tools and Resources section of this book for suggestions of where you can go for more information about home finances, investment, financial planning, and debt reduction.

LOOKING AHEAD

If you've read through all of part I to this point, I hope you feel prepared to begin your Daniel Fast. You've learned about the background and purpose of the fast, and you've started thinking about what a financial breakthrough could look like for you. You've studied Scriptures that lay some foundational truths about how God calls us to think about finances. You're ready to step out in faith into your fasting experience and see how God meets you.

As you begin your fast, make use of the tools and resources in part II, including the daily devotions that will help you keep your spiritual focus through the twenty-one days. Then, when your fast is drawing to a close, come back and finish with chapter 10.

May your Daniel Fast be a blessed time of closeness with your heavenly Father.

Faithful Servant Action Steps

1. Over the next few weeks, get a grip on where you are and where you want to go regarding your financial matters. Create your finance workspace and fill it with the physical tools you'll need to carry out your work as a steward.

2. Gather all your financial records and devote time to getting things in order. Make it a positive experience by sorting papers while you're watching a fun movie or developing your spending plan while you're sipping a healthy beverage and listening to uplifting music. Create a joyful atmosphere as you go about the work as a faithful servant and wise steward of the resources God has placed in your care.

3. Decide on a money management system that will work for you. Keep it simple, efficient, and effective. Remember, the only system that works is the one that you will do. Set up your system.

4. Decide on and plan for a specific time each day or each week you will manage your finances. Try devoting five or ten minutes daily.

CHAPTER TEN

Moving Forward in Joy

If we live in the Spirit, let us also walk in the Spirit.
GALATIANS 5:25

At this point you have either completed your twenty-one-day Daniel Fast or are close to that point. I pray that it has been a meaningful experience that has drawn you closer to God.

Knowledge and experience are both gifts that keep on giving. Now that you are on the other side of your fast, you have gained new insights and greater understanding. You know more about yourself. You've learned more about God and His ways. You have insights and revelations that only those who have ears to hear can know. With all these priceless gifts, you can move into your future with confidence and hope for a better life.

Fasting is a temporary, highly focused spiritual discipline that we use occasionally to present our needs and inquiries to the Lord. It's a short-term experience. However, the good habits we gain during the fast can remain.

During your Daniel Fast, it's very likely that you have developed or improved healthy habits in spending time with God and increasing your faith. You probably have been eating better than before you started the fast. Your body is happier, healthier, and operating more efficiently to produce more energy and vitality. You may also now have a better handle on tracking your spending, keeping your financial records, or setting financial goals.

When you conclude your twenty-one-day fast, you can decide what practices you will continue and what you will alter. I encourage you to keep the good habits that have served you well. You may want to alter your eating habits slightly, as you won't need to stay on the most stringent restrictions. You can have the occasional dessert, the cup of morning coffee, or the ham and cheese on rye! But even with loosening some restrictions, you can still maintain some healthier choices.

Continue with the core, faith-driven life changes you've gained. Adopt the good habits so they become your way of life—your lifestyle. And use them consistently so you continue to become more successful in all areas of your life.

YOUR FIRST DAYS AFTER THE FAST

Like most folks, you may have missed favorite foods and beverages while you fasted. For me, I can hardly wait to have a cup of extra hot, full-bodied, dark and intense French roast Starbucks coffee. Oh, life is good! For you it might be a sizzling, juicy steak, grilled to perfection and seasoned just right with your favorite spice blend. Or maybe you've been waiting patiently for a bowl of jamocha almond fudge ice cream with a dollop of rich whipped cream and topped with lightly toasted slivered almonds.

Here's the "learn from my experience" warning: Ease slowly into eating and drinking the once-forbidden fares. Your body is sparkling clean when you complete your Daniel Fast, and it's not accustomed to caffeine, sugar, and animal proteins. If you ask your system to consume too much too soon, it's likely to rebel with cramps, headaches, physical anxiety, and other symptoms.

Reintroduce the foods and beverages slowly so your body has the time it needs to adjust. Continue to care for your body by eating healthy meals. You may want to become "mostly vegan" or "almost vegetarian" if that suits you. Pay attention to your symptoms as you add foods back in, and think about what's best for you and your health.

Also, if during your Daniel Fast you planned and prepared your meals in advance, or ate more fresh produce than usual, you may want to continue that good habit. The same goes for any other good routines you developed during your fast. Carry forward those practices that served you well during your fast.

MAINTAINING YOUR WALK WITH GOD

The spiritual insights you've gained during your fast are too important to lose. Hold on to the growth, new understanding, and new closeness with God you now have.

If you've been journaling throughout your Daniel Fast, read back through your entries and think about the most significant things you learned. Can you distill this down to a few points? Do one or two Scripture passages come to mind? Make a record of these and come back to them periodically to remind yourself of these important insights.

If you developed a new discipline of prayer or Scripture reading during the fast, think about how you can keep it going. Keep looking for extra moments when you can listen to Christian music, memorize Scripture, or do other things that will draw you nearer to God.

YOUR FINANCIAL GROWTH

Take time after the fast is over to evaluate the financial changes you've made. In a journal, record your financial goals for the fast, and then reflect on how you're doing with those goals.

Which of the Faithful Servant Action Steps did you complete? Commit to continuing through the list and solidifying what you have learned. Periodically review these action steps to help you test your own attitudes toward money.

The fast was an opportunity to jump-start change in the area of finances. If you set new routines for keeping better track of your money, commit to maintaining those. You might consider scheduling a monthly or quarterly "check-in" so you can assess how you're doing. Review your goals—whether for budgeting, giving, saving, or money management—and set new ones as needed, asking God for discernment.

WELL DONE, MY GOOD AND FAITHFUL SERVANT

When you think of your life right now, with all your hopes, dreams, needs, and wants, what is a greater desire than to meet your Creator and hear Him say to you, "Well done, good and faithful servant; you were faithful over a few things, I will make you ruler over many things. Enter into the joy of your lord" (Matthew 25:21)? Is anything better than receiving this commendation from your God? Is there any greater reward than entering into His joy?

As you finish your Daniel Fast and move forward in better physical, spiritual, and financial health, let the idea of entering into the Lord's joy keep you on the right path.

The joy of the Lord is greater and more complete than we can imagine. Joy is much more than happiness. It's priceless. Joy isn't anything you can buy with your money; it's a reward from the Lord to one's heart.

Look at some of the ways Scripture refers to joy:

> *The kingdom of heaven is like treasure hidden in a field, which a man found and hid; and for joy over it he goes and sells all that he has and buys that field.*
> MATTHEW 13:44

The Kingdom of God is so valuable, so precious, that we experience joy when we attain it, no matter what we have to give up.

> *Then the angel said to them, "Do not be afraid, for behold, I bring you good tidings of great joy which will be to all people."*
> LUKE 2:10

> *"Go quickly and tell His disciples that He is risen from the dead, and indeed He is going before you into Galilee; there you will see Him. Behold, I have told you." So they went out quickly from the tomb with fear and great joy, and ran to bring His disciples word.*
> MATTHEW 28:7-8

Both the news of Jesus' birth and the news of his resurrection brought "great joy" because they heralded the beginning of God's redemption story.

These things I have spoken to you, that My joy may remain in you, and that your joy may be full.
JOHN 15:11

Therefore we also, since we are surrounded by so great a cloud of witnesses, let us lay aside every weight, and the sin which so easily ensnares us, and let us run with endurance the race that is set before us, looking unto Jesus, the author and finisher of our faith, who for the joy that was set before Him endured the cross, despising the shame, and has sat down at the right hand of the throne of God.
HEBREWS 12:1-2

I'll never forget how stunned I felt when I first read that because of the *joy* set before Jesus, He endured the Cross. The joy ahead of us as followers of Christ is so far beyond what we can imagine. Oh, the great invitation you and I have to follow the ways of our God. To live a Kingdom-of-God lifestyle. And to long to enter into the joy of our Lord.

We have a choice to make every day of our lives. Will we follow the way of the world and the deceitfulness it offers? Or will we submit ourselves to our loving God who treasures us, values us, and wants the very best for us so we can be the very best for Him? He has given us everything we will ever need to live a life for and in Him.

The apostle Paul articulated this choice of life so well:

I have been crucified with Christ; it is no longer I who live, but Christ lives in me; and the life which I now live in the flesh I live by faith in the Son of God, who loved me and gave Himself for me.
GALATIANS 2:20

Our God, who loved us so much that He gave His Son, offers us lives of love, joy, peace, and rest. He promises us everlasting life. And right now, we have the choice to live a carnal life by following the world or to be transformed by the renewing of our minds and live a Kingdom-of-God life. We can have the prosperous lives our Lord has for us if we choose to follow Him and live as stewards of what He has given us.

I've talked before about Bill Gates, one of the richest men in the world today. He credits his mother, Mary, for being the most influential person in his life. The seeds she planted in him from an early age continue to grow into a magnificent harvest. I remember hearing about Mary Gates because of the many charitable causes she supported with her time, talents, and dollars. She shared these truths in an address she presented to a crowd not long before she died:

> Each one of us has to start out with developing his or her own definition of success. And when we have these specific expectations of ourselves, we're more likely to live up to them. Ultimately it's not what you get or even what you give. It's what you become.[1]

I think Mary Gates would be immensely proud of who her son has become: a man who uses his vast wealth to make a good and oftentimes lifesaving difference for others. Bill Gates will most likely be remembered for being one of the most successful businessmen in the world as the cofounder of Microsoft. However, his legacy will be how he used that wealth to bless the lives of others.

You, as a steward of God's resources, can also leave a legacy. It all begins with your heart. Will you place your heart in the hand of our Lord? Will you trust Him as your Provider and your Source? Will you be the wise steward He's called you to be? And will you be the light in the world that He's made you to be, blessing others with what He has entrusted to you?

He has given you all you need . . .

Now may the God of hope fill you with all joy and peace in believing, that you may abound in hope by the power of the Holy Spirit.
ROMANS 15:13

YOU ARE BLESSED AND FAVORED

As you move forward after your fast, always remember who you are in God's eyes and walk in that identity. You are treasured. You are loved. You were created intentionally with certain gifts, talents, and qualities. Walk in the Spirit. Get to know yourself even better. And continue your journey as you move forward into your bright and successful faith-driven life.

I love hearing from women and men who have used the Daniel Fast for their method of fasting. Please visit the Daniel Fast website (Daniel-Fast.com) and share your experiences with me and with others. You will surely be a blessing and touch many lives as you express the goodness of God and how He works in our lives as we seek Him and His Kingdom.

Faithful Servant Action Steps

1. Imagine that a month from today, the Lord comes to you and examines how you're managing the resources He's placed in your care. He looks into your eyes with love and pleasure and says, "Well done, good and faithful servant; you have been faithful over a few things, I will make you ruler over many things. Enter into the joy of your lord." How do you feel? Write about that in your journal.

2. What had you done to receive this accolade from the Lord? Write down the actions you had taken to manage your finances wisely.

3. What kind of legacy do you want to leave for your loved ones or for the cause the Lord has put on your heart? Dream big. Remember, you have a Father with immeasurable riches.

4. What is the number one desire you have in your heart as God's child and the steward of His resources? Ask Him for this today.

part
two

The Daniel Fast Food List

The Daniel Fast is a totally plant-based, whole-food eating plan, and the only beverage is water. All foods are free of sweeteners, chemicals, and artificial colorings and flavorings. No processed foods are allowed. By processed foods, I mean those whole foods that have been altered by food manufacturers, such as white flour or white rice, where the original grain has been separated and the germ and hull removed, leaving only the starchy portion of the grain.

Unsweetened juice can be used in recipes; however, keep in mind that the only beverage on the Daniel Fast is water.

FOODS TO INCLUDE IN YOUR DIET DURING THE DANIEL FAST

All fruits. These can be fresh, frozen, dried, juiced, or canned, as long as they are not prepared with added sugar. Fruits include but are not limited to apples, apricots, bananas, blackberries, blueberries, boysen-berries, cantaloupe, cherries, cranberries, figs, grapefruit, grapes, guava, honeydew melon, kiwi, lemons, limes, mangoes, nectarines, oranges, papayas, peaches, pears, pineapples, plums, prunes, raisins, raspberries, strawberries, tangelos, tangerines, and watermelon.

All vegetables. These can be fresh, frozen, dried, juiced, or canned.

Vegetables include but are not limited to artichokes, asparagus, beets, broccoli, brussels sprouts, cabbage, carrots, cauliflower, celery, chili peppers, collard greens, corn, cucumbers, eggplant, garlic, gingerroot, kale, leeks, lettuce, mushrooms, mustard greens, okra, onions, parsley, potatoes, radishes, rutabagas, scallions, spinach, sprouts, squashes, sweet potatoes, tomatoes, turnips, watercress, yams, and zucchini. Veggie burgers or other vegan meat substitutes are also an option if you are not allergic to soy.

All whole grains, including but not limited to barley, brown rice, corn flour, cornmeal, grits, millet, popcorn, quinoa, rice cakes, wheat germ, whole wheat, whole wheat pasta, and whole wheat tortillas.

All nuts and seeds, including but not limited to almonds, cashews, flaxseeds, pecans, peanuts, pine nuts, poppy seeds, sesame seeds, sunflower seeds, unsweetened coconut, and walnuts. Also nut butters without added sugars, including peanut butter.

All legumes. These can be canned or dried. Legumes include but are not limited to black beans, black-eyed peas, cannellini beans, chickpeas, kidney beans, lentils, lima beans, navy beans, pinto beans, split peas, and white beans.

All quality oils, including but not limited to canola, coconut, grape seed, olive, peanut, and sesame.

Beverages: spring water, distilled water, or other pure waters.

Other: tofu, soy products, vinegar, seasonings, salt, herbs, and spices.

FOODS TO AVOID ON THE DANIEL FAST

All meat and animal products, including but not limited to beef, lamb, pork, poultry, fish, and eggs.

All dairy products, including but not limited to milk, cheese, cream, and butter.

All sweeteners, including but not limited to sugar, raw sugar, honey, syrups, molasses, date honey, and cane juice.

All leavened bread, including but not limited to Ezekiel Bread (most of which contains yeast and honey), pretzels, pita bread, and other baked goods made with leavening agents.

All refined and processed food products, including but not limited to artificial flavorings, food additives, chemicals, white rice, white flour, and foods that contain artificial preservatives.

All deep-fried foods, including but not limited to potato chips, french fries, corn chips.

All solid fats, including shortening, margarine, and lard, as well as foods high in fat.

Beverages besides water, including but not limited to coffee, tea, herbal teas, carbonated beverages, energy drinks, and alcohol.

Remember, READ THE LABELS and study the list of ingredients included in the packaged food to ensure that the contents comply with the Daniel Fast guidelines.

DON'T WANT TO COOK MUCH?

I hear from a lot of women, men, and especially students who want to use the Daniel Fast but are unable to cook many meals. Also, a lot of folks just don't like to cook and find many of the Daniel Fast recipes too complicated for their liking. If you are in this group of people, there are a couple ways to solve your conundrum.

Prepared Meals

More and more food companies are creating packaged and frozen meals that contain only natural ingredients and are free of sweeteners. They are more expensive than cooking at home (you're paying the company to do that for you), but they are a good solution. You can find them in the natural foods aisles and the natural food frozen section of your grocery store. You can also check your local or online health food stores and vendors.

Be sure to read the list of ingredients to make sure any packaged foods comply with the Daniel Fast guidelines.

Super Quick and Easy Meals at Home

If you decide to prepare your meals at home, consider some simple options that require few tools, few ingredients, and little cooking experience.

For example, you can purchase bottled marinara sauce and a box of whole grain pasta and have a meal ready for yourself in about fifteen minutes. Heat a big pot of water, add the pasta, and let it cook according to package directions. Meanwhile, heat the sauce in a pot or in your microwave. Voilà! Dinner is served!

You can also purchase prewashed salad greens at your supermarket along with bottled salad dressing. Just a tip here: When you consider dressings, be sure to read the list of ingredients on the label to make sure they are free of dairy, sweeteners, and chemicals. While I rarely recommend brands, one of the few dressings that is Daniel Fast compliant is Newman's Own Classic Oil & Vinegar Dressing. Add some rinsed and drained canned kidney beans for protein and you have an easy salad that requires minimal preparation.

Spend some time checking out what's available in your local stores or online. Keep your meals simple, and you can successfully use this method of fasting for your spiritual experience.

Daniel Fast Recipes

BREAKFASTS

Breakfast Burritos

These breakfast burritos are easy to make, filling, and very satisfying. I suggest you make a batch of the sautéed onions, bell peppers, and beans ahead of time. Then just warm them while you're cooking the tortillas, add the diced avocado, and you have a nutritious breakfast in minutes.

INGREDIENTS
- 2 tablespoons olive oil
- 1 large yellow onion, sliced
- 1 large green bell pepper, sliced
- 1 can (14 ounces) white beans, rinsed and drained
- 1 avocado, diced
- 1 package raw organic corn tortillas (try Mission brand—see note below)
- Prepared hot sauce

1. Heat the oil in a large skillet over medium-high heat. Add the onion and bell pepper and sauté until tender, about 8 minutes. Lower heat, add the white beans, and cook for 2 minutes more. Set aside and keep warm.

2. Prepare the tortillas according to the package directions. Fill each tortilla with the vegetables and then sprinkle with the diced avocado.

3. Serve two tortillas per person with prepared hot sauce.

Makes 4 servings

Note: Most prepared tortillas are packed with chemicals and sweeteners. However, Mission Organics White Corn Tortillas are Daniel Fast friendly. They are raw, so you cook them on your stovetop for a total of 90 seconds. So very good!

Buckwheat Granola

Buckwheat has a crunchy texture along with its nutty flavor. It's gluten-free and packed with nutrition. Adding the vanilla and the coconut flakes elevates the cereal for extra punch.

INGREDIENTS
- 1½ cups buckwheat groats
- 1½ cups rolled oats
- 1 cup coarsely chopped raw almonds
- 3 tablespoons coconut oil, melted
- 2 teaspoons pure vanilla extract
- ½ teaspoon salt
- 1 cup unsweetened coconut flakes
- Unsweetened plant-based milk, optional

1. Preheat oven to 325 degrees. In a large bowl, thoroughly combine buckwheat groats, oats, almonds, coconut oil, vanilla, and salt. On a nonstick baking sheet, evenly spread granola mixture, and bake about 20 minutes, or until golden.

2. Remove from oven and stir flaked coconut into granola mixture. Return to oven and bake 10–15 minutes more until granola is deeply golden. Serve individually in bowls with unsweetened plant-based milk or enjoy as a dry snack. Store excess granola up to one month at room temperature in an airtight container.

Makes 5 cups

Quick, Sweet, and Nutritious Smoothie

Mango is super sweet, and when it's mixed with the other ingredients, you'll taste layers of goodness. This is easy to make with ingredients you can keep on hand and makes a quick and healthy breakfast.

INGREDIENTS
- 2 cups frozen mango
- 1 medium carrot, trimmed, peeled, and diced
- 2 tablespoons apple cider vinegar
- 2 teaspoons lime juice
- 1 cup water
- ½ cup unsweetened plant-based milk

1. In a blender, place mango, carrot, vinegar, lime juice, and 1 cup water. Blend

until evenly smooth in consistency, scraping down sides as necessary until ingredients are liquefied.

2. Divide milk between two glasses and top with smoothie mixture.

Makes 2 servings

Note: While the only acceptable beverage on the Daniel Fast is water (see Daniel 1:12), smoothies are allowed since they are considered a "liquid meal" or meal replacement rather than a beverage.

Crunchy Sweet Melon Breakfast Bowl

Fruit is a tasty way to start your morning, and sprinkling it with granola and spices adds even more delight. This breakfast bowl is a quick and easy way to start your day!

INGREDIENTS
- ½ small ripe cantaloupe, seeds removed
- ½ to ¾ cup granola (made without sweeteners)
- ¼ cup blueberries, washed and drained
- ½ small banana, sliced into rounds
- ¼ teaspoon mace or nutmeg

1. Place cantaloupe in an individual serving bowl for stability, then place bowl on a serving plate. Add granola and make a trough in the center and tip in blueberries.

2. Poke banana rounds between the edges of cantaloupe and granola and add one or two into the blueberries. Sprinkle mace or nutmeg garnish evenly across fruit and granola.

Makes 1 serving

Green Berry Smoothie

Think of this recipe as a canvas on which you can add flourishes according to your own tastes and flavorful flair. The nuts/seeds provide additional protein, which I like as the recipe keeps me full until lunchtime. This smoothie isn't as silky as some other recipes, but that's okay with me. Very good and wholesome.

INGREDIENTS
- 1 cup spinach, tightly packed
- 1 cup unsweetened plant-based milk
- 1 cup frozen mixed berries
- 1 cup frozen pineapple chunks
- 1 banana
- ½ cup nuts or seeds, such as pecans, walnuts, or pumpkin seeds (optional)

1. Place the spinach and milk in a blender and puree until smooth.

2. Add the berries and blend until smooth.

3. Add the pineapple and banana, blending after each.

4. Add the nuts and seeds as desired and blend again.

5. Pour into a tall glass, Mason jar, or thermos cup to serve.

Makes 1 serving

Oatmeal and More

Oatmeal is a low-cost option that can become one of your core recipes, and there are ways to make it super easy and efficient. For example, you can place all the dry ingredients in a small lidded jar. Then in the morning, just add the boiling water or milk, cover, and let stand for 5 minutes or until the oats are ready to eat. Fast, easy, and filling.

INGREDIENTS
- 1 cup water or unsweetened plant-based milk
- ½ cup dry rolled oats
- Dash of kosher salt
- ¼ cup desired nuts, dried or fresh fruit, or 2 tablespoons unsweetened nut butter

1. Boil water or milk in a small pan; add the oats and salt and stir.

2. Cook uncovered for about 5 minutes over medium heat. Stir occasionally to prevent sticking.

3. Add nuts, dried or fresh fruit, or nut butter of choice.

Makes 1 serving

No-Brainer Overnight Oats

You know that I am a strong promoter of quick and easy meals to allow you to free up time for prayer, meditation, and study. This recipe fits that goal perfectly. Think about making your overnight oats while you're preparing your evening meal, or make several days of breakfasts in batches to save even more time.

INGREDIENTS
- ½ cup dry rolled oats
- ¼ cup coarsely chopped walnuts
- ¼ cup whole raisins
- ½ small apple, peeled and cored, cut into bite-size pieces
- ¾ cup plant-based milk
- ½ banana, sliced into bite-sized rounds
- Ground cinnamon and salt, if desired

1. In a medium serving bowl, combine dry ingredients. Mix in milk, stirring well; cover with small plate and refrigerate overnight.

2. Remove from refrigerator and add banana slices; sprinkle lightly with cinnamon and/or salt to taste.

Makes 1 serving

Brown Rice Breakfast Bowl

Give yourself a surprise with this nutritious concoction of rice, fruit, and nuts. The many flavors and textures make this breakfast interesting and enjoyable.

INGREDIENTS
- 1½ cups brown rice
- ½ teaspoon salt
- 3 cups water
- 1 cup fresh raspberries (or frozen berries, thawed and drained)
- ½ cup almonds, walnuts, or pecans, roasted, chopped, and lightly salted
- ½ cup unsweetened almond butter
- 1 cup unsweetened plant-based milk
- Fresh mint leaves, finely chopped, for garnish

1. In a medium pot, place rice, salt, and water. Bring to a boil and then reduce heat to low. Cover and cook 25–30 minutes until water is absorbed and rice is tender.

2. Divide rice among individual serving bowls and top with raspberries, nuts, and almond butter. Add milk and garnish with mint.

Makes 4 servings

CONDIMENTS

Walnut Cream

You can use walnut cream as a substitute in recipes calling for butter, cream, or milk. The walnuts are rich in protein and the cream can serve as an easy Daniel Fast–friendly ingredient replacement for many of your favorite recipes.

INGREDIENTS
- 2 cups walnuts, shelled
- 1 cup water, room temperature

1. In a blender or processor, puree nuts and liquid until consistency is entirely smooth, fluffy, and light.

2. Store in airtight container in refrigerator.

Makes 14 servings

Unsweetened Pickled Red Onions

Pickled onions are easy to make, yet they contribute such a big flavor to salads and are a nice addition to your antipasto plate. Usually made with sugar, this recipe is free of any sweeteners and is still rich in color and tangy in flavor.

INGREDIENTS
- 2 red onions, thinly sliced
- 1 cup apple cider vinegar
- 1 tablespoon kosher salt

1. Place the sliced onions in a large jar.

2. Whisk together vinegar and salt until the salt is dissolved. Pour over the onions and cover the jar with a tight-fitting lid. Let sit at room temperature for at least one hour before serving.

3. Store onions in the refrigerator for up to two weeks.

Makes about 2 cups

Homemade Bread Crumb Substitute

Bread crumbs are a nice addition to baked entrées and roasted vegetables. However, typical bread crumbs are made from leavened bread, so they aren't allowed on the Daniel Fast. This substitute is perfect for your meals, and you can make it in a batch to use in several meals over a week or more.

INGREDIENTS
- 1 cup whole wheat flour
- ⅛ teaspoon salt
- ⅓ cup olive oil
- ⅓ cup water

1. Preheat oven to 425 degrees.

2. Mix the flour, salt, and oil in a medium-size bowl. Add the water and blend until the dough is evenly mixed and soft.

3. Roll the dough on a lightly floured flat surface to about ¼-inch thickness. Cut the dough into about eight pieces (don't worry about the shape) and place on a baking sheet that is lined with parchment paper.

4. Bake in the preheated oven for 4–5 minutes. Turn the pieces over and continue to bake for another 4–5 minutes. Turn the oven off and let the pieces dry out and become crisp. Be sure to check often to make sure the pieces aren't getting too brown.

5. Remove from the oven. Using a rolling pin, roll the dried pieces into crumbs that are similar in size to typical bread crumbs. Store in an airtight container in the cupboard for up to 10 days.

Makes about 1 cup

ENTRÉES

Burrito Bowl

Quick. Easy. Affordable. Those three words have a nice ring to them, right? That's what I like about Burrito Bowls. You can make this recipe for lunch or as an entrée to serve with a simple salad. Burrito Bowls are also great to pack for when you have lunch away from home. Just place the hot rice, beans, and salsa mixture in a thermal container. Pack the other ingredients separately, then bring everything together for your meal. ¡Olé!

INGREDIENTS
- ¾ cup cooked brown rice
- ½ cup canned beans, drained (e.g., black, red, mixed)
- 4 tablespoons prepared salsa (sweetener- and chemical-free)
- Salt and pepper to taste
- 2 whole wheat flour or corn tortillas
- 1 tablespoon guacamole
- ¼ cup chopped tomatoes

1. Heat the brown rice, beans, and salsa in a small pan; season with salt and pepper to taste.

2. Divide mixture between the tortillas; garnish with guacamole and chopped tomatoes.

Makes 1 serving

Be Creative! Use this recipe as a model for concoctions you can design to your liking. Add shredded lettuce, corn, spices, or other veggies. This is also a great recipe for kids, as they enjoy designing their own meal.

Note: Whenever you use prepared products during your Daniel Fast, such as salsa or guacamole, be sure to read the list of ingredients to be assured that the contents are totally plant-based and free of any chemicals or sweeteners.

Butternut Squash, Quinoa, Bean, and Pear Bowl

Butternut squash is inexpensive, nutritious, and so versatile! In this recipe it serves as the star attraction. Along with the nuts and beans, the quinoa adds even more nutrients. Then comes the pear, which offers a sweet addition to the meal.

INGREDIENTS
- 1½ cups butternut squash, peeled and cubed into small chunks
- 1½ teaspoons olive oil, divided
- ¼ teaspoon salt, divided
- ¼ teaspoon black pepper, divided
- 2 cups vegetable broth
- 1 cup quinoa, washed
- 1 cup walnuts
- 1 teaspoon dried rosemary
- 9 cups mixed greens, chopped (spinach, romaine, or other leafy greens)
- 3 medium-size pears, peeled and cored, sliced thinly
- 1 can (15.5 ounces) white beans, rinsed and drained

BALSAMIC VINAIGRETTE
- ½ cup olive oil
- ¼ cup balsamic vinegar
- 1 teaspoon unsweetened Dijon mustard
- ¼ teaspoon dried rosemary
- ¼ teaspoon salt
- ⅛ teaspoon black pepper

1. Preheat oven to 400 degrees; line a baking sheet with foil. Place squash on baking sheet; drizzle with 1 teaspoon olive oil and sprinkle with ⅛ teaspoon each of salt and black pepper. Toss squash to coat evenly. Roast squash 25–30 minutes, turning pieces over after 15 minutes. Cook until tender and lightly caramelized. Remove from oven and reset to 350 degrees. Line a fresh baking sheet with foil for step 3.

2. In a medium saucepan over high heat, bring vegetable broth to a rolling boil and add quinoa; cover and reduce heat to medium-low. Cook 20–25 minutes until liquid is absorbed. Remove from heat and drain excess liquid. Set aside.

3. Arrange walnuts on the fresh, foil-lined baking sheet; drizzle with ½ teaspoon olive oil and sprinkle with rosemary plus ⅛ teaspoon each of salt and black pepper. Toss to coat and place walnuts in a single layer. Bake for 8 minutes until aromatic and toasted. Remove from oven and set aside to cool thoroughly. Chop walnuts coarsely and set aside.

4. For the vinaigrette dressing, combine olive oil, vinegar, mustard, rosemary, salt, and pepper in a tightly lidded jar; shake vigorously to combine ingredients. Set aside.

5. Layering ingredients, place greens, pears, white beans, squash, quinoa, and walnuts into individual serving bowls or on dinner plates. Drizzle with vinaigrette dressing and serve immediately.

Makes 8 servings

Carrot and Chickpea Stir-Fry

Colorful and tasty, this stir-fry is quick to prepare and packed with nutrition. Serve with a simple green salad and you have a pleasant and satisfying meal.

INGREDIENTS
- 3 tablespoons olive oil, divided
- 2 cans (15 ounces each) chickpeas, rinsed and drained
- 1 pound carrots, peeled, halved, and sliced into ¼-inch rounds
- 2 cups cauliflower florets
- 1 teaspoon paprika
- 1 teaspoon ground cumin
- ½ teaspoon salt
- 1 cup vegetable broth
- ½ cup orange juice
- Fresh mint, finely chopped for garnish

1. In a large skillet over medium heat, heat 2 tablespoons olive oil and chickpeas; cook and stir occasionally until peas are lightly browned. Remove chickpeas from skillet and set aside.

2. In the skillet, add 1 tablespoon olive oil, carrots, cauliflower, paprika, cumin, and ½ teaspoon salt. Cook and stir occasionally until vegetables are barely tender. Stir in broth and orange juice, reduce heat, and continue to cook uncovered for about 10 minutes until most of the liquid is absorbed and the vegetables are done to your preference.

3. Add chickpeas to skillet and stir until all ingredients are evenly heated. Serve with mint garnish if desired.

Makes 4 servings

Cauliflower Steak with Hummus Sauce

Cauliflower is becoming a favorite as folks find creative ways to serve this nutritious and economical vegetable. Use these steaks for your entrée and let cauliflower become the star of your meal. The hummus sauce elevates the dish with flavor and nutrients.

INGREDIENTS
- 1 to 2–pound head cauliflower, trimmed
- ¼ cup olive oil
- Kosher salt
- Freshly ground black pepper
- ¼ cup sliced almonds

HUMMUS SAUCE
- ¼ cup plain hummus
- 2 teaspoons Dijon mustard
- 1 large clove garlic, peeled and minced
- ¼ cup chopped dates
- 3 tablespoons water
- Kosher salt to taste

1. Make the hummus sauce by blending all ingredients in a blender, adjusting thickness of sauce by adding more hummus or extra water. Set the sauce aside to serve with cauliflower steaks.

2. Cut cauliflower head in half from top to bottom. Lay each half cut-side down and create "steaks" by cutting each half crosswise into ¾-inch slices. Brush the steaks with oil and season with salt and pepper.

3. Heat a cast-iron skillet over medium heat until very hot; add the steaks in batches, cooking 8–10 minutes or until lightly browned and tender. Remove from skillet and keep warm while cooking remaining steaks.

4. Adjust seasoning for the steaks. Drizzle with hummus sauce, garnish with sliced almonds, and serve as entrée with green salad, roasted veggies, and cooked brown rice or quinoa.

Makes 4 servings

Atakilt Wat—Ethiopian Cabbage, Carrot, and Potato Dish

One of my favorite international cuisines is Ethiopian. I've been to the country a few times, plus my adopted son was born there. While I've eaten many kinds of dishes, I included Atakilt Wat because it's easy to prepare and very affordable. The key is the Ethiopian berbere spice blend, which is a mix of twelve different spices and has a unique flavor. While you can make your own, it is available in most supermarkets and online. Ethiopia is known for this multi-spice blend, which is unique and very flavorful.

INGREDIENTS

- 2 tablespoons olive oil, divided
- 4 cloves garlic, peeled and minced
- 2 tablespoons fresh ginger, minced
- 1 medium onion, coarsely chopped
- 1 tablespoon Ethiopian berbere spice blend
- 4 carrots, peeled and sliced into ¼-inch disks
- 4 medium potatoes, skin on and cut into bite-size cubes
- 1 head green cabbage, coarsely chopped
- 1 teaspoon kosher salt, divided
- Freshly ground black pepper

1. Heat 1 tablespoon of the oil in a large skillet over medium heat. Add the garlic, ginger, and onion; sauté until the onions become translucent, about 5 minutes. Add the berbere spice blend and sauté 1 minute more.

2. Add the carrots, potatoes, cabbage, and ½ teaspoon salt, along with a splash of water. Cover and cook for 10 minutes, checking occasionally to make sure nothing sticks to the pan.

3. Add 1 tablespoon of oil to the pan and gently stir the mixture. Reduce heat to low, cover the pan, and continue to cook until the potatoes are tender. Adjust seasoning with salt and pepper before serving.

Makes 4 servings

Traditionally, this tasty dish is served along with Ethiopian injera flatbread. Injera is made from whole grain teff flour, water, and salt. Each diner is served one piece of injera, which looks like a large crepe. Instead of using a fork or spoon, the diner tears off a bit of the flatbread and uses it to pick up a bite of the food, then neatly puts the whole bite in their mouth. Making injera is an art. However, if you live near an Ethiopian restaurant, they usually will prepare injera and offer it for sale. It is truly worth the effort to find and try it!

Fresh Veggie Sushi Roll

Sushi is becoming a favorite meal for me. There are so many variations, and it's packed with fresh flavors and lots of vitamins and minerals. Making sushi is also a fun family sharing time, and if you have youngsters or picky eaters, it's a great way for them to try new foods. It's helpful to have a bamboo mat or similarly flexible surface to help form sushi rolls.

INGREDIENTS

- 2 sheets nori (approximately 10-inch square), raw and untoasted (see note below)
- 1 cup cooked brown rice, cooled to room temperature
- 1 carrot, shredded
- 1 green onion, bulb finely sliced, greens sliced into short strips
- ½ avocado, cut in thin slices
- Sunflower or other sprouts
- Sesame seeds

1. Place a small bowl of water and kitchen towels near your work area for cleaning sticky hands. Place one nori sheet, glossy side down, on a bamboo mat and press a handful of rice on the lower two-thirds of the sheet. At the bottom of the rice, place a small portion of each topping ingredient. (Do not overfill.) Use the bamboo mat to tuck and roll the nori, then use the mat to gently shape the roll. Place seam side down and set roll aside. Repeat this step for assembling the remaining roll.

2. Use a sharp knife to cut sushi into 1-inch-thick rounds, wiping knife clean with dampened towel between slices. Serve immediately.

Makes 2 servings

Note: Nori is made of edible seaweed that is shredded and then pressed into sheets to use for sushi. You can find nori in the international foods area of most grocery stores.

Fruit and Veggie Sushi Roll

Combining flavors from fruits and vegetables for your sushi makes a pleasant experience for your appetite. Use the ideas here or come up with your own combinations. Also, consider making batches of sushi that you can use for packed lunches or snacks.

SUSHI RICE INGREDIENTS
- 2 cups water
- 1 cup short-grain brown rice, thoroughly rinsed and drained
- 1 tablespoon olive oil
- 2 tablespoons rice vinegar
- 1 teaspoon sea salt

ROLL INGREDIENTS
- 4 nori sheets (approximately 10-inch square)
- 1 cucumber, peeled and cut into long strips
- 1 mango, peeled and cut into vertical strips
- 1 ripe avocado, skin removed and cut into slices
- ⅓ cup raw greens of choice, coarsely chopped
- 2 tablespoons sesame seeds, if desired
- Tamari or peanut sauce, if desired

1. In a medium saucepan over high heat, heat water, rice, and olive oil; bring to a rolling boil. Cover, reduce heat, and simmer for 45 minutes. Remove lidded pot from heat and let sit 10 minutes before fluffing rice with a fork and folding in vinegar and salt. Cover and set aside.

2. Place a small bowl of water and kitchen towel near your work area for cleaning sticky hands. Place one nori sheet, glossy side down, on a bamboo mat and press a handful of rice on the lower two-thirds of the sheet. At the bottom of the rice, place a small portion of each topping ingredient. (Do not overfill.) Use bamboo mat to tuck and roll the nori, then use the mat to gently shape the roll. Place seam side down and set roll aside. Repeat this step for remaining rolls.

3. Use a sharp knife to cut sushi into 1-inch-thick rounds, wiping knife clean with dampened towel between slices. Serve immediately, sprinkled with sesame seeds and with tamari or peanut sauce (available at supermarkets or online), if desired.

Makes 4 servings

Chard and Pesto Linguine

Pasta is a perfect entrée for your Daniel Fast. You can easily find pasta made from either whole wheat or whole grain (my preference) in your grocery store. The basil in this recipe adds a fresh flavor and the chard is highly nutritious. The roasted almonds provide great flavor and crunch.

INGREDIENTS
- 2 teaspoons salt, divided
- 12 ounces whole grain linguine
- ½ cup fresh basil leaves
- 1 cup fresh flat-leaf parsley leaves
- 1 bunch chard, stems/ribs removed, leaves coarsely chopped
- 1 cup unsalted roasted almonds
- 2 cloves garlic, peeled and pressed
- 1 tablespoon olive oil
- 1 tablespoon lemon zest
- 2 tablespoons lemon juice
- Kosher salt and freshly ground pepper to taste
- Red pepper flakes (optional)

1. Add teaspoons salt to a large pot of water and bring to a boil. Add pasta and cook according to package directions.

2. While the pasta is cooking, boil water in another medium-sized pot. Place basil and parsley in a strainer and dip in boiling water to wilt herbs, then immediately place strainer in a bowl of ice water. Add chard to boiling water and cook for 1 minute; scoop out with strainer or tongs and transfer to another bowl of ice water. Drain and press excess water from the chard.

3. In a food processor, pulse almonds until chopped. Add garlic, oil, lemon zest, lemon juice, and ½ teaspoon salt; pulse to combine. Add wilted herbs and chard to the mixture and puree until smooth. This forms your pesto.

4. Reserve 1 cup cooking water. Drain pasta, and return it to cooking pot. Add pesto and ½ cup cooking water, and toss pasta to coat, adding more water as necessary to thin sauce.

5. Season with salt and pepper; serve with a sprinkle of red pepper flakes if desired.

Makes 4 servings

Loaded Sweet Potatoes

Sweet potatoes are perfect for the Daniel Fast, and I eat them throughout the year. They are packed with nutrients and so versatile. Loaded sweet potatoes make for a full meal with added nutrition, color, and flavors.

INGREDIENTS
- 4 medium sweet potatoes
- ½ cup fresh grapefruit juice
- 5 tablespoons olive oil, divided
- ⅛ teaspoon ground allspice
- 1 teaspoon salt, divided
- 2 bunches kale, stems/ribs removed and leaves coarsely chopped
- 1 serrano chili, seeds removed and sliced thinly
- 1 can (14 ounces) unsweetened coconut milk, well shaken
- 2 teaspoons fresh lime juice
- ½ teaspoon curry powder
- ¾ cup unsweetened coconut flakes, toasted

1. Scrub sweet potato surfaces and prick uniformly with a fork. Place in a microwave-safe dish, cover with plastic wrap, and microwave 5 minutes on high. Remove dish and turn potatoes over for even cooking; microwave 5 minutes more until potatoes are tender. Set aside and let cool.

2. Using a large bowl, sharp knife, and spoon scoop, cut sweet potatoes lengthwise into two halves. Scoop potato pulp into the bowl and set aside intact skin shells. Mash potato pulp together with grapefruit juice, 2 tablespoons olive oil, allspice, and ½ teaspoon salt until the mixture is evenly smooth.

3. Heat 3 tablespoons olive oil in a large skillet. Add kale and chili and cook until barely wilted, about 3 minutes, stirring frequently. Add coconut milk and bring mixture to a boil. Reduce heat to low immediately and cook until kale is tenderly creamy, about 6 minutes. Remove skillet from heat and stir in lime juice, curry powder, and ½ teaspoon salt.

4. Fill potato shells with mashed mixture and top with cooked kale and toasted coconut.

Makes 4 servings

Pasta with Marinated Tomato Sauce

I really enjoy simple pasta dishes. I like the bold flavors of the different vegetables and the ease of preparation. You can make this pasta dish in just a few minutes. Pair it with a simple salad and your meal is ready to go!

INGREDIENTS
- ½ medium sweet onion, thinly sliced
- ½ fennel bulb, cored and thinly sliced
- ¼ cup apple cider vinegar
- 3 tablespoons olive oil
- 1 pound cherry tomatoes, halved
- 12 ounces whole grain penne pasta
- 2 tablespoons fresh marjoram leaves, chopped
- Kosher salt and freshly ground black pepper

1. In a large bowl, mix together sliced onions, fennel, vinegar, olive oil, salt, and pepper; add tomatoes and gently toss. Set aside.

2. Cook the pasta according to package directions. Drain and toss with tomato mixture; adjust seasoning and transfer to serving dish. Sprinkle with marjoram and serve.

Makes 4 servings

Italian Flag Pasta

I celebrate my Italian friends whenever I make this recipe because the ingredient colors remind me of the green, white, and red Italian flag. The green spinach, white cannellini beans, and red tomatoes may be humble ingredients, but together over whole wheat pasta they are transformed into a flavorful, pleasing, and nutritious meal.

INGREDIENTS
- 3 tablespoons olive oil
- 4 cloves garlic, peeled and diced
- 1 medium yellow onion, finely chopped
- Salt and pepper
- 1½ pounds baby spinach, stemmed
- 1 cup vegetable broth
- 1 can (14.5 ounces) diced tomatoes, drained
- 1 can (15 ounces) cannellini beans, drained
- 1 cup pitted kalamata olives, coarsely chopped
- 1 pound whole wheat linguine pasta

1. In a deep skillet over medium heat, sauté olive oil and garlic; cook until garlic turns golden, 2–3 minutes, stirring frequently. Add onion and cook until softened and just beginning to brown. Add salt and black pepper to taste. Add half the spinach and cook, tossing occasionally until it begins to wilt, about 2 minutes.

2. Add the broth, tomatoes, and the remaining spinach. Bring to a simmer, then cover and cook, stirring occasionally, until the spinach is completely wilted, 8–10 minutes. Mix in the beans and olives. The mixture will be somewhat watery at this point. Remove from heat, cover, and keep warm until the pasta is ready.

3. Meanwhile, prepare the pasta according to package directions, cooking until nearly tender. Drain the pasta and return it to the pot. Stir in the spinach mixture and cook over medium heat until all the water is absorbed and the pasta is tender, about 2 minutes. Serve.

Makes 4–6 servings

Red Curry Vegetables with Brown Rice

Red curry dishes are perfect any time of the year, but I especially like them in the winter when the temperatures drop and I need a little warmup. Being of Scandinavian descent, I prefer the mild to medium variety of curry paste. Choose the level of heat that works for you and then enjoy this quick and easy dish. This is another great recipe to double so you can eat the leftovers for lunch or a repeat dinner performance the next day.

INGREDIENTS

- 1 tablespoon olive oil
- 1 red onion, sliced
- 2 tablespoons minced fresh ginger
- 3 tablespoons Thai red curry paste
- 6 to 7 cups cut fresh vegetables of your choice, such as broccoli florets, red and/or yellow bell peppers, carrots, celery, sugar snap peas, white or yellow onion, water chestnuts, green onions, or baby corn
- 1 can (15 ounces) chickpeas
- 1 can (13.5 ounces) unsweetened coconut milk
- Kosher salt
- 3 cups cooked brown rice

1. Heat the oil in a large skillet over medium-high heat. Add the red onion and sauté for 2–3 minutes; add the ginger and sauté until fragrant, about 30 seconds. Stir in the red curry paste and cook for 1–2 minutes more.

2. Add the vegetables and chickpeas, stirring to make sure they are covered with the red curry paste. Cover and cook for 4–5 minutes, adding a little water if necessary.

3. Add the coconut milk and gently stir until well mixed; cook uncovered for 2 minutes. Season with salt if necessary.

4. Remove from heat and serve over brown rice.

Makes 6 servings

Roasted Whole Cauliflower

How in the world did we miss out on cauliflower all those years? I remember my mother serving it occasionally; however, it was usually the frozen variety or was mixed with broccoli and carrots. Now cauliflower is all the rage and used in lots of different ways. Here it's a stand-in for a roast of meat—but so much lighter, and great for your Daniel Fast.

INGREDIENTS
- 1 large head of cauliflower
- ½ cup olive oil
- Kosher salt and freshly ground black pepper

1. Preheat oven to 400 degrees.

2. Trim the cauliflower and remove some of the core, keeping the head intact.

3. Place the cauliflower in a roasting pan; drizzle with olive oil and massage the oil into the head of cauliflower with your hands.

4. Sprinkle with salt and cover tightly with foil before placing in preheated oven. Roast for 10 minutes.

5. Remove the foil and return to the oven to roast for 45–60 minutes or until the cauliflower is golden brown and tender.

6. Remove from the oven and carve into slices or wedges; season with salt and pepper before serving.

Makes 4 servings

Spicy Black Bean Loaf

Black bean loaf is a welcome entrée for meat-lovers. While it's not exactly like the typical ground beef meatloaf, the flavors and texture create a pleasant alternative. Serve it with a side of baked or air-fried french fries and a green salad for an appetizing and pleasant Daniel Fast meal.

INGREDIENTS
- 2 cans (15 ounces each) black beans, rinsed and drained, divided
- 1½ cups cooked brown rice
- 2 tablespoons tomato paste
- 2 teaspoons ground cumin
- 1 medium onion, finely chopped
- 4 cloves garlic, peeled and minced
- 1 red bell pepper, chopped
- 1 carrot, peeled and grated
- 2 stalks celery, finely chopped
- Kosher salt and freshly ground black pepper

1. Preheat the oven to 350 degrees.

2. Line a loaf pan with parchment paper (layered with one sheet of paper overlapping each side, and one sheet of paper overlapping each end), and set aside.

3. Measure 1 cup of the black beans into a large bowl; add the brown rice, tomato paste, and cumin. Gently mix ingredients and set aside.

4. Place the remaining black beans into a food processor and pulse until the beans begin to smooth. Add the onion and garlic and pulse to mix well. Next, add the bell pepper, carrot, and celery and pulse to mix.

5. Add the pulsed bean mixture to the bean and rice mixture in the bowl and blend; adjust seasoning with salt and pepper.

6. Spoon the bean mixture into the prepared loaf pan; smooth the surface. Place the pan in preheated oven and bake for 30 minutes or until a crust forms on the top of the loaf.

7. Cut into portions and season as you would meatloaf with unsweetened soy sauce or Daniel Fast–compliant ketchup. Serve with steamed vegetables and a salad for a complete and hearty meal.

Makes 6 servings

Stuffed Bell Peppers

Bell peppers make the perfect edible dish for an easy-to-prepare meal. I like to mix up a flavorful filling, stuff the bell peppers, bake, then add a topping and broil. Nice color, flavors, and textures.

INGREDIENTS
- 4 bell peppers (red, yellow, orange, or green)
- 2 tablespoons olive oil
- 1 large yellow onion, chopped
- ½ cup fresh or frozen green peas
- ½ cup sliced mushrooms
- 1 bay leaf
- 1½ teaspoons salt
- ¼ teaspoon freshly ground pepper
- 3 cups cooked brown rice
- 1 teaspoon marjoram
- 1 teaspoon tarragon

1. Preheat the oven to 350 degrees.

2. Cut the top off each pepper and set aside. Scoop the seeds and the membranes from inside the peppers and discard.

3. Heat the oil in a large skillet over medium heat. Add the onion and sauté until softened and translucent. Add the remaining ingredients and gently stir to mix. Continue to cook so the flavors blend, about 5 minutes.

4. Divide the mixture into four portions. Fill each of the bell peppers and then cap with the pepper tops. Place the peppers on a baking sheet that's been lined with parchment paper. Bake for 25–30 minutes until the peppers begin to slightly brown on their sides.

Makes 4 servings

Sweet and Fruity Stuffed Acorn Squash

Acorn squash is a favorite in my meal plans for the creamy and rich flavor it offers. When it's stuffed with veggies, apples, raisins, and nuts to entertain your taste buds, the simple squash becomes a star.

INGREDIENTS
- 3 acorn squash, seeds removed and halved from top to bottom
- 2 tablespoons olive oil
- 3 stalks celery, diced
- 1 medium onion, diced
- 3 carrots, peeled and diced
- 2 tart apples, seeded, peels on and diced
- 1 teaspoon cinnamon
- ½ cup raisins
- ½ cup raw pecans, coarsely chopped
- 3 cups cooked brown rice

1. Preheat the oven to 350 degrees.

2. Place the squash cut side down on a rimmed baking sheet. Fill the baking sheet with ½ inch water and carefully place in preheated oven. Roast for 40 minutes.

3. Meanwhile, heat the oil in a skillet over medium heat; add the celery, onion, carrots, and apple. Cook for 10–15 minutes or until the vegetables are softened; add the cinnamon, raisins, and pecans. Gently fold in the rice and blend until well mixed.

4. When the squash are baked, turn them cut side up. Remove any remaining water from the pan. Fill squash with the rice mixture; return to the oven to heat for 15 minutes.

5. Serve as an entrée with a dinner salad.

Makes 6 servings

Stuffed Portobello Mushrooms

What does a baby button mushroom become when it grows up? A portobello! And these granddaddy mushrooms are so good! Packed with flavor and goodness, they provide a delicious foundation for the stuffing they hold. Portobellos are perfect for entrées. If you haven't had them before, prepare for a special treat.

INGREDIENTS
- 4 large portobello mushrooms, stems removed and brushed clean
- 1 tablespoon olive oil
- 1 medium carrot, coarsely shredded
- 1 medium red bell pepper, diced
- 5 to 6 spears fresh asparagus, trimmed and cut into bite-size pieces
- 1 teaspoon chili powder
- 1 teaspoon ground cumin
- 1 teaspoon kosher salt
- 1 cup cooked quinoa
- 1 cup canned black beans, rinsed and drained
- Salt and pepper to taste

1. Preheat oven to 425 degrees and place the portobello mushrooms on a baking sheet. Bake 10–12 minutes until mushrooms soften and release juices. Transfer mushrooms and juices to individual serving plates.

2. Meanwhile, heat the oil in a skillet over medium heat. Add the carrots, bell pepper, and asparagus; cook for 10–15 minutes or until the vegetables are softened. Add the chili powder, cumin, and salt; gently fold in the quinoa and black beans until well mixed and heated.

3. Spoon the filling into the mushroom caps. Salt and pepper to taste and serve.

Makes 4 servings

Mediterranean Veggie Wraps

If you want to reduce calories and still have the fun of food wraps, then lettuce is your new best friend. The filling for these wraps is full of flavor, protein, and vitamins. Easy to make and fun to serve and eat.

FILLING INGREDIENTS
- 2 cups walnuts, shelled
- ½ cup yellow onion, chopped
- ½ cup cauliflower, chopped
- ½ cup carrot, shredded
- ½ cup olive oil
- 2 tablespoons white wine vinegar
- 1½ tablespoons paprika
- 1½ teaspoons dried thyme
- 1½ teaspoons dried marjoram
- ¾ teaspoon sea salt
- ½ teaspoon black pepper
- 4 cloves garlic, peeled and minced
- 1 cup cannellini beans, rinsed and drained

WRAP INGREDIENTS
- ¼ cup walnut filling mixture
- 2 tablespoons soy cheese, shredded
- 2 large Bibb or romaine lettuce leaves
- 4 tablespoons hummus
- 24 tablespoons whole grain couscous, cooked
- 2 tablespoons cherry tomatoes, diced
- 2 teaspoons green onions, sliced

1. In a food processor, place all filling ingredients and pulse until uniformly chopped. Transfer to a large nonstick skillet over medium heat and cook 5–7 minutes, stirring frequently until vegetables are tender and lightly browned. Add soy cheese to pan and stir well until cheese is barely melted. Let cool.

2. Place lettuce on individual serving plate. Spread each leaf with 2 tablespoons each of hummus, couscous, and walnut filling mixture, and then add a few tomatoes and green onions. Fold bottom edge of leaf up and over filling; then wrap left and right edges across filling one atop the other and top edge down to complete wrap. If desired, pin the wrap with a wooden toothpick to hold shape. Serve immediately. Any leftover filling can be enjoyed the next day.

Makes 1 serving

Vegan Tostadas with Fruit Salsa

Tostada means "toasted" in Spanish—and that's one of the main features of this dish. The tortillas are browned and then filled with salsa and other ingredients to make what is a tasty entrée, albeit kind of messy to eat.

SALSA INGREDIENTS
- 1½ cups mango cubes taken from firmly ripe, peeled, and pitted fruit
- 2 tablespoons red onion, minced
- ½ small jalapeño pepper, seeds and stem removed, minced
- 2 tablespoons fresh cilantro leaves, finely chopped
- 3 tablespoons lime juice
- 2 teaspoons lime zest
- Pinch of salt

FAUX MEAT INGREDIENTS
- 2 cups walnuts, shelled
- 1 cup chopped cauliflower
- 1 to 1½ teaspoons chipotle chili powder
- 1½ teaspoons chili powder
- ½ teaspoon onion or garlic powder
- 1 teaspoon ground cumin
- ½ teaspoon salt or to taste
- Juice of 1 lime
- 6 tablespoons olive oil, divided

TOSTADA INGREDIENTS
- Cooking spray
- 6 corn tortillas
- Salt
- ½ cup refried beans
- 1½ cups romaine lettuce, coarsely chopped
- Lime wedges for garnish

1. Preheat oven to 400 degrees. In a medium bowl, place mango, red onion, jalapeño, and cilantro. Add lime juice, lime zest, and salt and toss to combine; set aside.

2. In a food processor, place walnuts, cauliflower, chipotle chili powder, chili powder, onion or garlic powder, cumin, salt, lime juice, and ¼ cup olive oil. Pulse until ingredients look like ground meat. In a large skillet on medium heat, put 2 tablespoons olive oil. Transfer walnut mixture and cook for 10 minutes, stirring

frequently, until vegetables are tender and ingredients are uniformly and lightly browned.

3. Coat 2 baking sheets with cooking spray and spray both sides of tortillas lightly before arranging in a single layer on the baking sheets. Sprinkle with salt. Bake tortillas for 5 minutes, turn them over, and continue baking for 5–10 minutes more until crisp.

4. Assemble tostadas by spreading refried beans thinly across warm tostada shells. Add a layer of walnut mixture. Top with romaine lettuce and mango salsa; garnish with lime wedges.

Makes 6 servings

Indian Chickpea Casserole

One way to make meals more satisfying is to see that they are rich in flavors, colors, and textures. That's what makes this casserole a hit for your Daniel Fast menus. This recipe also serves as good leftovers for lunch the next day.

INGREDIENTS
- Olive oil spray
- 3 medium Yukon Gold potatoes, scrubbed and cut into ½-inch slices
- 1 small red onion, chopped
- 2 medium zucchini, cut into ½-inch dice
- Salt and pepper
- 1 medium jalapeño pepper, seeds removed and minced
- 1 teaspoon grated ginger
- 1 tablespoon ground coriander
- 2 tablespoons garam masala
- ½ teaspoon salt
- 2 tablespoons tomato paste
- 1 can (14 ounces) diced tomatoes, undrained
- 1 can (15 ounces) chickpeas, drained and rinsed
- 3 tablespoons Homemade Bread Crumb Substitute (page 154)
- Chopped cilantro for garnish

1. Preheat the oven to 425 degrees; spray two large 9 x 13 x 2–inch baking pans with oil.

2. Spread the sliced potatoes and onion in one of the baking pans and the zucchini in the second. Spray the vegetables with oil and season to taste with salt and pepper. Place the pans into the oven and roast for 30 minutes. Remove the zucchini from the oven and set aside. Toss the potatoes and onions and continue to roast for 10 more minutes.

3. Meanwhile, in a small bowl blend the jalapeño, ginger, coriander, garam masala, and salt. Stir in the tomato paste. Add the tomatoes with their juices and gently stir until well blended.

4. Remove the potatoes and onions from the oven and reduce the oven temperature to 375 degrees.

5. Add the zucchini to the pan containing the potatoes and onions. Add the tomato mixture and the chickpeas and gently stir to combine. Return to the oven for 15 minutes.

6. Remove from the oven and turn the oven to broil. Sprinkle with bread crumb substitute and chopped cilantro. Return to the oven and broil for 2–3 minutes. Serve.

Makes 4 servings

Veggie Poké Bowl

You may not get to Hawaii while on your Daniel Fast, but you can bring Hawaii to you by preparing a poké bowl for your meal. The word actually means "sliced" in Hawaiian, and a poké bowl is a basin of goodness for each diner. Use this recipe as your base, then add ingredients that suit your taste.

INGREDIENTS
- 1 cup cooked brown rice
- ¾ cup tofu, cut into 1-inch cubes, seasoned with salt and black pepper to taste
- 1 green onion, coarsely chopped
- ½ teaspoon black sesame seeds
- ½ to 1 small red chili, seeds removed and chopped finely
- 2 teaspoons soy sauce
- 2 teaspoons sesame oil
- Extra black sesame seeds for garnish
- Topping options: sliced avocado, edamame beans, grated carrot, cucumber chunks, sliced radishes, shredded cabbage sliced paper-thin, coarsely chopped white onion, and an endless list of fresh vegetables to taste

1. In an individual serving bowl, arrange a bed of rice. Top with tofu circled with green onion, sesame seeds, and red chili around edges. Sprinkle with soy sauce and sesame oil; garnish with black sesame seeds and other toppings of your choice.

Makes 1 serving

West African Peanut Soup with Brown Rice

The unique flavors in this nutritious soup served with brown rice make it a Daniel Fast favorite for me. It's also packed with protein, which will satisfy your tummy while you enjoy the spicy tastes of this special international dish.

INGREDIENTS
- 1 tablespoon coconut oil
- 1 medium onion, finely chopped
- 2 tablespoons minced ginger
- 3 to 4 cloves garlic, peeled and minced
- 1 teaspoon kosher salt
- 1 tablespoon coriander
- 2 teaspoons cumin
- ¼ teaspoon cayenne pepper
- ¼ cup tomato paste
- 2 sweet potatoes, peeled and cut into 1-inch cubes
- 1 can (15 ounces) chickpeas, drained and rinsed
- ¾ cup unsweetened creamy peanut butter
- 4 cups vegetable broth
- 3 cups spinach, stems removed
- 3 cups cooked brown rice, warmed

1. Using a large soup pot or Dutch oven, heat the coconut oil over medium heat. Add the onion, ginger, garlic, and salt; sauté until onion becomes translucent, about 3 minutes. Add the coriander, cumin, and cayenne and cook for 2 minutes more.

2. Add the tomato paste, sweet potatoes, chickpeas, peanut butter, and vegetable broth. Increase heat to bring soup to a boil, then reduce heat to medium-low and simmer for 15–20 minutes. Add the spinach and cook for 15 minutes more.

3. Using individual soup bowls, pile ½ cup brown rice on one half of each bowl. Then spoon the soup into the other half of the bowl to serve.

Makes 6 servings

SALADS

Apple and Farro Salad

Farro is an ancient grain that's making a comeback as diners prefer healthier meals with whole grains. This grain is packed with nutrients and makes a distinctive ingredient for heartier salads. The grapes and apple in this recipe add a sweet punch to a pleasant salad you can serve as a meal.

INGREDIENTS
- 1½ cups farro
- 2 tablespoons red wine vinegar
- ½ teaspoon salt
- ½ teaspoon black pepper
- ½ small red onion, chopped coarsely
- 2 stalks celery, strings removed and thinly sliced
- 1 cup red seedless grapes, cut in half
- 1 firm ripe red apple, cored and cut in 1-inch pieces
- 2 tablespoons olive oil
- 1 bunch arugula, thick stems removed, torn
- More salt and black pepper, if desired, to taste

1. Preheat oven to 425 degrees. Prepare farro using package instructions.

2. In a large mixing bowl, mix vinegar and ½ teaspoon each of salt and black pepper; add onion and stir well to coat. Set aside for 5 minutes before stirring in celery, grapes, and apple. Add farro, drizzle with oil, and combine well. Gently fold in arugula.

3. Transfer salad to a large platter or serve on individual salad plates; season to taste with salt and pepper.

Makes 4 servings

Roasted Beet, Spinach, and Quinoa Salad

I am a big fan of beets, and their natural sweetness is beautifully released when they're roasted. This salad is one of my very favorite and is so filling and nutritious. The spinach and quinoa add lots of protein, making this a perfect complete meal.

INGREDIENTS
- 8 medium beets (red and/or golden), scrubbed and trimmed of top and root
- Olive oil
- Kosher salt
- 2 cups baby spinach leaves, packed to measure
- 2 cups cooked red quinoa
- 1 cup Unsweetened Pickled Red Onions (see page 153)
- ½ cup raw pecans, broken

DRESSING INGREDIENTS
- ½ cup extra-virgin olive oil
- Juice of 1 lemon
- 2 tablespoons white wine vinegar
- Kosher salt
- Freshly ground black pepper

1. Preheat the oven to 350 degrees.

2. Lay a large sheet of aluminum foil on a large rimmed baking sheet. Place the beets on the foil, drizzle with oil, and sprinkle with salt. Wrap the foil around the beets to seal. Roast for 40–60 minutes or until fork tender. Remove the beets from the oven and the foil. Run cold water over the beets and slip off the skins with your hands. Cut the beets into bite-size dice and set aside to cool completely.

3. Place all salad dressing ingredients in a small bowl and emulsify with a whisk; set aside.

4. When the beets are completely cooled, assemble four salads on individual plates: Lay down a layer of spinach leaves. Add a mound of ¼ cup quinoa. Add one-fourth of the beets to each plate and top with pickled red onions and pecans. Drizzle with salad dressing and season to taste with salt and pepper.

Makes 4 servings

Butternut Noodle Salad

A vegetable spiralizer (a kitchen tool that cuts vegetables into long, spaghetti-like strands) is a handy friend for your Daniel Fast—and all your meal plans if you want to cut back on calories and carbs. If you made this recipe with whole grain noodles, it would have almost three times as many calories! Plus, the flavor from the butternut squash is superior.

INGREDIENTS
- 1 medium butternut squash, peeled and spiralized into either wide or medium-wide noodles
- Olive oil spray
- Kosher salt
- 1 sweet apple, cored and seeds removed, spiralized into thin noodles
- 2 cups baby spinach leaves, packed to measure
- ½ cup pomegranate seeds
- ½ cup golden raisins
- ½ cup raw pecans, broken

DRESSING INGREDIENTS
- ¼ cup white wine vinegar
- ½ cup olive oil
- 2 tablespoons unsweetened Dijon mustard
- 1 tablespoon fresh lemon juice
- ½ teaspoon kosher salt
- ½ teaspoon freshly ground black pepper

1. Preheat the oven to 400 degrees.

2. Cover a large rimmed baking sheet with parchment paper. Spread the butternut noodles in one layer on the sheet pan; spray with the olive oil cooking spray and sprinkle with salt. Roast to al dente doneness, 8–10 minutes.

3. Meanwhile, prepare the remaining salad ingredients and lightly toss in a large salad bowl; set aside.

4. Place all salad dressing ingredients in a small bowl and emulsify with a whisk; set aside.

5. When the butternut squash noodles are roasted, remove from oven and cool to room temperature. Add to salad bowl and gently toss to mix. Drizzle with salad dressing.

Makes 6 servings

Daniel Fast Cobb Salad

This salad is a take on the traditional Cobb salad, replacing some of the ingredients so it works for the Daniel Fast. One of the rewards of a Cobb salad is the variety of colors, textures, and flavors. It's also so pretty on the plate!

INGREDIENTS
- 2 sweet potatoes, peeled and diced into ½-inch cubes
- 1 tablespoon olive oil
- Kosher salt and freshly ground black pepper
- 1 avocado, peeled, pit removed, and diced into ½-inch cubes
- 12 cherry or grape tomatoes, cut in half lengthwise
- 1 cucumber, peeled, seeds removed, and cut into ½-inch half disks
- 1 can (15 ounces) chickpeas, drained and rinsed
- 2 green onions, trimmed and cut into rounds
- 1 can (15 ounces) whole beets, diced into ½-inch cubes
- ¼ cup sliced almonds

DRESSING INGREDIENTS
- ¼ cup white wine vinegar
- ½ cup olive oil
- 2 tablespoons unsweetened Dijon mustard
- 1 tablespoon fresh lemon juice
- ½ teaspoon kosher salt
- ½ teaspoon freshly ground black pepper

1. Preheat oven to 400 degrees.

2. Place the cubed sweet potatoes in a bowl; drizzle with olive oil and sprinkle with salt and pepper. Place on rimmed baking sheet and roast in preheated oven for 35–40 minutes, turning once.

3. Meanwhile, prepare the other vegetables.

4. When sweet potatoes are tender and cooled to room temperature, decoratively position all the vegetables on a large platter in rows or wedges; sprinkle with sliced almonds.

5. Place all the dressing ingredients in a small bowl and whisk until emulsified; drizzle over salad and serve, allowing each diner to dish up their own plate.

Makes 6 servings

Whole Grain Spelt, Bean, and Veggie Salad

Spelt, also called dinkel wheat, has been cultivated since 5000 BC. The grain fell off the preferred grain chart, but it's slowly climbing as it's being rediscovered by many health-conscious consumers. Pair spelt with beans and you have all the amino acids that make a complete protein. Adding colorful and flavorful vegetables makes this salad dazzle.

INGREDIENTS
- 2½ cups spelt berries
- 1 cucumber, peeled and seeded, cut into ½-inch thick half disks
- 1 red bell pepper, stem and seeds removed, diced
- 1 yellow bell pepper, stem and seeds removed, diced
- 1 medium jicama, trimmed, peeled, and julienned
- 1 can (15 ounces) kidney beans, rinsed and drained
- ½ cup chopped Italian parsley
- ¼ cup chopped fresh dill

DRESSING INGREDIENTS
- ¼ cup fresh lemon juice
- ¾ cup olive oil
- 2 tablespoons unsweetened Dijon mustard
- ½ teaspoon kosher salt
- ½ teaspoon freshly ground black pepper

1. Prepare spelt berries according to package directions; cool to room temperature.

2. Place all the salad dressing ingredients in a small bowl and emulsify with a whisk; set aside.

3. When ready to prepare salad, place the spelt berries, cucumber, bell peppers, jicama, beans, parsley, and dill in a large salad bowl. Toss gently and drizzle with salad dressing. Toss again before serving.

Makes 6 servings

Hearty Sweet Potato Salad

This salad is bursting with color, textures, and flavors, making it a hearty salad for your lunch or dinner. Serve with a small dish of fresh pineapple or other fruit for a pleasant meal.

INGREDIENTS
- 2 large sweet potatoes, peeled and chopped into 1-inch pieces
- ⅓ cup plus 2 tablespoons olive oil
- ¾ teaspoon chili powder
- Kosher salt and freshly ground black pepper to taste
- 1 teaspoon grated lime zest
- 3 tablespoons lime juice
- ¼ cup roughly chopped cilantro leaves (reserve some for garnish)
- 2 romaine lettuce hearts, chopped
- 1 can (15 ounces) black beans, rinsed and drained
- Garnish mixture (sliced radishes, chopped avocado, pumpkin seeds, chopped nuts)

1. Preheat oven to 450 degrees.

2. Place sweet potato pieces in a single layer on a rimmed baking sheet; drizzle with 2 tablespoons olive oil and sprinkle with chili powder, salt, and pepper. Roast until tender and browned, about 20 minutes, stirring a couple of times during roasting. Let cool to warm.

3. While potato pieces are roasting, whisk together lime zest, lime juice, cilantro, and remaining ⅓ cup olive oil; season with salt and pepper.

4. Place the romaine lettuce in a large bowl. Drizzle about ¼ cup of the dressing over the lettuce and toss; season with salt and pepper. Divide the lettuce among four bowls, top with beans and sweet potatoes, and garnish as desired. Drizzle with remaining dressing and sprinkle with cilantro leaves.

Makes 4 servings

Quinoa Tabbouleh Hearty Salad Bowl

Tabbouleh is a wholesome salad that comes to us from Lebanon. This salad is tangy to the taste and really good for your health.

QUINOA INGREDIENTS
- 2 tablespoons olive oil
- 2 shallots, diced
- 3 cloves garlic, peeled and diced
- 1 teaspoon sea salt
- 1 pinch black pepper, freshly ground
- 1 teaspoon ground cumin
- 1½ cup quinoa, washed
- 1½ cup water or vegetable stock, boiling

SALAD INGREDIENTS
- 3 packed cups fresh flat-leaf parsley, chopped
- 1 packed cup fresh cilantro, chopped
- ½ cup fresh mint, chopped
- 2 cucumbers, diced
- 3 plum tomatoes, ends trimmed and diced
- 1 large fennel bulb, cored and diced; reserve a few fronds for garnish
- 1 large hot chili pepper, if desired, seeds removed and coarsely chopped
- 1 small red onion, diced
- 3 scallions, green parts coarsely chopped
- ½ cup olive oil
- ½ cup lemon juice
- 1 teaspoon sea salt, or add to taste
- 1 pinch black pepper, freshly ground

1. In a deep skillet over medium heat, heat olive oil and shallots; cook until shallots turn golden, 2–3 minutes, stirring frequently. Add garlic and cook until scent rises. Add salt, black pepper, cumin, quinoa, and boiling water (or stock) and bring the mixture to a boil. Reduce heat and simmer until quinoa is cooked, about 10–12 minutes. Remove from heat and spread quinoa mixture evenly across a baking sheet to cool.

2. Place quinoa mixture in a large serving bowl and add parsley, cilantro, mint, cucumber, tomatoes, fennel, chili, onion, and scallions. Thoroughly combine by gently tossing. Drizzle olive oil and lemon juice evenly over mixture and season with salt and pepper. Garnish with fennel fronds and serve.

Makes 8 servings

Rainbow Fruit Bowl

You probably know from experience that you eat with your eyes first. Foods that look appealing tend to taste better to us. And this lovely fruit bowl will look so scrumptious that you'll want to eat every bite. Colors, textures, and flavors are the trifecta of this salad.

INGREDIENTS
- ½ cup strawberries, stems removed, cut in half
- ½ cup peeled orange, segments cut small and seeds removed
- ½ cup peeled pineapple, cut into bite-size pieces
- ½ cup peeled kiwi fruit, cut into bite-size pieces
- ½ cup whole red grapes, stems removed

1. In a medium-sized serving bowl, arrange fruit in side-by-side rows of individual ingredients to create a graduated rainbow-color spectrum effect.

Makes 1 serving

Rice Noodle Salad

A fresh addition to your menus, this noodle salad goes well with entrées that feature Asian flavors. The work is well worth the effort.

INGREDIENTS
- 8 ounces uncooked rice noodles
- ½ cup fresh lime juice
- 1 tablespoon grated fresh ginger
- 1 teaspoon kosher salt
- 4 medium cucumbers, sliced
- 4 green onions, thinly sliced
- ½ red bell pepper, diced small
- ½ cup chopped fresh cilantro, loosely packed
- ½ cup chopped fresh mint, loosely packed

1. Cook the rice noodles according to package directions. Rinse under cold water to cool, then drain and transfer to a large bowl.

2. In a separate bowl, whisk together the lime juice, ginger, and salt. Add the cucumber, green onion, bell pepper, cilantro, and mint.

3. Add the vegetable mixture to the rice noodles, toss, and serve.

Makes 4 servings

Tomato and Onion Salad

Tomatoes are the star of this salad. If tomatoes are in season and you can get them from a local farmer, your salad will be even better since the flavor will be so much stronger. Vidalia onions come with a sweetness that makes this salad a special addition to your recipe collection.

INGREDIENTS
- ½ cup unsweetened balsamic vinegar
- 1½ cups fresh basil leaves, trimmed of the stems
- 1 cup olive oil
- Kosher salt and freshly ground black pepper
- 6 large tomatoes, cut into 1-inch slices
- 1 large bunch arugula
- 1 large Vidalia onion, thinly sliced

1. Heat the vinegar in a small pan over medium to low heat. Simmer until it is reduced and thick enough to coat the back of a spoon; set aside to cool.

2. Puree the basil and oil in a food processor; season with salt and pepper to taste. Set aside.

3. Divide the sliced tomatoes, the arugula, and the onion on six plates. Drizzle with the cooled vinegar and then with the basil oil.

Makes 6 servings

SIDES

Herbed Brown Rice

I switched over to using brown rice way back in the 1970s. That was when I could only get it at the rare health food store in my area, which was more than 25 miles away. I like brown rice so much that I actually crave it sometimes. Dressing it up with herbs just adds to the goodness. And this recipe has lots of goodness going for it!

INGREDIENTS
- 1 tablespoon olive oil
- 2 medium onions, diced
- 2 medium bell peppers, diced
- 2 teaspoons dried thyme
- 2 teaspoons dried sage
- 2 teaspoons dried marjoram
- 4 cloves garlic, peeled and minced
- 2 cups brown rice, rinsed three times
- 4 cups water
- 1 bunch green onions
- ½ cup finely chopped fresh parsley

1. In a large pot, heat the oil over medium heat. Add the onions and bell peppers and sauté for 5 minutes. Add the herbs and garlic and sauté for an additional 5 minutes.

2. Gently stir in the rice and mix with the herbs. Add the water and bring to a boil, stirring only briefly to keep the rice from sticking. Cover and simmer for about 30 minutes or until all the liquid is absorbed. If the rice is not tender, add a little more water and continue to cook.

3. Remove from heat. Use two forks to fluff the rice along with the green onions and parsley; adjust seasoning and serve.

Makes 6–10 servings

Mashed Sweet Potatoes and Carrots

Mashed potatoes just got better with the sweetness of sweet potatoes and the unique flavor of cooked carrots. This bright orange mash pops with the flavor of almond from the milk, along with vanilla and cinnamon.

INGREDIENTS
- 1½ pounds small sweet potatoes, peeled and cut into 1-inch pieces
- 1 pound carrots, peeled and cut into 1-inch pieces
- 1¼ teaspoon salt, divided
- ½ cup unsweetened almond milk
- ¼ teaspoon vanilla extract
- 2 to 3 tablespoons light olive oil
- 1 teaspoon ground cinnamon
- ½ teaspoon black pepper
- Minced fresh thyme or dried thyme for garnish

1. In a large pot of water over high heat, heat potatoes and carrots. Correct water level until it is 1 inch above the vegetables. Add ¾ teaspoon salt and bring water to a rolling boil. Reduce heat to medium and simmer vegetables until tender, 15–20 minutes. Drain and return vegetables to cooking pot. Cook and stir until remaining liquid evaporates, about 2 minutes.

2. Remove pot from heat. Add almond milk, vanilla, olive oil, cinnamon, ½ teaspoon salt, and ½ teaspoon black pepper; mash the mixture with potato masher or electric beater until consistency is smooth and creamy. Serve garnished with a sprinkle of thyme.

Makes 4 servings

Roasted Asparagus with Peppers and Onions

I am so blessed to have wild asparagus on my little farm in Central Washington. I enjoy it in the spring and prepare it in multiple ways, but roasted is my favorite. When the wild asparagus season is over, I get it from my local grocery store. Roasted asparagus is so easy to prepare and serves as a perfect snack or side dish.

INGREDIENTS
- 3 pounds asparagus, trimmed
- 1 medium yellow onion, thinly sliced
- 2 red bell peppers, seeded and thinly sliced
- ¼ cup olive oil
- 2 cups water
- Kosher salt and freshly ground black pepper

1. Preheat the oven to 400 degrees.

2. Using a rimmed baking sheet, lay the asparagus in a single layer. Lay the onion and bell pepper evenly over the asparagus and drizzle with oil. Add water and season with salt and pepper.

3. Cover with foil and bake for 30–40 minutes or until the asparagus is softened; remove the foil and continue to roast until the vegetables are all fork tender.

4. Serve the asparagus topped with the onions and bell peppers; drizzle with liquid from the pan.

Makes 6 servings

Spanish-Style Green Beans

Green beans are a favorite vegetable and are rich in vitamins, including A, C, K, B_6, and folic acid. Plus, they are an excellent source of fiber and micronutrients. Green beans are easy to dress up with various flavors, including this simple Spanish style.

INGREDIENTS
- 1½ pounds green beans, trimmed
- 2 tablespoons olive oil
- 4 cloves garlic, peeled and minced
- 1 dried whole chile de arbol pepper
- Kosher salt and freshly ground black pepper

1. Bring a large pot of salted water to a boil over high heat. Add the beans and cook until crisp-tender, about 5 minutes. Drain well and set aside.

2. In a large skillet, heat the olive oil over medium heat. Add the garlic and the whole chili and cook, stirring constantly, for 1 minute. Add the green beans and toss so they are all coated with the oil and well heated, about 2 minutes. Remove and discard the chile pepper. Serve.

Makes 4 servings

Baked Falafel Patties

These little gems can be used in so many ways, including for breakfast with fruit, for lunch crumbled atop a hearty salad, or for dinner along with chili and a green salad. Make them in batches, store in the fridge, and use as needed. Also, form the patties into the size you want for your meals. For example, this recipe will make 4 large patties for entrées or 8 small patties for sides.

INGREDIENTS
- 2 cups fresh parsley, coarsely chopped
- 4 cloves garlic, peeled
- 2½ tablespoons fresh lemon juice
- 1¼ teaspoon ground cumin
- ½ teaspoon kosher salt
- 1 can (15 ounces) chickpeas, rinsed and drained
- ⅓ cup raw nuts (walnuts, pecans, or almonds), coarsely ground

1. Preheat oven to 375 degrees. (If you have made the patties ahead, you can preheat the oven when the patties are in the fridge or freezer.)

2. Using a food processor, mix the parsley, garlic, lemon juice, cumin, and salt until blended. Add the chickpeas and pulse until combined with other ingredients. The mixture should still be slightly chunky.

3. Transfer the mixture to a large bowl. Add the nut meal and stir until a dough forms that's firm enough to shape into patties. Adjust seasoning to taste.

4. Divide the dough into as many units as you desire (4–8 depending on how large you want the patties). Form the portions into round patties about ½ inch thick. Place the patties on a baking sheet; put the baking sheet in the refrigerator or freezer for about 15 minutes.

5. Bake for 30–40 minutes, flipping at the halfway point. Serve warm as a side or with sauce or toppings for an entrée.

6. Store leftover falafel patties, layered with parchment paper, in an airtight container in the refrigerator for up to 5 days or in the freezer for up to 1 month.

Makes 4 large or 8 small patties

Roasted Bell Peppers

This is another easy-to-prepare recipe that is rich in flavor, colorful, and useful in so many ways. I especially like to use these peppers in salads or in a simple pasta meal.

INGREDIENTS
- 6 large bell peppers, any color
- ½ cup olive oil
- 2 teaspoons kosher salt
- 2 teaspoons freshly ground pepper

1. Preheat the oven to 450 degrees.

2. Using a large bowl, toss the whole peppers with the oil, salt, and pepper, making sure they are all well coated.

3. Place the peppers on a large rimmed baking sheet or in a large roasting pan; drizzle any remaining oil over the peppers. Set the bowl aside to use later.

4. Place the peppers in the oven and roast until their skins begin to blister, then turn them over. Continue roasting the peppers until all sides are blistered, about 30 minutes. Remove from the oven.

5. Return the peppers to the bowl and drizzle any liquid from the roasting pan over them. Cover the bowl tightly with plastic wrap, place in a cool place, and allow to cool for 45–60 minutes.

6. Gently remove and discard the stem from each pepper (taking as many of the seeds with it as possible), reserving any liquid that may be inside. Peel and discard the skin and return the peppers to the bowl.

7. Finally, inspect each of the whole peppers and remove and discard any seeds that may remain. Slice and serve as a side dish. Leftover peppers can be stored in a glass container for up to two weeks.

Makes 6–10 servings

Roasted Ratatouille

My bestie, Toni, is a stunning home chef. She's the kind who can start with whatever her fridge may have to offer and within minutes serve an exquisite meal. She is also a lover of France and its cuisine. Toni was the first to serve me ratatouille, a vegetable stew from the region of Provence. Ratatouille may be tricky to spell, but it's actually easy to make and very tasty.

INGREDIENTS
- 2 medium eggplants, skin on and diced small (see prep note in item 1 below)
- 1 medium zucchini, diced
- 1 small yellow squash, diced
- 2 red bell peppers, diced
- 6 cloves garlic, peeled and minced
- 2 large tomatoes, diced
- 2 medium onions, diced
- ¼ cup olive oil
- 1 tablespoon fresh thyme, chopped
- 2 tablespoons fresh basil, chopped
- Kosher salt and freshly ground black pepper

1. Prepare the diced eggplant by soaking in 1 quart of cold, salted water for 15–20 minutes; drain.

2. Preheat the oven to 400 degrees.

3. Place the drained eggplant in a large roasting pan; add the zucchini, yellow squash, bell peppers, garlic, tomatoes, and onions. Drizzle with oil and sprinkle with thyme, basil, salt, and pepper. Then gently stir to mix and coat all the vegetables.

4. Roast in the preheated oven for 60 minutes. Carefully toss the vegetables from top to bottom so the vegetables cook evenly and then roast for 30 minutes more. Adjust seasoning as needed before serving.

Makes 6–8 servings

Sautéed Broccolini with Brown Rice

I can eat this recipe multiple times each week, either for lunch or dinner. Broccolini, which is baby broccoli, has thinner stalks than regular broccoli, is rich in flavor, and pairs perfectly with brown rice and soy sauce. The citrus in this recipe adds a sparkle to the flavor profile. This dish is simple to prepare and easy to make in batches so you can eat it for several days. Make for dinner and then use the leftovers for lunch the next day. Oh, and it packs easily to take to work, too.

INGREDIENTS
- 1 tablespoon olive oil
- 1 large clove garlic, peeled and thinly sliced
- 1 teaspoon soy sauce
- ½ cup water
- 1 bunch broccolini, washed, trimmed, and cut in 4-inch lengths; separate firm and tender pieces
- 4 cups cooked brown rice
- Fresh citrus fruit (lemon, lime, and/or orange) sliced in wedges, seeds removed
- Salt and black pepper to taste

1. In a large skillet over medium heat, heat oil, garlic, soy sauce, and water; bring to a steaming simmer. Add firm broccolini parts, reduce heat to medium-low, cover, and cook until barely beginning to soften, about 5 minutes. Add tender broccolini parts, cover, and cook 3–5 minutes more. Reduce heat to low.

2. Add rice and mix thoroughly with broccolini. Cover and cook until ingredients are evenly warmed and pan juices are absorbed into the mixture.

3. Transfer to a serving dish and place citrus wedges around edges, or make individual side servings on dinner plates with citrus wedges placed beside. Garnish with squeezed citrus juice and, if desired, a light sprinkle of salt and pepper.

Makes 4 servings

Roasted Brussels Sprouts and Carrots

Like most kids, I wasn't too keen on the funny-looking brussels sprouts when I was young. However, when my taste buds matured with adulthood, I began to enjoy them. Roasting the vegetables with carrots is an easy way to prepare this nutritious and tasty dish.

INGREDIENTS
- 1 pound brussels sprouts, trimmed
- 1 pound carrots, peeled and trimmed
- 2 teaspoons olive oil
- 1 teaspoon kosher salt
- ½ teaspoon freshly ground black pepper

1. Preheat oven to 400 degrees. Line a large rimmed baking sheet with parchment paper.

2. Place the brussels sprouts and carrots into a gallon-size ziplock bag. Add the olive oil, salt, and pepper. Seal the bag and maneuver so that the vegetables are well coated. Transfer the vegetables to the baking sheet.

3. Place the baking sheet into the oven and roast the vegetables for 40–50 minutes, tossing every 7 minutes to assure even cooking. If carrots cook faster, remove them from the baking sheet and set aside. The brussels sprouts are cooked when dark in color and fork tender.

4. Return any carrots that you may have removed to the pan for the last 5 minutes of roasting to heat well. Adjust seasoning with salt and pepper. Serve.

Makes 4 servings

Roasted Potatoes with Oregano and Lemon

Potatoes are an excellent choice for your Daniel Fast meals. With plenty of fiber, potassium, and vitamins C and B_6, potatoes are good for your body. Dress them up with some herbs and lemon, and let the humble vegetable delight your palate.

INGREDIENTS
- 2 pounds large russet potatoes, scrubbed, unpeeled, quartered lengthwise
- 2 tablespoons olive oil
- 2 teaspoons dried oregano
- Kosher salt
- Freshly ground black pepper
- ½ cup vegetable broth
- ½ cup water
- 1 medium lemon, juiced

1. Preheat oven to 450 degrees. Line a large rimmed baking sheet with parchment paper. Add the potatoes and drizzle with olive oil, tossing as necessary to coat each quarter. Sprinkle with oregano, salt, and pepper.

2. In a small bowl combine the broth, water, and lemon juice. Pour around the potatoes. Roast, uncovered, for about 50 minutes, tossing periodically to prevent sticking. Add more water to the pan if necessary. Roast until the potatoes are tender and golden. Serve.

Makes 6 servings

Air-Fryer Roasted Veggies

Air fryers are a healthy, efficient, and easy way to cook many foods, including vegetables. They use rapidly circulating air and a small amount of oil to give foods a crispy taste. If you have an air fryer, you'll likely use it often during your Daniel Fast and after.

VEGETABLE INGREDIENTS
- 3 cups vegetables, either tender (zucchini, summer squash, sweet pepper, mushrooms, cauliflower, asparagus) or firm (new potato, carrot, turnip, parsnip, winter squash, celeriac, sweet potato), prepared according to type and cut into 1-inch pieces
- 1 tablespoon olive oil
- ¼ teaspoon kosher salt
- ¼ teaspoon freshly ground black pepper
- 1 tablespoon fresh herbs of your choice
- 1 tablespoon white wine vinegar
- 1 tablespoon minced shallot

SAUCE INGREDIENTS
- 1 clove garlic, peeled and minced
- 1 teaspoon Dijon mustard
- ⅛ teaspoon salt
- ⅛ teaspoon pepper

FOR SERVING
- Kosher salt
- Freshly ground black pepper

1. Preheat air fryer to 360 degrees. In a large bowl, combine vegetables, oil, salt, pepper, herbs, vinegar, and shallot; toss to coat ingredients evenly. Arrange in fryer basket and cook tender vegetables about 10 minutes, stirring halfway through. Cook firm vegetables for 15 minutes, stirring every 5 minutes until tender.

2. Meanwhile, prepare the sauce by combining garlic, mustard, salt, and pepper in a small bowl.

3. Serve vegetables sprinkled with kosher salt and freshly ground pepper; enjoy with garlic-Dijon dipping sauce.

Makes 4 servings

Air-Fryer French Fries

Cook potatoes in an air fryer and then use them as a blank canvas to which you can add the flavors you enjoy. Here's just a sample. Be creative!

POTATO INGREDIENTS
- 1 pound white or sweet potatoes, peeled, if desired, and cut into sticks about ½ inch thick
- 1 teaspoon olive oil
- ¼ teaspoon salt
- ¼ teaspoon seasoning of choice

SEASONING INGREDIENTS
- Option 1: ½ teaspoon rosemary, dried and crushed, combined with ¼ teaspoon garlic salt
- Option 2: 1 tablespoon parsley, dry flakes or freshly chopped, combined with 1 tablespoon grated soy cheese and Italian seasoning to taste
- Option 3: 1 tablespoon grated soy cheese combined with smoked paprika to taste

1. In a large pot, cover potatoes in cool water and soak for 30 minutes. Drain and pat dry with paper towels. Place potatoes in a bowl, drizzle with oil, and toss to distribute an even coating.

2. Preheat air fryer to 400 degrees. Arrange a double layer of potato sticks in the fryer basket and begin cooking until golden brown, about 15–20 minutes, tossing potatoes at 5-minute intervals to ensure even cooking. Place in serving bowl and garnish with salt or prepared seasoning of choice.

Makes 4 servings

SNACKS

Popcorn Five Ways

The go-to nutritional superstar here is simply white, yellow, or multi-colored popcorn kernels. Using an air popper, pop ½ cup popcorn. Then give it a delicious touch using one of the following options.

SEASONING INGREDIENTS AND PREPARATION

1. Sriracha-Lime Popcorn: In a large bowl, sprinkle 1 tablespoon lime zest and ½ teaspoon salt over finished popcorn. In a small bowl, mix together 1 tablespoon light olive oil and 1 tablespoon of Thai sriracha sauce, then drizzle over popcorn mixture and toss to evenly distribute seasoning.

2. Popcorn Curry: In a small saucepan over medium heat, warm 3 tablespoons of coconut or olive oil. Add 2 large peeled and minced cloves of garlic and ¼ teaspoon each turmeric, curry, and cumin; stir and cook for 1 minute. Reduce heat to low and simmer for 1 minute more. Add 3–4 dashes hot sauce, stir, and pour over finished popcorn in a large bowl. Sprinkle with ½ teaspoon salt and toss well to coat evenly.

3. Garlic Popcorn: In a large bowl, spray aerosol olive oil cooking spray over finished popcorn and toss to coat evenly. Sprinkle popcorn with grated soy cheese, ¾ teaspoon garlic salt, and 1 teaspoon dried rosemary or 1 tablespoon chopped fresh rosemary. Toss the mixture to distribute ingredients.

4. Zippy Popcorn: In a microwave-safe bowl, mix together 2 tablespoons olive oil, 1 teaspoon paprika, ¾ teaspoon salt, ½ teaspoon cayenne pepper, and ¼ teaspoon black pepper. Microwave for 30 seconds, remove, stir, and drizzle over a serving bowl of finished popcorn. Toss well to evenly coat before serving.

5. Nutty Popcorn: In a medium bowl, mix together ½ cup each of unsalted, roughly chopped walnuts, almonds, and peanuts; whole pumpkin and sunflower seeds; and dried prunes cut in small pieces. Add nuts, seeds, and dried fruit to a serving bowl of finished popcorn and combine well. If desired, season with salt and black pepper to taste.

Makes 4 servings from 12 cups finished popcorn

Antipasto Platter

Your grill can be a valuable tool for your Daniel Fast. The key to getting those great grill marks is to not shift the vegetables too frequently once they've been placed on the hot grill.

INGREDIENTS
- 1 medium zucchini, cut lengthwise in ¼-inch strips
- 4 carrots, peeled and cut lengthwise in ¼-inch strips
- 1 yellow bell pepper, stem and seeds removed, cut lengthwise into 8 wedges
- 8 to 12 mushrooms, stems removed
- 4 to 8 green onions, tops trimmed and roots cut off
- ¼ cup olive oil
- Kosher salt and freshly ground black pepper
- 1 avocado, seeded, peeled, and cut into 8 wedges
- 12 cherry or grape tomatoes, whole
- 1 (8-ounce) jar of marinated artichoke hearts
- 2 dill pickles, cut lengthwise into quarters
- 4 to 8 deli-style peperoncini peppers
- 12 to 16 kalamata or Greek green olives
- Tajín Clásico Seasoning (optional)

1. Heat an outdoor grill or a stovetop cast-iron grill over medium-high heat. Brush the zucchini, carrots, bell peppers, mushrooms, and green onions with olive oil and place on grill; sprinkle the vegetables with salt and pepper. Grilling in batches, cook the vegetables until tender and lightly charred all over, about 4 minutes for the green onions, 7 minutes for the zucchini and mushrooms, and 8–10 minutes for the carrots and bell peppers. Cool to room temperature.

2. Arrange the grilled vegetables, avocado, tomatoes, artichoke hearts, pickles, peperoncini peppers, and olives in an artful way on the platter. Sprinkle with salt and pepper, and offer the Tajín Clásico Seasoning on the side.

Makes 4 generous servings

Tomato-Stuffed Avocado Snack

This simple, healthy snack or side dish serves your taste buds and your body's desire for nutrition. Keep the ingredients on hand and reach for them when you're tempted to eat foods not allowed on the fast.

INGREDIENTS
- 1 avocado, cut in half and seeded
- 1 vine-ripened tomato, seeded and chopped
- 1 tablespoon finely chopped fresh basil
- 1 teaspoon balsamic vinegar
- Kosher salt and freshly ground black pepper

1. Place each avocado half on an individual serving plate. Sprinkle with a bit of salt and set aside.

2. In a small bowl, gently toss the tomato, basil, and balsamic vinegar. Add salt and pepper to taste.

3. Spoon the tomato mixture over the avocado halves and serve.

Makes 2 servings

Crispy Kale Chips

You may find yourself missing "crunch foods" on your Daniel Fast. These chips are a nutritious choice. Make a batch and then keep them on hand for those "Ruffles" temptation moments.

INGREDIENTS
- 1 fresh bunch kale, stems and blemishes trimmed, washed and patted dry with paper towels
- 1 cup olive oil
- ½ cup distilled white vinegar
- 1 teaspoon finely ground salt

1. Preheat oven to 375 degrees and prepare a nonstick or lightly oiled baking sheet. Prepare a cooling rack near your oven work area. Cut kale greens into medium-sized pieces and set aside.

2. In a large crock or glass bowl, whisk together oil, vinegar, and salt. Add kale and work the oil mixture well into greens by hand.

3. Arrange kale greens across baking sheet, not allowing edges to touch. Bake 7–10 minutes, paying attention to make sure chips don't turn brown, as that leads to a bitter taste. Transfer crisp chips from oven to cooling rack.

Makes 4 servings

Daniel Fast Nut and Dried Fruit Mix

Make a batch of this healthy mixture and store it in an airtight container. You can also portion it into snack-sized ziplock baggies. Quarter-cup portions are easy to keep in your purse, your desk drawer, your glove compartment, or your cupboard.

INGREDIENTS
- 2 cups raw walnut pieces
- 2 cups raw pecan pieces
- 2 cups cashews, broken
- 1 cup golden raisins
- 1 cup coarsely chopped dates
- ½ cup sunflower seeds
- ½ cup pumpkin seeds

1. Place all ingredients in a large bowl and gently stir until thoroughly blended.

2. Store the mix in an airtight container.

Makes about 25 snack servings of ¼ cup each

Fresh Veggies with Hummus

I never buy hummus anymore. This homemade recipe tastes so much better, is free of chemicals, and is a fraction of the cost. Prepare a variety of veggies and see how this can be a great replacement for chips and dip!

VEGGIES
- 2 carrots, peeled and diagonally cut into ¼-inch slices
- 2 stalks celery, trimmed and cut into sticks
- 8 radishes, trimmed leaving a bit of the stem, and cut in half lengthwise
- 8 sugar snap peas
- 8 steamed and chilled green beans
- 1 jicama, peeled and cut into ¼-inch sticks
- 1 or 2 bell peppers (any color), stem and seeds removed, cut lengthwise into strips
- 1 zucchini, trimmed and diagonally cut into ¼-inch slices
- 8 cauliflower florets
- 8 broccoli florets

HUMMUS INGREDIENTS
- 1 can (15 ounces) chickpeas, drained and rinsed
- 2 to 4 tablespoons fresh lemon juice

- ¼ cup tahini (sesame seed paste, available at most grocery stores)
- 1 teaspoon cumin
- 1 teaspoon garlic powder
- ¼ cup water
- Kosher salt and freshly ground black pepper

1. Prepare the fresh vegetables and place on a serving platter in a pleasing design.

2. Place all the hummus ingredients in a food processor and blend until smooth. Adjust the consistency by adding more water 1 teaspoon at a time, and adjust the seasoning with salt and pepper to taste. Place in a small bowl and serve with cut vegetables.

Makes 4 generous servings

Spicy Pumpkin Dip

A collection of flavors makes up this unique dip recipe. I like serving it with vegetables and fruit for breakfast, for a simple meal, in place of a salad, or as a snack.

INGREDIENTS
- 6 to 8 cloves garlic, peeled
- ¼ cup fresh cilantro
- ¼ cup lime juice
- ¼ cup tahini
- 2 tablespoons olive oil
- 1 can (15 ounces) pumpkin
- 3 teaspoons cumin
- ½ teaspoon chili powder
- ½ teaspoon chipotle chili powder
- ½ cup pumpkin seeds, whole and chopped
- Salt, if desired

1. In a food processor, pulse-chop garlic finely. Add cilantro, lime juice, tahini, olive oil, pumpkin, cumin, chili powder, and chipotle chili powder; blend until evenly smooth. Transfer to a covered bowl and refrigerate to cool and to blend savory flavors.

2. Before serving with celery and carrot sticks, cucumber rounds, crisp romaine lettuce ribs, or slices of sweet apples, drizzle with additional olive oil and sprinkle pumpkin seed garnish across surface. Salt individual servings to taste.

Makes 4 servings

SOUPS

Easy Cajun Bean and Rice Soup

A lesson for your Daniel Fast meals—and for all healthy meals—is that rich flavors are more satisfying. This recipe provides a lot of nutrition, and it's also satisfying to your tastes. Simple, yet exactly what you need.

INGREDIENTS
- 2 tablespoons olive oil
- 1 medium onion, chopped
- 1 medium green bell pepper, diced
- 4 cloves garlic, peeled and minced
- 2 tablespoons Cajun seasoning
- 6 cups vegetable broth
- 3 cans (15 ounces each) red kidney beans, rinsed and drained
- 1 cup cooked brown rice
- Kosher salt and freshly ground black pepper

1. Using a large pot, heat the oil over medium-high heat. Add onion, bell pepper, and garlic, and sauté for 5–6 minutes. Add the Cajun seasoning and cook for 1 minute more; then add the vegetable broth and beans. Bring to a boil, reduce heat, and simmer for 15 minutes.

2. Add the cooked brown rice to the soup and cook for 5 minutes more. Season with salt and pepper as desired.

Makes 6 servings

Easy Minestrone Soup

Branded as the king of Mediterranean cuisine, the mixture of vegetables, beans, and pasta in minestrone soup results in a well-balanced and healthy collection of flavors, textures, and colors. Minestrone is a hearty meal to meet your body's need for nutrition. Plus, it's easy to make and a pleasure to eat.

INGREDIENTS
- 3 tablespoons olive oil
- 1 large onion, finely chopped
- 3 leeks, trimmed and coarsely chopped
- 3 stalks celery, coarsely chopped
- Kosher salt
- 1½ cups whole grain elbow or small shell pasta
- 1 pound red or white potatoes, cut into ½-inch cubes
- 8 to 10 sprigs fresh thyme
- Freshly ground black pepper
- 1½ pound fresh asparagus, trimmed and cut into 1-inch pieces
- ½ pound sugar snap peas, trimmed and cut in half crosswise
- 1 can (15 ounces) white beans, rinsed and drained

1. Heat the oil in a large soup pot or Dutch oven on medium heat. Add the onion, leeks, celery, and ½ teaspoon salt. Cover and cook until tender, stirring occasionally, 5–7 minutes.

2. Add the pasta, potatoes, thyme, ½ teaspoon salt, ½ teaspoon pepper, and 9 cups of water. Bring to a boil, then reduce heat to a simmer.

3. Add the asparagus, peas, and beans and continue to simmer until all the vegetables are tender, about 4–5 minutes.

4. Adjust seasoning and serve.

Makes 6 servings

Fast and Easy Tortilla Soup

Flavorful soups are excellent for your Daniel Fast menus, and Tortilla Soup is a perfect choice. Consider doubling the recipe so you can use leftovers for lunches or other dinner meals. This recipe is easy to prepare and plentiful in colors, textures, and flavors.

INGREDIENTS
- 1 tablespoon olive oil
- 1 cup chopped onion
- 1 poblano chili pepper, stemmed, seeded, and chopped
- 4 cups vegetable broth
- 1 can (15 ounces) black beans, rinsed and drained
- 1½ cups chopped tomato
- 2 tablespoons ground cumin
- 4 corn tortillas, cut into ½-inch strips
- 1 cup frozen corn kernels
- Salt and pepper to taste
- 2 avocados, halved, seeded, peeled, and chopped
- 1 lime, juiced

1. Preheat the oven to 375 degrees.

2. Heat the oil in a large saucepan over medium heat; add the onion and poblano and cook about 4–5 minutes or until tender.

3. Stir in the broth, black beans, tomatoes, and cumin; bring to a boil and then reduce heat to a simmer. Continue to cook uncovered for 15 minutes, stirring occasionally.

4. While the soup is cooking, spread the tortilla strips in a single layer on a baking sheet. Bake in preheated oven for about 10 minutes or until crisp; watch carefully so they don't burn.

5. Stir the corn into the soup and continue to cook for just 1–2 minutes. Adjust seasoning with salt and pepper. Just before serving, stir in avocados and lime juice. Serve with tortilla strips.

Makes 6 servings

Note: Whenever you use prepared products during your Daniel Fast, be sure to read the list of ingredients to be assured that the contents are totally plant-based and free of any chemicals or sweeteners.

Quinoa and Bean Chili

This chili has it all! Whole grains and beans, being complete proteins, make this hearty dish a perfect standard for your meals. Plus, the flavors are pleasing. When paired with a simple green salad, you have a wonderful meal.

INGREDIENTS
- 1 tablespoon olive oil
- 1 medium yellow onion, chopped
- 1 medium zucchini, chopped
- 3 cloves garlic, peeled and minced
- ½ pound mushrooms, chopped
- 2 tablespoons chili powder
- ½ teaspoon ground cumin
- ½ teaspoon dried oregano
- Kosher salt and freshly ground black pepper
- ½ cup uncooked red quinoa, rinsed and drained
- 2 cans (14.5 ounces each) diced tomatoes, undrained
- 1 cup vegetable broth
- 1 can (15.5 ounces) black beans, rinsed and drained
- 1 can (15.5 ounces) kidney beans, rinsed and drained
- 1 can (15.5 ounces) pinto beans, rinsed and drained

1. In a large pot, heat the oil over medium heat. Add the onion and zucchini; cover and cook until tender, about 5 minutes. Add the garlic and mushrooms and cook for 2 minutes. Stir in the chili powder, cumin, and oregano, plus salt and pepper to taste. Add the quinoa, tomatoes, and broth. Increase the heat and bring to a boil. Then reduce the heat to a simmer, cover, and cook for 15 minutes.

2. Add the beans and gently stir to blend all ingredients together. Simmer uncovered for 30 minutes. Adjust seasoning with salt and pepper before serving.

Makes 4 servings

Hearty Vegetable Soup

A good vegetable soup recipe is perfect for any personal collection. This recipe has all the basic ingredients. Make it and adjust it to your liking; then make it again and adjust it again so that it gets even better. Soon you will have a favorite that will be your own special Hearty Vegetable Soup that you'll use for your Daniel Fast and beyond.

INGREDIENTS
- 2 tablespoons olive oil
- 1 medium yellow onion, chopped
- 1 medium leek, trimmed, white and light green portion cut into ½-inch disks
- 4 cloves garlic, peeled and minced
- 2 carrots, peeled and diced
- 2 stalks celery, diced
- 2 teaspoons dried Italian herbs
- 8 cups vegetable broth
- 3 to 4 white or red potatoes, peels on and diced into bite-size pieces
- 3 cans (15 ounces each) red beans, rinsed and drained
- 1 cup spinach leaves, stems removed
- Kosher salt and freshly ground black pepper

1. Using a large pot, heat the oil over medium-high heat. Add the onion, leek, garlic, carrots, and celery. Sprinkle with salt and then sauté for 4–5 minutes, stirring occasionally to prevent sticking. Add the Italian herbs and cook until fragrant, about 1 minute.

2. Add the vegetable broth, potatoes, and beans. Bring to a boil, then reduce heat and simmer for 10–12 minutes or until the potatoes are softened. Add the spinach and cook for 2 more minutes.

3. Adjust seasoning with salt and pepper before serving.

Makes 6 servings

Black Bean and Sweet Potato Soup

A hearty soup can be a complete meal, and this recipe surely fills the bill. The colors and textures are pleasing along with the satisfying flavors. Plus, the ingredients are nutritious.

INGREDIENTS
- 1 tablespoon olive oil
- 1 medium yellow onion, chopped
- 3 cloves garlic, peeled and minced
- 1 large sweet potato, peeled and diced
- 2 cans (15 ounces) black beans, rinsed and drained
- 1 can (14.5 ounces) diced tomatoes, undrained
- 1 teaspoon ground cumin
- ½ teaspoon ground coriander
- ½ teaspoon paprika
- 4 cups vegetable broth
- Kosher salt and freshly ground black pepper
- 6 cups chopped kale leaves (free of stems)

1. Using a large pot, heat the oil over medium-high heat. Add the onion and cook until softened, about 5 minutes. Add garlic and cook for 1 more minute. Stir in the sweet potato, black beans, tomatoes, cumin, coriander, paprika, broth, and salt and pepper to taste. Bring to a boil, then reduce the heat to simmer until the vegetables are tender, about 20 minutes.

2. Stir in the kale. Adjust seasoning with salt and pepper and simmer for an additional 10 minutes before serving.

Makes 4 servings

Spicy Lentil Soup

I never ate lentil soup until I started using the Daniel Fast method of fasting. Then, as I searched for hearty, economical, and easy-to-make recipes, lentil soup emerged as one of my favorites. I also decided to purchase my first immersion blender so I could make lentil soup more efficiently. Now it's one of my most-used kitchen utensils.

INGREDIENTS
- 2 tablespoons olive oil
- 1 medium onion, chopped
- 4 cloves garlic, peeled and minced
- 2 carrots, peeled and diced
- 2 stalks celery, diced
- 2 teaspoons cumin
- 2 teaspoons curry powder
- 1 can (28 ounces) diced tomatoes
- 6 cups vegetable broth
- 1 cup green lentils, picked and rinsed
- 1 cup spinach, stems removed and packed
- Kosher salt and freshly ground black pepper

1. Using a large pot, heat the oil over medium-high heat. Add the onion, garlic, carrots, and celery and sauté for 5–6 minutes. Add the cumin and curry powder and cook for 1 minute more until fragrant.

2. Add the tomatoes and the vegetable broth and bring to a boil. Stir in the lentils, then reduce the heat to low; cover and cook at a low simmer until the lentils are tender, approximately 35–40 minutes.

3. Unless you like a chunkier soup, use a handheld immersion blender to puree soup to your preferred consistency. Add the spinach and cook until well heated; adjust seasoning and serve.

Makes 6 servings

Basic Split Pea Soup

This wholesome, nourishing soup is a good core recipe for your Daniel Fast. Make a double batch while you're cooking another meal; then serve some the next day and freeze the rest for later.

INGREDIENTS
- 16 ounces dry green split peas, rinsed and drained
- 6 cups vegetable stock
- 2 leeks, chopped (white and pale-green parts only)
- 3 carrots, peeled and chopped
- 2 celery stalks, chopped
- 3 cloves garlic, peeled and chopped
- 1 teaspoon dried thyme
- 1 bay leaf
- Salt and ground black pepper to taste
- Red pepper flakes, optional garnish

1. In a large bowl, cover split peas with water to 1 inch above surface and soak for 4 hours; drain.

2. In a 4-quart slow cooker on low heat, add split peas to remaining ingredients; stir to combine. Cover and cook for 8 hours on low.

3. Remove lid and bay leaf. Serve immediately for a chunkier texture, or let cool a half hour before processing mixture in a high-speed blender until smooth. Reheat, then serve in individual bowls with red pepper flake garnish.

Makes 4 servings

Quick and Easy Black Bean Chili

I'm all for the quick and easy meals, and this recipe fits the description perfectly. Make it while preparing other recipes for super efficiency, and then freeze portions for meals in your near future. Flavorful and nutritious, this recipe is great for lunches. Or pair with a green salad and tortillas for your dinner meal.

INGREDIENTS
- 2 medium-size red bell peppers, chopped
- 1 medium-size yellow onion, chopped
- 6 cloves garlic, peeled and minced
- 2 to 3 tablespoons olive oil
- 2 tablespoons chili powder
- 2 teaspoons ground cumin
- 2 teaspoons dried oregano
- ½ teaspoon cayenne pepper
- 3 cans (15 ounces each) black beans, juice and all
- 1 can (16 ounces) diced tomatoes
- Salt and pepper to taste
- Chopped fresh cilantro and chopped green onions for garnish

1. In a large pot over medium-high heat, sauté the peppers, onions, and garlic in oil until the onions are translucent and the peppers begin to soften. Add the chili powder, cumin, oregano, and cayenne pepper, heating until fragrant.

2. Stir in the beans and tomatoes. Bring to a boil and then reduce the heat. Let simmer uncovered for 15–20 minutes, stirring occasionally to prevent sticking. Season to taste with salt and pepper.

3. Garnish individual soup bowls with cilantro and green onions.

Makes 4 generous servings

Susan's Vegetarian Chili

Over the years, I've created and presented hundreds of Daniel Fast recipes. This one is by far the most popular, and it's appeared in both *The Daniel Fast* and *The Daniel Fast for Weight Loss*. Actually, I started making it for my family long before I ever knew about the Daniel Fast. It's quick and easy to make, economical, great to make in large batches, and freezes well. I fill gallon-size ziplock bags and lay the filled bags flat in my freezer until frozen; once they're hardened, I can position them differently. The bags thaw quickly for a fast meal.

INGREDIENTS
- 2 medium-size green peppers, chopped
- 1 medium-size yellow onion, chopped
- 2 tablespoons olive oil
- 1 zucchini, sliced
- 1 yellow squash, sliced
- 2 tablespoons chili powder (adjust to your liking)
- ¾ teaspoon salt
- ¼ teaspoon ground red pepper (optional)
- 2 cups corn kernels (fresh or frozen)
- 2 cans (15 ounces each) tomatoes, juice and all
- 2 cans (15 ounces each) pinto beans, juice and all
- 2 cans (15 ounces each) black beans, juice and all
- 1 can (4 ounces) mild green chilies
- 1 can (6 ounces) tomato paste

1. In a large saucepan, sauté the peppers and onions in oil. Add the sliced zucchini and yellow squash, chili powder, salt, ground red pepper, and corn; stir and heat. When all the vegetables are soft but still slightly firm, add the tomatoes, all the beans, the green chilies, and the tomato paste. Stir until just blended.

2. Bring to a boil and then reduce the heat. Let simmer for 15–20 minutes, stirring occasionally to prevent sticking. Serve hot.

Makes 6 generous servings

Meal Planning

Food manufacturers are now providing more prepared foods that are free of sugar, processed ingredients, and man-made chemicals. However, you will find you need to prepare most of your meals at home if you want a reasonable variety of meal choices.

Invest a little time one day a week to plan your menus and your shopping list.

1. Create a simple chart like the menu planner on page 216 to use for your personal planning.

2. Review the foods you have on hand, first checking your perishables and then your cupboard and pantry items.

3. Review your schedule for the week to make allowances for time away from home, meals out, or other engagements that will impact the number of meals you will prepare. Remember to include leftovers in your planning, especially if you are fasting on your own. Most of the recipes make multiple servings.

4. To make the fast more affordable, consider building menus around food items that may be on sale. Check the weekly ads and other coupons you may have on hand.

5. Choose recipes from the collection here or others you like. Adjust your own recipes to make sure they comply with the Daniel Fast and will be enjoyed by you and your family members.

6. Plan what you will eat for breakfasts, lunches, dinners, and snacks, and add it to your meal-planning chart. Make a grocery list with all the ingredients you need. Try to plan times when you can cook once and eat twice, or prepare lunch meals while cooking breakfast or dinner.

7. Place your meal plans in a folder or notebook in the kitchen for easy access during the week.

8. Now work your plan! Go to the grocery store for your weekly shopping trip, and post your menu plan in the kitchen where you can access it easily. Each evening or morning (whichever works best for you), review the recipes you will use so you can plan for thawing time and preparation.

9. Use the time when you prepare meals to listen to teaching CDs or podcasts, visit with family members, memorize Scripture, pray, listen to music, or whatever you like to make the time enjoyable and pleasant.

10. At the end of the week, review how your meal plan worked for you and your family and make adjustments. Give thanks for the order in your life, for the improving health of you and your family, and for the money you've saved by planning meals instead of grabbing expensive prepared foods. Then repeat the process!

Use this sample weekly meal plan for your first week of fasting or as a model so you can create your own set of menus. You will be so pleased and relieved if you plan your meals ahead of time. You can go to Daniel-Fast.com/mealplanner for a handy worksheet to print out.

Day	Breakfast	Lunch	Dinner	Snack
1	No-Brainer Overnight Oats	Roasted Beet, Spinach, and Quinoa Salad	Susan's Vegetarian Chili with a green salad	Tomato-Stuffed Avocados
2	Green Berry Smoothie	Susan's Vegetarian Chili (leftovers)	Loaded Sweet Potatoes with Apple and Farro Salad	Fresh Veggies with Hummus
3	Brown Rice Breakfast Bowl	Pasta with Marinated Tomato Sauce	Burrito Bowl with sliced fresh fruit	Popcorn Five Ways (as you like it)
4	Quick, Sweet, and Nutritious Smoothie	Whole Grain Spelt, Bean, and Veggie Salad	West African Peanut Soup with Brown Rice with dinner salad	Antipasto Platter
5	Breakfast Burritos	West African Peanut Soup with Brown Rice (leftovers)	Roasted Whole Cauliflower with beets and Swiss chard	Daniel Fast Nut and Dried Fruit Mix
6	Quick, Sweet, and Nutritious Smoothie	Chard and Pesto Linguine	Sweet and Fruity Stuffed Acorn Squash with sliced fresh fruit	Crispy Kale Chips
7	Oatmeal and More	Red Curry Vegetables with Brown Rice	Atakilt Wat— Ethiopian Cabbage, Carrot, and Potato Dish	Apple slices with peanut butter

Day	Breakfast	Lunch	Dinner	Snack
1				
2				
3				
4				
5				
6				
7				

Other Tips

- When you return from a shopping trip, wash, prepare, and store all your salad ingredients so they are handy throughout the week when you create your meals. You will be amazed at how quickly you can make a salad when all the ingredients are already sliced and ready to go!

- Consider having a cooking day when you prepare several meals that you can then store or freeze for later in the week. This cook-once-eat-several-times approach to meals will save hours of time during the week.

- Make your own snack bags by filling small snack-size ziplock plastic bags with one serving each of a favorite snack, such as ¼ cup raw or seasoned nuts, sliced veggies, or sliced fruit.

- Make sure you have Daniel Fast food available so you can stay within the guidelines when you are short on time or experiencing cravings. If you plan for those challenging moments, you will be prepared when they occur.

- Engage the family in meal planning and preparation. Having children prepare vegetables and fruits for their meals can increase their desire to consume them.

- When you come to the end of the fast, don't immediately jump into eating and drinking whatever you want. Your body will not be used to sugar, caffeine, dairy, or meat. Consuming too much too fast can cause cramps, headaches, anxiety, or other symptoms.

Frequently Asked Questions

How can I afford the Daniel Fast? Preparing simple meals for your Daniel Fast can be very affordable. Beans, whole grains, in-season fresh vegetables, frozen and canned vegetables, salad greens, and frozen fruit can be purchased at reasonable prices. Prepared foods can be more expensive, so I encourage you to make batches of chili and soup to keep on hand for your meals.

Keep in mind that while you will be spending more money on Daniel Fast foods, you will also be spending less in other categories. You'll be eliminating meat and dairy, which are typically some of the more expensive parts of a grocery budget. If you're not purchasing a package of chicken breasts or ground beef for a meal, you'll have that money available for other ingredients.

You will also likely find yourself spending less money eating out during your fast, as much restaurant fare is not Daniel Fast–friendly. In our busy culture, take-out food or meals out can be a significant portion of the food budget.

If you don't typically cook from scratch, you may find yourself spending more money buying spices and other ingredients you don't usually buy. The good news is that those spices will last long after you finish the fast. You may be surprised to find that you want to continue to use them and cook more of your meals at home!

If you're concerned about the cost, I encourage you to look at grocery ads and check on prices. You might plan your menus around whatever vegetables are on sale that week. In addition, some of the staples for the Daniel Fast are quite inexpensive, such as brown rice, beans and other legumes (especially bags of dried beans or lentils), and potatoes. Plan meals around these options for lower costs.

Do I have to buy only organic and natural food for the Daniel Fast? No, although if they are available and suitable for your food budget, I believe they are healthier and safer for your body. Also, organic foods are becoming more widely available at good prices as consumers demand better-quality food.

Is the Daniel Fast always twenty-one days? Can I do fewer or more days? Most people use the Daniel Fast for twenty-one consecutive days; however, it's not a requirement. A partial fast is best used for a minimum of seven consecutive days. Many people choose to extend the fast up to forty days. Seek God's guidance and choose the number of days that is best for you.

What happens if God doesn't answer my prayer during the fast? We're instructed to ask and then believe we'll receive before we can touch or experience the outcome. Our part is to ask and believe. God fulfills His promises, and He's in charge of the "how and when." Continue to build your trust in God. Continue to thank Him for the work He is doing on your behalf. And be patient. If you're concerned that you've asked amiss, seek the Lord, alter your request, and then present it again to the Lord.

What do I do if I keep doubting? The Bible teaches us that we are transformed with the renewing of our minds (see Romans 12:2). Doubting is a sign that we're not trusting God, but instead falling back into worldly or carnal thinking (see 1 Corinthians 3:1-3). If you're doubting, spend time with your Father. Meditate on His truths. And allow your mind to be changed as you feed it with the bread of heaven. Your faith is like a muscle. You can strengthen your faith muscle by using it and nourishing your mind with the truth.

What should I do if I give in to temptation during the fast? Immediately resume the fast, unless you have totally walked away for several days. (If that's the case, then start again.) Also, examine your behavior and your heart to discover why you decided to give in to the temptations. You can learn valuable lessons about yourself. Think through what you will do differently next time so you don't repeat the mistake you made. Use the experience to learn and grow.

Honey is a natural food, so can I use it as a sweetener on the Daniel Fast? No, we avoid all sweeteners on the Daniel Fast. In Daniel 10:3, the prophet notes that he "ate no pleasant food, no meat or wine came into my mouth." Honey falls in the category of "pleasant." Also, going without sweetened foods is part of the fasting experience of withholding food for spiritual purposes.

Can I drink tea on the Daniel Fast? No, tea and coffee (including any kind of substitutes) are not allowed on the Daniel Fast. For the purists, water is the only acceptable beverage, while some people also drink 100 percent fruit or vegetable juice. It's most likely that Daniel drank only water.

What about people with special dietary needs? How do they do the Daniel Fast? Teens, women who are pregnant, diabetics, athletes, and others who may need special diets should check with their health providers before starting any fast, including the Daniel Fast. However, most health providers will find the Daniel Fast an excellent way to eat since it includes all vegetables, all fruits, all whole grains, no sugar, no alcohol, no caffeine, and no animal products. You might be instructed to add chicken or fish into the mix, which would be fine for a special-needs diet. Remember, there is no power in the foods themselves; rather, fasting is about consecrating yourself to the Lord so that you can focus on Him in a more specific and concentrated way. So if your health provider wants you to add animal protein into the diet, you can still have a successful fast.

How about corn chips and tortillas? When you read through the blog on my website, you will find that I am constantly encouraging people to READ THE LABEL so they can see the ingredients in prepared foods. I was amazed the first time I read the list of chemicals in prepared tortillas! Corn chips are usually deep-fried, and no deep-fried and processed foods are allowed during the Daniel Fast. However, there is a recipe on the blog for natural tortillas, and it's easy to use this same recipe to make your own chips. The tortillas are made from whole wheat flour, olive oil, salt, and water. You can easily substitute finely ground cornmeal. The tortillas are then warmed in a dry pan with little or no oil.

What about cramping in my legs and in my stomach? If cramping persists and you sense a concern, be sure to contact your health professional. The cramping is most likely a symptom of your body detoxing. The typical diet is packed with sugar, caffeine, and chemicals. So when these are eliminated, the body is a little confused and responds with cramps. The best remedy is to drink lots of water (the best detox there is), increase your vitamin C, and eat extra bananas and cantaloupe until the cramping subsides. This usually ends in a few days. Headaches are also very common—usually a symptom of caffeine withdrawal.

If you have other questions, visit Daniel-Fast.com/blog. Most of your questions will be answered, plus you will gain great encouragement as you read comments from thousands of other men and women around the world who are seeking God with prayer and fasting! If you still have a question, leave a comment on the blog and most often you will receive an answer within twenty-four hours.

Tools and
Resources

BOOKS ABOUT PERSONAL FINANCE

Smart Women Finish Rich: 9 Steps to Achieving Financial Security and Funding Your Dreams by David Bach

The Automatic Millionaire: A Powerful One-Step Plan to Live and Finish Rich by David Bach

The Latte Factor: Why You Don't Have to Be Rich to Live Rich by David Bach and John David Mann

Rich Dad Poor Dad: What the Rich Teach Their Kids about Money—That the Poor and Middle Class Do Not! by Robert Kiyosaki

The Total Money Makeover: A Proven Plan for Financial Fitness by Dave Ramsey

Your Money or Your Life: 9 Steps to Transforming Your Relationship with Money and Achieving Financial Independence by Vicki Robin and Joe Dominguez

The Millionaire Next Door: The Surprising Secrets of America's Wealthy by Thomas J. Stanley and William D. Danko

SOFTWARE AND DIGITAL TOOLS

Quicken

Mint

Acorns

Twenty-One-Day
Daniel Fast Devotional

As you begin your Daniel Fast, plan to set aside at least thirty minutes every day to meet with God for prayer and time in His Word. This is the most important, most transformative part of the fast. I pray that these devotionals will call you deeper into the fasting experience and, more importantly, into trust in God.

I've found it best to give God the very first part of my day, before distractions can rob me of this special time. During the Daniel Fast I prepare a cup of boiling hot water with a slice of lemon. Then I nestle into my overstuffed easy chair. As I sip on the hot water I talk with my Father. I tell Him whatever is on my mind and relax with Him. And then I dig into my Bible, devotions, and study materials.

I encourage you to follow a similar practice. I've created each of the devotions with you in mind. My hope is that you will more deeply grasp the awesome and loving nature of God. That you will see more clearly your identity as His child and as a citizen of His Kingdom. And that you will continue to grow in the love and knowledge of Jesus Christ.

DAY ONE

Be Thankful in All Circumstances

Be thankful in all circumstances, for this is God's will for you who belong to Christ Jesus.

1 THESSALONIANS 5:18, NLT

If you're experiencing challenges with money, you're likely feeling anxious, stressed, and even scared. I get it. I've been there. I told you my story in part I, so you know that when I was at rock bottom back in 2007, I was more fearful than I had ever been in my life. Yet, looking back now, I can see that that dark and scary time was also one of the best times for me. Because of the desperate place I was in, I learned to depend on God like never before. I learned how to use my faith in a way I had never known. I grew in my understanding of the Scriptures and experienced a spiritual transformation that changed my life forever. I underwent a life-altering breakthrough.

I'm not sure I would have ever learned the lessons I did if I hadn't gone through the desperate circumstances of that period. So I am thankful. I praise God for being with me, for ministering to me, and for being patient with me as I turned to Him and learned to trust Him.

I don't believe for a second that God caused the financial trauma that brought havoc into my life. I do believe He was with me the whole time, ready to come to my aid, and that He was protecting me from further pain. And the same is true for you.

Turn to God and you will gain insights, truths, and revelations that would otherwise remain hidden from you. Hidden not because they are secrets, but because they are spiritual understandings that can be seen only with spiritual eyes.

You now have an opportunity to take the hand of God's Holy Spirit and enter into a different way of living. You have an invitation to enlist in the school of higher learning with your Lord. And you have a loving summons to put your trust in God, who treasures you and wants to equip you with the spiritual tools that will see you through whatever challenges you are facing. You are taking this time of prayer and fasting to bring your financial concerns to God, so lay those before Him now. Ask Him for wisdom and thank Him for His leading and direction.

Be thankful for this circumstance, as God calls you to do in His Word. See it as an opportunity to grow in knowledge and understanding. Receive the gifts your Father wants to give as you open your heart to Him and His powerful ways.

Even now, as you start your Daniel Fast, thank God for what you will learn over these twenty-one days. Lay down your fear. Wrap yourself in the robe of God's love, and receive the crown that comes with being a child of the Most High. Walk with Him in the Spirit, and thank Him for what He is already doing in your heart and soul. Be thankful in this circumstance, for this is God's will for you who belong to Christ Jesus. And put your trust in your Father, who will see you through.

You are your heavenly Father's precious child. He adores you, and He wants the very best for you. You are not all on your own; you are His. And as you enter into this fasting experience, He will be with you. Take hold of His hand, be with Him, and let Him guide you as you walk this part of your journey in faith.

Prayer: *God, please help me to enter into this Daniel Fast with thanksgiving, knowing that whatever my circumstances or my financial needs, You are with me and have things to teach me.*

Fasting tip: If you haven't already planned meals for the first few days of your fast, take time to do it today. It can seem difficult to find quick options that are Daniel Fast–compliant, so preparing ahead will set you up for success.

DAY TWO

Five Smooth Stones

Saul clothed David with his armor, and he put a bronze helmet on his head; he also clothed him with a coat of mail. David fastened his sword to his armor and tried to walk, for he had not tested them. And David said to Saul, "I cannot walk with these, for I have not tested them." So David took them off. Then he took his staff in his hand; and he chose for himself five smooth stones from the brook, and put them in a shepherd's bag, in a pouch which he had, and his sling was in his hand. And he drew near to the Philistine.

1 SAMUEL 17:38-40

You're likely familiar with the epic story of the young shepherd boy David facing the formidable Philistine giant Goliath. Clearly, based on mere physical presence, Goliath had the convincing advantage as he towered over David, plus he had a matchless reputation as an intrepid warrior.

When we're facing a giant challenge like mounting debt, unpaid bills, and calls from collection agencies, we can feel so small. And on the surface, or according to the world's system, we are too weak and disadvantaged to be able to fix our problems. But we have a distinct way of facing our giant, just as David did when he faced Goliath.

David's background was unlike Goliath's. The shepherd's training came from his many days in the wilderness protecting his father's herd of sheep. He must have spent many hours in prayer, because we know from his psalms that David knew how to depend on God. He also knew how to muster his courage. He had fought against a bear and won. He had fought against a lion and triumphed. He knew how to fight, and he knew how to trust in God and keep Him as the invisible force for his success.

King Saul wanted to prepare David for battle using Saul's own armor and weapons. David went with the plan at first, but then he checked in with what he knew. He didn't feel comfortable with the armor and the sword. He had a better way.

Yes, you and I want to use sound principles and solid practices for money management and wise stewardship. But at times, those strategies don't match up with what can seem like an overwhelming force coming against us. And so, like David, we turn to what we know will work. We trust in God and put our faith in His ways.

David stripped himself of the armor and the helmet. He set aside the sword. And instead, he armed himself with what appeared to be a simple, feeble tool: his slingshot. Then he went to the nearby brook, knelt down, and chose five smooth stones. I envision the young man speaking softly to the God he knew so well. He opened his heart to God so he could be filled with the matchless courage that only the Most High can provide.

David stood, armed with his familiar and trusted weapons.

Then David said to the Philistine, "You come to me with a sword, with a spear, and with a javelin. But I come to you in the name of the LORD of hosts, the God of the armies of Israel, whom you have defied. This day the LORD will deliver you into my hand, and I will strike you and take your head from you."
1 SAMUEL 17:45-46

Do you see it? Yes, David had his slingshot and the five smooth stones. But greater than the physical instruments was his faith that God was with him and that God would fight his battle.

We know the outcome. Goliath was down before he knew what hit him. And David, with the Lord, triumphed over what appeared to the natural eye to be insurmountable odds. However, David knew he had access to a power that is not of this world. He knew God and His character, and he trusted God.

How about you? Do you trust God to be the force that defeats the giant you may be facing now? Do you know that your Father wants you free of the burden and stress? And most important, do you know God and know that He is stronger, mightier, and better prepared than any enemy you could ever face?

You, too, can prepare for your battle. Put your trust in God. Then get into the "brook" you have available to you, the living Word of God, and select five promises to use as your smooth stones. Declare them over your situation. In these days of fasting, follow the practice Jesus taught the disciples when He told them to "say to the mountain" (see Matthew 21:21) and hoist the powerful truth of God's Word at your challenge. Then call it finished as you wait for the giant to fall and for you to receive the victory that is yours in Christ.

Prayer: *Father, Your Word is rich in wisdom, encouragement, and instructions for living a grounded life that's secure in You. Thank You for Your assurance that You are the same now as in the days of David. Thank You that I can count on Your Word to lead and direct me as I navigate this leg in my journey.*

Reflection: Spend some time with your Bible or a concordance and write down five promises from God's Word that you will rely on during your Daniel Fast.

DAY THREE

Walk in the Spirit

If we live in the Spirit, let us also walk in the Spirit.
GALATIANS 5:25

Have you ever heard the title "life coach"? Trained individuals with skills and insights help people with life issues, including financial pressures and decisions. Sometimes life coaches help solve problems. Sometimes they help their clients set and achieve goals. And sometimes they help their followers find clarity and understanding.

In today's world, the apostle Paul, who spent the last several years of his life planting new churches and helping believers grow in the faith, could be called a life coach. He was helping people understand how to live their new lives in Christ.

In his letter to the many congregations in the area of Galatia, Paul was encouraging the followers of Jesus to live out their faith and to practice the things they were learning. He was saying, "If you call yourself a Christian . . . if you believe in Christ, then take the necessary steps to fulfill your new life in Christ."

You and I can hear the same instruction from the apostle. If we indeed call ourselves Christians, if we live in the Spirit, then let us also behave in such a way. Just as the congregations in Galatia were learning a new way of life, we too can learn a new way to live. There is a difference between life in the Spirit and life in the world, or life in Christ and life in the flesh. There is a difference between being rich in spirit and being rich according to the world's standards.

A bit earlier in the epistle, Paul tells us, "Walk in the Spirit, and you shall not fulfill the lust of the flesh" (Galatians 5:16). This speaks to the separated life that we have the opportunity and the privilege to live.

This sanctified life, or a life that is set apart for the purposes of God, has distinct ways of operating. This isn't something to add on to the way we live now. Instead, we're to look to the Lord and the ways of the Kingdom and allow our lives to be brand new. We seek first the Kingdom of God. That is our opportunity. That is our call.

Take a sheet of paper and draw a line from top to bottom. On one side at the top, write "The World." Over the other column, write "Kingdom Living."

Now think about behaviors and attitudes that characterize the worldly way of living compared to the Kingdom-of-God way of living. For example, in the world there is fear, whereas in the Kingdom of God there is hope. In the world there is strife, but in the Kingdom of God there is peace. In the world there is selfishness and envy, while in the Kingdom of God there is service and encouragement.

I long to see the body of Christ walking in the Spirit and living in the way of the Lord to such a degree that we truly shine in this dark world. My hope is that one day people will be so encouraged by and attracted to the Christian life that they will be lining up at churches to receive this knowledge. How do we do that? One life at a time. Your life. My life. We start with ourselves.

If you live in the Spirit, then also walk in the Spirit. If you believe in Christ, then behave like Christ. Follow His ways. Allow Him to be your Model for right living. Let your beliefs affect every part of your life.

As you live your day-to-day life and continue the Daniel Fast, check in with yourself. Are you operating in the Spirit, or are you operating in the ways of the world? This is all part of our growth process. We're learning a new way of living, just like the Galatians.

As you experience the challenges, the hopes, and the joys of this life, do so in a manner that is consistent with the ways of the Lord. That is your joy. That is your happiness. That is your fulfillment to living in the Spirit.

During these days of extended prayer and fasting, you have the opportunity to consider this way of life even more. Open your heart to the Lord. Let Him teach you. Let Him guide you. And listen for how He is encouraging you to make changes in your life. Bit by bit. Step by step. If you live in the Spirit, then also walk in the Spirit.

Prayer: *Lord, I pray that what I believe would be more than just words. May my beliefs affect everything I do and say. As I go through the fast, teach me to walk more and more in Your Spirit.*

Reflection: How are you doing with the Faithful Servant Action Steps? Set yourself up for success. Walk toward your solutions. Commit to working through the Action Steps as you go through the twenty-one days of your fast.

DAY FOUR

Be Blessed

> *The blessing of the LORD makes one rich,*
> *and He adds no sorrow with it.*
> PROVERBS 10:22

As you go through your Daniel Fast experience, my prayer is that it will be filled with revelation and growing understanding about yourself and about God. My hope is that you're well on your way into a new mode of living—into a Kingdom-of-God lifestyle that is filled with expectancy, confidence, a stronger faith, and a deeper trust in God.

I believe today's verse from Proverbs 10 relates back to the beginning, when God blessed his people and provided everything they needed and more. They were rich with God's blessing and presence. That was what He wanted for all of humankind, but then, because of Adam's sin, there was the curse, which brought sorrow. Now the Lord is saying to you that His blessing, which is yours, makes you rich, and He brings no sorrow with it!

Remember who you are. You're that prodigal child who came back into the father's house, where you were given the robe and the ring and the sandals so that you could walk in this holy place of God's design. You're the seed that was planted by the Son of Man. You're the light of the world created to shine so that those who don't yet know the love of Christ will be attracted to you and the lifestyle you lead, and ultimately to Christ. You're a child of God, treasured by Him, loved by Him, and blessed by Him.

You're an heir to the Kingdom and a citizen of heaven. Keep in mind that God's hope is that "Grace and peace be multiplied to you in the knowledge of God and of Jesus our Lord, as His divine power has given to us all things that pertain to life and godliness, through the knowledge of Him who called us by glory and virtue, by which have been given to us exceedingly great and precious promises, that through these you may be partakers of the divine nature, having escaped the corruption that is in the world through lust" (2 Peter 1:2-4).

I know that sometimes all of this seems too good to be true. But again, that's because we're looking at these amazing benefits of being a child of God through our natural eyes. Our quest is to renew our minds to the truth of God. Your God wants you to be well equipped and ready to serve in any way that He calls you to act. As long as you feel weak, debilitated, and even paralyzed because of money worries, you can't serve Him fully.

You and I, as children of God, are examples of what it is to be in His family. Think about it: How do we look to others as they see the way we behave or observe the way we live? How do people we know view the way we give and the way we love? Are we generous? Are we the leaders of good or the weak and needy?

According to the Word of God, our part is to believe, to trust, to follow His ways, and then to behave in the same way that our Master did when He was on the earth. He is our Model. He is our Example. And God has equipped us with everything we need to walk in His way.

We're taught from the Scriptures that we were once in the darkness, but now we're in the light (see Ephesians 5:8). Let's behave as the light-charged children of God that we are called to be. Let's be the powerful witnesses and examples of the overcomers, the victorious ones, and the grand royal family under the leadership of our King Jesus.

All of this calls us to open ourselves to be transformed. To be changed. To repent and think a new way . . . and then to live the life that Jesus came to give us. This life is yours now. It's the priceless gift from your loving Father. Step in. Partake. Live the good life of the gospel.

Prayer: *Father, thank You for the work You are doing in my heart and mind to help me see myself as You see me. Thank You for the immeasurable* *love and grace You pour over me and into my life. Help me to uncover any untruths that are not aligned with Your ways so I can shine brightly for Your purposes.*

Fasting Tip: The only beverage on the Daniel Fast is water, which is one of the hardest parts of the fast for most people. Instead of focusing on the deprivation your flesh experiences, be thankful for the good work water is performing in your body as it washes out toxins, enables your muscles and joints to work better, and promotes good circulation.

DAY FIVE

Seed in the Ground

While the earth remains, seedtime and harvest, cold and heat, winter and summer, and day and night shall not cease.
GENESIS 8:22

Let's take the complexity out of some of our thinking and take a simple approach to reasoning the ways of God. I want to help us move toward understanding as we see the clear-cut message in God's truth.

We learn in Genesis 8:22 that what God created in the beginning will remain. Period. He is the Creator—and not just of physical things. God created those things we see with our natural eyes, but He also created unseen things. His Word declares, "In the beginning was the Word, and the Word was with God, and the Word was God. He was in the beginning with God. All things were made through Him, and without Him nothing was made that was made" (John 1:1-3).

All things were made through Him! Not just things in the earth, but everything in our solar system. Not just our solar system, but everything in our galaxy. Not just the Milky Way, but all the billions of galaxies in the universe.

When God, through His Son, created "all things," He set up systems that would operate forever. He established natural laws, like gravity and friction, and He also instituted spiritual laws. According to His Word, His laws shall not cease, just as He will not cease and will remain the same for eternity. Hebrews 13:8 tells us, "Jesus Christ is the same yesterday, today, and forever."

In the same way scientists study the laws of gravity so they can create instruments that will work within that consistent property, you and I can study the laws of the Kingdom so we can operate our lives successfully. One of the never-changing laws that operates in both the natural realm and the heavenly realm is seedtime and harvest.

Think for a moment about a seed. Let's imagine an acorn, which is the seed of an oak tree. Picture an acorn that's about one inch long and can easily fit in the palm of your hand. The acorn isn't very heavy. In fact, each one weighs only a few ounces. You could easily lift a bag of 100 acorns with one hand.

The seeming simplicity of the acorn could surely diminish our belief in its greatness. However, let's take a deeper look at the unassuming seed's complexity. Within that acorn is all the information it needs to transform from a small seed into a mighty oak tree. Unless the seed is destroyed or its life is disrupted in another way, it will fulfill its call.

The seed knows how to send an embryonic root into the soil so it will be anchored and able to absorb nutrients. It knows how to create the wood. The protective bark. The limbs. The leaves. The flowers. And it knows how to create more seeds so it can be reproduced many times over.

Seedtime and harvest. The acorn seed goes into the ground, and then it's transformed to fulfill its purpose. It becomes the strong, sturdy tree it was designed to be.

Our tithes and offerings are also seeds. We don't always know what they will become, but we can trust that God has a plan. When we give to the causes and ministries we're directed to support, we're sowing seeds that will transform into more and more life. Life for the ministry and its purpose. Life for those people helped by the ministry. And also life for us as we grow in generosity and love toward others.

God calls us to sow into His good works, and He tells us there will be a harvest. We don't always know how long the harvest will take. An acorn can take years before it matures into an oak tree and starts producing more acorns. Yet within just a few weeks of a kernel of corn being planted, multiple ears of corn are created, each having hundreds of kernels that can reproduce into more stalks of corn. A $50 donation to Global Ministries will help their efforts to combat human trafficking, yet the dismantling of the horrific trafficking networks will likely take decades. In contrast, a $50 gift to feed a boy or girl in an impoverished country will have immediate results as the child will receive nourishing food for their growth and well-being. Some seeds will take longer to result in a visible harvest.

Our part in the growing season is to trust God and plant the seed. We patiently await the harvest, knowing that the seed we sow embodies all the wisdom of God to become exactly what He intends it to be.

Seedtime and harvest . . . shall not cease.

Prayer: *Lord God, thank You for multiplying our small gifts into something more fruitful than we can even imagine. Through this Daniel Fast, please help me to grow in generosity and direct my giving so that it may bring a great harvest.*

Reflection: Consider ways you can become a habitual seed planter. Plant seeds of care in the lives of your loved ones. Plant seeds of hope by donating to a local homeless shelter. Plant seeds of justice by supporting the oppressed. Plant seeds of trust by consistently giving to the causes your Father presents to you for support.

DAY SIX

I Have Come to Give You Life

The thief does not come except to steal, and to kill, and to destroy. I have come that they may have life, and that they may have it more abundantly.
JOHN 10:10

Anyone studying the Scriptures will quickly see that there are two distinct realms: the realm of the Spirit, which is the Kingdom of God, and the realm of the world, which is under the authority of the enemy, or the thief.

Jesus says in John 10 that He came that we may have life, and that we may have it more abundantly. Life is so much more than breathing and walking and talking. Life from Jesus is powerful, full of goodness, and full of joy. Abundant life that comes from Jesus spreads to others. We are His light in the world because His life brings everlasting light.

Meanwhile, we live in a world ruled by an enemy. His purpose is to kill, steal, and destroy anything that is good in your life. He is the enemy of your soul. He wants to keep you from growth and from the good life that Jesus has already made possible.

Jesus says, "I have come to give you life!" He wants each of us to have a good, purposeful, meaningful life. And in that life, He gives peace. Having His peace means that nothing in your life is missing and nothing is broken. The good life that Jesus came to give you is not what you experience only on Sunday while you're in church. You don't only have the good life when you know your bills are paid or when you're well-fed and well-clothed. The good life is rich in God's peace and presence. It reproduces goodness and joy, shining into the dark world. It's a life that is attractive to others because it is well-lived.

The life that Jesus offers you is His life. You have an opportunity to put aside all that has happened before and allow Christ to give you His life, which is waiting for you. He says, "I am the way, the truth, and the life" (John 14:6). He also teaches us, "If you cling to your life, you will lose it; but if you give up your life for me, you will find it" (Matthew 10:39, NLT).

The life of Jesus awaits you. It means choosing Jesus and choosing His good life. It means choosing to open your heart and receive Him in all of His greatness.

Satan has always been the thief. He stole the birthright from Adam, and now he wants to steal all that is good from you. He wants you to worry, fret, and fear about your financial stability. He wants you to doubt that God cares or will provide.

But you have the life of Jesus inside you, and Jesus has defeated the enemy. Yes, the thief comes to steal, kill, and destroy, but Jesus came so that you could have life and have it abundantly. A rich, beautiful, fulfilling life is yours. Your part is to receive the great, powerful, and wonderful life that Jesus has already provided for you. He has given you life with Him, your Creator. Life with the Holy Spirit.

You're a new creation in Christ. The life you have now is the life of Christ in you. Celebrate your new life. Realize the many blessings that are already yours because you have Christ's life in you. Be blessed. Put your trust in the truth of the Lord. He came to give you life—a more abundant life.

Prayer: *Dear God, thank You for promising to give me abundant life. As I go through the Daniel Fast, teach me to set aside fear and doubt from the enemy and instead seek this life of joy and peace that comes only from trusting You.*

Fasting Tip: Your fast is a time when you have separated yourself from your typical daily life. It's a time for gaining understanding, renewal, and transformation. What would need to change in your life for you to begin feeling secure, stable, joyful, and at peace? Your answers to this question are all requests you can present to God so you can fully experience the life He wants you to have. Allow your Father to lead you into the transformation Christ came to give you.

DAY SEVEN

Father, Forgive Me

> *If we confess our sins, He is faithful and just to forgive us our sins and to cleanse us from all unrighteousness.*
> 1 JOHN 1:9

Have you always been responsible with your money? Perhaps you've made some mistakes or have even been reckless. Perhaps you've spent beyond your means and made some poor decisions, or spent money on things that didn't honor God.

If that's the case for you, this is your opportunity to turn over a new leaf. This is your chance to change from the path you've been on to the path that reflects the way of the Lord. It all starts with understanding your mistakes and making the decision to change. The Word says that if we confess our sins, God will forgive us and cleanse us from all unrighteousness. What does that mean? It means you have a new day—a new opportunity to begin again.

When we confess our sins, we're not only acknowledging to God that we've made mistakes. We're also acknowledging to ourselves the errors of our ways. This is how we can learn and change.

When we confess our sins, we're repenting. There are two parts of repentance: first, to acknowledge to God that we've made mistakes and seek His forgiveness; and second, to change. We're to change the way we think. We're to change what we believe. We're to change how we behave. We change from mistakes and unwise living to wise stewardship and following the ways of the Lord.

If you're like me, you may not have been taught how to manage money in an appropriate and godly manner. As a child I didn't learn about tithing, saving, or following a spending plan. I was raised with the philosophy "If you want it, you buy it. If you want it, you eat it." In other words, I, like so many others, was raised in the ways of the world, which caters to the flesh. But we who follow Christ are called to live a different way. Paul teaches in Romans 12:2, "Do not be conformed to this world, but be transformed by the renewing of your mind, that you may prove what is that good and acceptable and perfect will of God."

The perfect will of God is the best way to live. And where do we learn how to follow His will? We start with His Word and His Kingdom principles and laws. We learn by retraining our minds. We learn His ways. We learn His truth. And we change from the inside out.

Changing what we think leads to changing what we believe. That leads to changing how we behave and how we live our lives. We haven't repented completely if we haven't changed our ways to align with the ways of God.

As you think about the financial future that you want for yourself, in what areas do you need to change so you can walk into that bright future? Repent! Change the way you think. Learn what God teaches about wise stewardship. About giving. About responsibility.

Spend some time in prayer with the Lord. He is so eager for you to come to Him and to confess. He wants to hear your heart, and He wants to help you. He doesn't shame or punish; neither of those are His character. However, He will encourage you and teach you. Open your heart to your Father. He loves you. He wants the very best for you. And He will show you the way.

Your Father has designed a bright and safe future for you—a future filled with peace, rest, and provision. Walk into that future. Get to know what the Father wants for you. And then make the changes that are necessary for you to walk into your new life.

My hope and prayer is that you'll choose the wonderful and great new life that is available to you. Make the decision to repent. Make the decision to confess your sins to your Father. And then make the decision to receive His forgiveness and the righteousness that He offers you.

Prayer: *Father, when I consider the ways I've used money in my past, I realize I've made mistakes. I seek Your forgiveness and I ask You to continue to point me in the direction You would have me go. Help me to shed any shame or blame I may be feeling. Help me to forgive myself so I can move into the hopeful future You have provided for me.*

Fasting tip: By the end of the day, you'll have finished the first week of the Daniel Fast! Take a moment to reflect on how things are going on all levels. How are you focusing on your finances and remembering the purpose for the fast? What about your dedicated time with God? How are you doing with food choices and preparation? Celebrate what is going well and make a plan to address any things that could be improved.

DAY EIGHT

Rest in the Lord

Come to Me, all you who labor and are heavy laden, and I will give you rest. Take My yoke upon you and learn from Me, for I am gentle and lowly in heart, and you will find rest for your souls.
MATTHEW 11:28-29

In the beginning, God spent the first six days creating the heavens, the earth, and everything in the earth needed to support life. He also created human beings. He created Adam and Eve. And then, on the seventh day, God rested. He didn't rest because he was tired; He rested because He was finished. Everything that was necessary for life was available to all of creation. Everything was complete. There was nothing else to do. So He stopped creating and rested.

When Adam sinned, he contaminated the perfect life that God had created and brought a curse upon his life. That curse went on to affect all of humankind born after Adam. Part of that curse was difficult labor. Adam went from having everything that God created—more than enough—to the curse of needing to provide for himself by the sweat of his brow.

Take a moment and think about what God wanted for men, women, children, and families before the Fall. He wanted families to have everything they needed. He wanted men and women to have their needs met so they could fulfill their deeper purpose in life and not have to worry about being their own providers.

Even now, we probably all know people whose dream is to be far from everyday toil. People who play the lottery want to win to escape the often boring or stressful routines of their jobs. People who want to escape going to work every day long for riches. Many people look forward to retirement because they want to be free of the weighty day-to-day toil.

We have a natural inclination to be away from the toil. That doesn't mean away from any work or from fulfilling our purpose. But we would like to use our skills, talents, gifts, and resources to live a meaningful life without the responsibility of being our own providers.

We read throughout the Old Testament that people's work was difficult. In the ancient world, people worked ceaselessly to provide food and support their families. That's what makes Jesus' words in Matthew 11 so remarkable.

Jesus gave an invitation to you and to me and to all who would believe: "Come to Me, all you who labor and are heavy laden, and I will give you rest. Take My yoke upon you and learn from Me, for I am gentle and lowly in heart, and you will find rest for your souls." The rest Jesus is talking about is the same rest that God experienced on the seventh day. Everything was complete. Everything was provided. This rest is available to you and me and all who believe when we enter into a relationship with Jesus and live by the laws of His Kingdom.

Jesus is inviting us to get out of the toil, get out of the heavy-laden life, and rest because we know He will provide for us.

Jesus is calling us to learn His ways. To learn about the Kingdom. To learn about His character and His love for us.

He promises that we will find rest for our souls. Think of that! Rest for your soul. No worry. No stress. No sleepless nights.

You have an invitation to learn from Jesus and about Jesus. To learn about the King and His Kingdom, and learn how to walk in His ways.

When we learn how to do this—when we learn what the Word of God teaches about the Kingdom of God, when we submit to the Lord and seek first the Kingdom of God—then we will have everything we need, just as God intended in the very beginning.

Think about Jesus on the cross at Calvary. Jesus paid the supreme sacrifice of His life so that you and I could have the opportunity to live in the Kingdom of God. When He gave His last breath on the cross, He said, "It is finished." Once again, because Jesus had restored what the enemy had stolen, everything was in place so that women and men and families could return to their relationship with God and live with Him as their complete Provider.

His part is to provide what we need. Our part is to open our hearts and receive the Kingdom of God. We are called to believe in the gospel. The Kingdom of God is the gospel of Christ.

This gospel of the kingdom will be preached in all the world as a witness to all the nations, and then the end will come.
MATTHEW 24:14

Do you believe? Open your heart. Enter His rest.

Prayer: *Lord, I often exhaust myself trying to make things happen on my own. Teach me how to come to You and rest. Show me how to carry Your easy yoke instead of my heavy one, and to trust that You care for me.*

Fasting Tip: Develop a new habit during your fast. Each morning, as soon as you open your eyes, thank God for the day you're about to begin. Thank Him for how He cares for you and for the provision He brings into your life.

DAY NINE

Only Believe

*My brethren, count it all joy when you fall into various trials, know-
ing that the testing of your faith produces patience. But let patience
have its perfect work, that you may be perfect and complete, lacking
nothing.*

JAMES 1:2-4

There are some lessons we can learn only in a time of trial. Perhaps you're
under a great deal of stress and in a challenging time right now. This
verse speaks to that issue, as James tells us to count it all joy.

Maybe your inner voice is shrieking, "What! Joy in the middle of a
crisis? Get real!"

Your Lord is saying to you, "Yes, experience the joy, my dear one."

You experience joy when you develop a deep faith in God. Because
you trust Him, you have the assurance that He will see you through.
This isn't a fake type of joy where you put on that smiley-face mask so
others will think all is well in your house. This is true joy—the joy that
comes from the Lord and gives you strength. This is the joy you feel
because you're so confident in your Lord and His love and care for you
that worry and stress don't come near you.

Our fallen world has plenty of trials for us to experience. Remember
what Jesus said: "These things I have spoken to you, that in Me you may
have peace. In the world you will have tribulation; but be of good cheer,
I have overcome the world" (John 16:33).

Yes, the world will hand you tribulation and pressure. The world,
under the authority of the enemy, will offer you lies, stress, doubt, and
anguish. But Jesus says that we are to be of good cheer. Why? Because
we put our trust in Jesus. And we know, because He told us, that He
has overcome the world.

My friend Hannah told me about the time when her kitchen cupboards were literally bare of any food to feed her four young children.
Hannah's husband, Blair, had been out of work for six months. They
had used up all their savings. Their credit cards were maxed out. They

had borrowed money from her parents and from his. Plus, they had already been served with a foreclosure notice from the bank. "I didn't even have a box of pasta to boil and mix with a can of tomatoes for the kids," Hannah recounted. She had no idea what she would do.

Blair returned home after another day of job searching and saw that Hannah was down. Immediately after she explained the bleak situation, the kids rushed into the kitchen with a burning question: "What's for dinner, Mom?"

Blair and Hannah looked into each other's eyes, and then she replied, "It's a surprise. I'll call you when it's ready."

Within seconds, there was a knock on the door. A friend was on his way home, and through an uncommon circumstance he had been given a big bag full of food. He didn't need it, and so he thought, since he was passing by, that maybe Hannah, Blair, and their kids could put it to good use.

After thanking their friend profusely and closing the door, Hannah burst into tears. She felt God's presence in a new way, and it was this turning point that set Blair and her on a new path of trusting God as their Provider. Today, life is totally different for this family. They have financial security and are making a huge difference in the world. The enemy tried to crush them, but God was there to lift them up.

Challenges can be like weights. When you go to the gym and lift weights, your muscles grow stronger. In the same way, when you meet challenges in life, your faith muscles get stronger. You learn to trust, and your faith muscles strengthen. You experience God's goodness, and your faith muscles strengthen. You patiently wait on the Lord, and your faith muscles strengthen.

When you go through tribulations or challenges, examine your heart. Strengthen those faith muscles and lean into God. What is He teaching you during this time? What do you notice about the way you handle stress? What can you learn to do better?

Are you developing patience? Are you turning to God and putting your trust in Him even though it feels as if He is taking you to the edge? Count it all joy as you work those faith muscles. Let patience have its perfect work in you. Through this experience you'll become a stronger, more mature, and better equipped follower of Jesus Christ.

You're being prepared for your future and for a testimony of God's goodness and provision that you can share with others. Let the joy of the Lord be your strength. Learn from Him, grow in Him, develop patience, and trust in Him.

Prayer: *Lord, as I look back at the challenges I've faced this year, I can see how they have made my faith stronger. As I continue on my fast, help me to remember that my trials and temptations—big and small—are growing me and preparing me to share about Your goodness.*

Fasting Tip: Before you are tempted, think about the ways you could encounter challenges with food. Plan ahead for how you can avoid breaking the fast. Keep appropriate snacks on hand in your cupboards, workplace, purse, and car. Have ingredients for quick and easy meals you can prepare. Plan ahead so you'll be ready when temptation comes knocking on your door.

DAY TEN

Your New Life in Christ

> *Therefore, if anyone is in Christ, he is a new creation; old things have passed away; behold, all things have become new.*
> 2 CORINTHIANS 5:17

I believe 2 Corinthians 5:17 is one of those passages that people often take at face value when they're meant to be understood much more deeply than that. Let me explain what I mean.

It's true that this verse hearkens back to the fact that we were once lost and now we're found. We once were separated from God, but now we have free access to Him and are reconciled with our Father. But the apostle Paul is also teaching the Corinthian believers that if they are in Christ, they are a new creation. What does it mean to be in Christ?

Being in Christ is so much more than just believing in Him. Many people believe that Christ was a real person who walked the earth and that He is the Son of God, but holding those beliefs is not being "in

Christ." Being in Christ is a profound, deep, and transforming status. It's putting away our will . . . putting away our beliefs . . . and totally sacrificing all of who we are so we can live in all of who He is.

In Galatians 2:20, Paul teaches that he's been crucified with Christ. No longer is it Paul who lives, but Christ who lives in him. We crucify ourselves by submitting in a deep and profound way to the truth of our Lord. We honor Him for who He is, and we also follow Him because He is the way, the truth, and the life.

Think about a time when you've accepted the role of a student under the tutelage of an expert. Recently I attended a four-day conference led by one of the world's leading personal development experts. I knew of his reputation as a bestselling author and a highly respected influencer, and I was so thankful that I was able to attend the conference along with about a thousand other enthusiastic admirers.

During the meetings I eagerly listened to every word this man spoke. I took notes. I thought about specific ways that I could use the lessons I was learning from him. I put my trust in his teachings because he was the proven expert. He knew so much more than I did about the subjects he was teaching that I gave in and soaked in all that he could instill in me.

Even more, we want to give in to Jesus, accepting His wisdom and authority. We want to put aside all that we know or feel or believe from our own reasoning and instead subject ourselves to what He's teaching us.

When we are in Christ, all of our old worldly ways melt away. We become new creations, and our spirits come alive. That which was once dead has now been reborn. Old things have passed away, and all things have become new. Jesus says, "If you try to hang on to your life, you will lose it. But if you give up your life for my sake, you will save it" (Matthew 16:25, NLT). Surrendering to Christ is what brings us new life.

You're a new creation in Christ. All of the old systems, boundaries, weights, and pressures that you were forced to face in the worldly way of living have now evaporated because you have a new way of life. You have a Kingdom way of living. That's good news.

Scripture teaches that all things will be made new (see Revelation 21:5). As you put your faith in God as your Provider, all can be brand new for you. His Holy Spirit will serve as your Guide. He will direct you and help you become a wise steward of the resources the Lord provides for you.

Become a law-abiding citizen of the Kingdom of God, where old things have passed away and you're no longer subject to the laws of the world under the headship of Satan. Instead, you're under the laws of the King—King Jesus. He is the Ruler. All things have been given to Him by the Father. And now Jesus passes on to you the authority, the power, the benefits, the rights, and the citizenship that you have because you're in Christ.

What keeps you from fully accepting this new reality for your life? Doubt and unbelief. Don't allow the enemy to lie to you and deceive you. Instead, learn about the Kingdom of God. Learn the truth from the Word of God and allow it to set you free. You're a new creation in Christ. This is your new life. Receive it.

Prayer: *Father, help me to more fully understand and embrace the new life I can have as a citizen in Your Kingdom. Help me to see that it's now and not later. That this very day I am a citizen of Your Kingdom and have access to all the blessings You provide for Your people.*

Reflection: As you think about fasting with a financial focus, what does it mean that you are a new creation? How might you change the way you think about and handle money to reflect your status as a citizen of the Kingdom of God?

DAY ELEVEN

Just Do It

> *Be doers of the word, and not hearers only, deceiving yourselves.*
> JAMES 1:22

I have high regard for chefs who have mastered their craft of preparing delicious, healthy meals. One of my favorites is Gordon Ramsay. I subscribe to a collection of video tutorials, which I enjoy watching. Ramsay breaks down what can seem like complex recipes into easy steps that can be followed by home cooks. The video lessons are well done, and he makes it all look so easy. But you know what? None of what Ramsay teaches me will have any effect on my cooking unless I put the lessons into action. If I don't change the way I cook, I've only received knowledge. I would be deceiving myself to think I was a Gordon Ramsay–trained cook if I didn't practice what he preaches from his kitchen.

The same goes for you and me as we learn about adopting a Kingdom-of-God way of thinking and lifestyle. You can sit on the edge of your seat at your church, listen to every word your pastor speaks, and take copious notes. But unless you apply what you learn to your life, it does no good. You could memorize every word in this book, but unless you take the principles and put them into action, they have little value to you. So often, we are hearers only. And so often, we may say to ourselves, *Oh, I already know that.* Or *I've heard that before.* Then we discount the teachings. But unless you're acting on the Word, you're deceiving yourself and missing out on the great impact valuable lessons can have on your life.

Paul seemed to be concerned that the Christians in Philippi needed to have a deeper understanding of his teachings. He wrote this to them: "And now, my brothers and sisters, be filled with joy in the Lord. It is no trouble for me to write the same things to you again. I want to be sure that you are prepared" (Philippians 3:1, ERV).

For years, I had friends who told me how much impact using a vision board or a prayer board made in their lives. Finally I created one, and wow! What a difference this simple tool has made in my prayer life. The usefulness of the prayer board was always available to me, but the usefulness of it was only activated when I became a doer and not a hearer only.

Imagine you want to learn tennis. You hire an experienced coach to help you learn so you can grow in knowledge and enjoy the sport. During your first lesson, your coach notices that your serve is weak. You need help. You need to exercise in a specific way to build muscle, flexibility, and accuracy. Your coach tells you to work on your serve for thirty minutes over the next week. You get where I'm going with this. You can either follow the instruction of the coach—who knows more about tennis than you do and knows how to help people succeed—or you can ignore your coach. What's the result of these two choices? If you take action, you learn, improve, and get closer to your goal of learning the sport. If you ignore your coach, your game will stay at the same ol' weak status. And you know what else gets weaker? Your resolve and the trust you have in yourself.

So here I am, coming to you as your Daniel Fast coach. My instruction to you is to use this book as your plan to invite God into the center of your finances. Going through the fast is your opportunity to grow in your faith and in your relationship with the Lord. It's your chance to be transformed by the renewing of your mind and be forever changed for the better. Again, it's up to you. Will you use the Faithful Servant Action Steps? Will you spend time with God each day? Will you use your journal or create a prayer board? The choice is yours, and the result is yours. The great news is that when you take action and become a doer and not just a hearer, the Holy Spirit joins with you. He's there to lead and direct you. He'll cheer you on. He'll counsel you and give you tips.

Make a commitment to yourself that you'll become a doer and not a hearer only. Like the Nike motto declares, "Just do it!" And take joy in the process, the understanding you gain, and the results you desire.

Prayer: *Lord Jesus, thank You for being the best Coach I could ever want. And thank You for helping me see that I can't just keep knowledge in my head. I want the knowledge to seep down into my hands so that I can take action and realize the changes I want in my life.*

Reflection: Our habits are deeply entrenched in our beings. We get into patterns or grooves that feel comfortable and normal. Yet sometimes a groove can become a rut or a ditch that doesn't help us. As you think about your habits around money, what are some that you want to erase and replace with practices that will lead you to the security you desire?

DAY TWELVE

Live in the Spirit

Those who are Christ's have crucified the flesh with its passions and desires. If we live in the Spirit, let us also walk in the Spirit.
GALATIANS 5:24-25

I'll never forget that day, early in the morning, as I lay in bed in more despair than I had ever known. My bank accounts were nearly empty. I had thousands of dollars' worth of bills that needed to be paid. I had prayed. I had studied the Word. I'd tried to figure out whatever I could do to get out of this mess. Finally, with tears streaming down my cheeks, I said to my Father, "I've done all I can! Are You going to let me go down even deeper?"

What I realize now, as I look back on that moment, is that this was the day I died to myself. Up until that time I had been able to figure things out on my own. Yes, I believed in God, but my dependence on Him had never been tested like this. The world had always provided what I needed for my everyday life. And as I lay in bed, weeping once again, my aching soul turned to my God as I came to the end of myself.

I can't remember now how many days there were between that breaking point in my life and the breakthrough that God gave me. I do remember that God's light shined in my soul, and I heard Him speak to me in my spirit. That still small voice gave me an assignment to write about the Daniel Fast. This one assignment gave me hope and got me started on a path that I never expected to travel.

God knows our beginnings and our ends. He had a plan for me, and He has a plan for you.

What is our part? Our part is to obey. To put our trust in Him. And to come to the end of ourselves so He can lead us and direct us, and so we can hear that still small voice that speaks to our spirit.

Again, as I look back on that period of my life I see now that I had faith *in* Jesus, but I didn't have faith *like* Jesus. Jesus was so deeply connected with the Father that in every cell within His human body He believed in the power of God to work in the earth. He believed wholeheartedly in the fullness of the Kingdom of God. And what was the result? He healed the sick. He fed the hungry. He walked on water. He raised the dead. He calmed the storm. He made fish come to the right side of the boat for fishermen who had labored all night and caught nothing.

Hear the words of Jesus describing His seamless connection with His Father:

*Most assuredly, I say to you, the Son can do nothing of Himself,
but what He sees the Father do; for whatever He does, the Son also
does in like manner. For the Father loves the Son, and shows Him
all things that He Himself does; and He will show Him greater
works than these, that you may marvel. For as the Father raises
the dead and gives life to them, even so the Son gives life to whom
He will.*

JOHN 5:19-21

Jesus, who was fully God yet on earth in the nature of a human being, was sold out to God and His principles in every way possible. And He tells us, who are also in the nature of a human being, that we can live in this same way. "Most assuredly, I say to you, he who believes in Me, the works that I do he will do also; and greater works than these he will do, because I go to My Father. And whatever you ask in My name, that I will do, that the Father may be glorified in the Son. If you ask anything in My name, I will do it" (John 14:12-14).

Since that time it's been my quest to learn how to believe like Jesus. I'm not there yet, but my faith muscles are getting stronger each day to help me develop an unwavering trust in God. To believe in the promises He gives to us in His Word. To expect that my every request is answered. And to pray that my life, as a child of the Most High God, will be "on earth as it is in heaven."

This is the transformation that our Lord wants us to experience. Take the step. As you continue your Daniel Fast, take the opportunity to examine your heart. Identify areas where you're still leading with your own will or your natural senses, and where you're depending on things in the world. Step into a Kingdom lifestyle and receive the many blessings that God has for you.

I promise you that His way is the better way!

Prayer: *Father, I know in my heart of hearts that I believe in Jesus and that I have everlasting life with You. What I am seeing is that I don't believe like Jesus, and that's what I want to develop for my life. Jesus wasn't overcome by fear or worry, because He trusted You. He didn't question His* *future, because He trusted You. I want to trust You more each and every day. Thank You for the trust that's growing in me as I keep looking to You.*

Reflection: If you're in financial crisis right now, cry out to God for His help. Tell Him you know you're not capable on your own, and declare your dependence on Him. Trust His good plan for your life.

DAY THIRTEEN

Stand

Finally, my brethren, be strong in the Lord and in the power of His might. Put on the whole armor of God, that you may be able to stand against the wiles of the devil. For we do not wrestle against flesh and blood, but against principalities, against powers, against the rulers of the darkness of this age, against spiritual hosts of wickedness in the heavenly places.
EPHESIANS 6:10-12

One of my most cherished songs is "Stand," performed by gospel singer Donnie McClurkin. The lyrics, written by Sylvester Stewart (known by music fans as Sly Stone), serve as a powerful call for us to stand firm even in hard times—not to give up or give in, but just to stand in trust and watch the Lord see us through the challenge and on to victory. I recall many times, including times of financial pressures, when I listened to the song, sang the lyrics, and meditated on Ephesians 6 to help me put on God's armor and stand firm until He saw me through.

This is the message that Paul was giving the believers in Ephesus. It's not an evangelistic message; they already knew Christ. But they were also facing struggles and attacks of the enemy.

One thing I've found over the years is that when we start making progress in our faith and in our relationship with God, the enemy will fight back. We're claiming territories that are already ours, but that the enemy has occupied in our lives. For example, when you begin to trust in God as your Source and Provider, you're reclaiming a territory that the enemy has held with his lies. He wants to keep you in bondage, so he'll fight to keep you there. What are his weapons? Fear, circumstances, deception, and any other kind of lie that he can put in your mind. That's what was happening with the Ephesians, and that's what Paul was addressing.

What was his instruction? To stand. To use the tools and resources of God to resist the common tricks of the enemy. Remember that the devil is a defeated foe; because of Christ, Satan and his demons are under your feet. Christ has the victory and you're in Christ, so His victory is your victory!

However, even with this knowledge we still have battles to fight. So we are to arm ourselves with the spiritual tools that are available to us. Remember, God will never allow you to face a trial that you cannot win. First Corinthians 10:13 tells us that He will always provide a way out: "No temptation has overtaken you except such as is common to man; but God is faithful, who will not allow you to be tempted beyond what you are able, but with the temptation will also make the way of escape, that you may be able to bear it." He has equipped you with everything you need to fulfill His purposes for you. But in the same way that a soldier must pick up a weapon, we must pick up our sword, which is the Word of God.

Donnie McClurkin sings out the battle cry through these song lyrics: "When you've given your all and it seems like you can't make it through, well you just stand when there's nothing left to do . . . watch the Lord see you through."[1]

You don't stand passively. No, you're active. You're declaring the truth of God in the midst of your circumstances. You're building your faith. You're leaning on your Father. You're not standing still; you're standing active and alive. You're standing in faith and dressing yourself in the whole armor of God.

When you stand, you're in your fighting position. You're ready and active. You're focusing your attention on the truth of God's Word and putting your trust in Him. Don't let doubt seep into your thinking. Don't let the lies of the enemy take you off course. Don't let worldly circumstances or financial stresses seem more powerful than the ways of God. Even if fear and doubt come knocking at the door of your mind, don't open to that defeating kind of thinking. Stand. Stay focused on the Lord and His truth.

Stand, my friend. Stand and let the Lord see you through. Have confidence in Him. Have confidence in His ways. Have confidence in His Word. And have confidence that Jesus Christ has defeated the enemy. Satan is under your feet. He has no power over you unless you give him entry into your thinking.

Stay strong and the Lord will always see you through. That is His promise to you.

Prayer: *Lord, You will see me through. I am so very thankful for Your faithfulness that never changes. Even when I am weak, You are strong. I can stand because You are faithful and You are always with me. Thank You for Your love, Your grace, and Your forever faithfulness.*

Reflection: What challenges are you facing right now—in your Daniel Fast, in your finances, in other areas of your life—where you can stand firm and resist the devil?

DAY FOURTEEN

Be Free

Stand fast therefore in the liberty by which Christ has made us free, and do not be entangled again with a yoke of bondage.
GALATIANS 5:1

One of the most significant lessons that you can learn during your Daniel Fast is to overcome the flesh and begin stepping into a new lifestyle as a citizen of heaven. However, as I've learned through my own experiences and the experiences of others, the world is clamoring for your attention—and so is your flesh. So even though you're learning new things and experiencing new freedoms, you will also see, feel, and hear a steady stream of invitations to go back to the old ways.

We must constantly make the choice to stay in the freedom that Christ has given us. It's an ongoing decision that we can make because although we're in this world, we're not of this world (see John 17:16).

Because of Christ, you have rights, privileges, abilities, and benefits. These are all part of the liberty you have through Him. Christ has made you free of the bondage that all those who don't yet know Him are under—the same bondage that you were under before you accepted Christ as your Savior. Christ has freed you to live in everlasting life—life that is rich, filled with joy and love and care and confidence. But even though you're out of bondage, God knows your heart. He knows the challenges that you face in the world. And that's why He calls you to take up your cross daily.

What is that cross? It's the crucifixion of our flesh and the old ways. Remember, you're a new creation in Christ. Old things have passed away; all things are new. So crucify all that is of the old nature. Get rid of all the old, defeated thinking. Each and every day, take up your cross. Live in Christ. Allow Him to lead you. Allow the Holy Spirit to guide you. Allow God to give you the direction you need for the faith-driven life that is always available to you.

On every occasion when you sense that you're returning to old ways, pause. Maybe you find yourself spending too much for selfish reasons or worrying that God won't provide for your family's needs. Think about the truth. Think about the freedom that is yours, and walk that way. Walk in the freedom that is always available to you.

Remember this promise from God's Word: "He [God] is a rewarder of those who diligently seek Him" (Hebrews 11:6). Every day, crucify the flesh and seek Him. Every day, put your trust in the Lord. Every day, make the choice to follow in the ways of Jesus. That is how you pick up your cross daily. It's a discipline. It's a way of life. It's the way of faith.

As you go through the Daniel Fast, you have the opportunity to make this choice in a tangible way every day. You choose to get up and spend time in the Word, even though your old habits urge you to turn on the television or check out what's new on Facebook. You choose to continue the Faithful Servant Action Steps and pursue your financial breakthrough even though it is hard work to make changes. You choose to follow the food restrictions even though you might crave sugar or coffee. You choose to seek God in the midst of your fast.

I know there are times when you'll feel like you've taken three steps forward and two steps back. But remember, you can always keep moving forward. Be the overcomer. Examine your heart. Be the inspector of your own life, and make the adjustments necessary to experience the rich and rewarding life that's already yours.

Picture in your mind your before and after. Before, you were in bondage, just as if you were bound by chains in a prison cell. You had no choices, no strength. You were subject to the ruler of this world, the devil.

Praise God that you're now free. That is your after! You have all of the power of heaven available to you to work on your behalf. When Jesus was teaching his disciples how to pray to the Father, he declared, "Your kingdom come. Your will be done on earth as it is in heaven." That is your prayer. That is your promise. That is your opportunity.

You're free. Don't fall for the ways of the enemy. Stand fast and remain in the liberty that you have.

Prayer: *Father, I am so very thankful that You are mine and that I am Yours. Oh, I am Yours. What a measureless blessing it is to be Your child and to be loved and cared for by You. You have already designed a future for me that is secure and forever. My part is to seek You and Your Kingdom first, and then all I need will be provided. Thank You, Father.*

Fasting tip: At the end of the day, your fast will be two-thirds complete! Take another opportunity to review how it's going—physically, spiritually, and with your finances—and make any adjustments needed. Review your progress on the Faithful Servant Action Steps. Journal about what God is doing in your life, and thank Him for it.

DAY FIFTEEN

Get Understanding

> *Wisdom is the principal thing; therefore get wisdom. And in all your getting, get understanding.*
> PROVERBS 4:7

Our life in Christ is a new and different life. And as new creations, our lives are separated from the ways of the world. During your Daniel Fast, as you learn about God, yourself, and how to depend on the Lord as your Provider, you can begin making the shift in your thinking and what you believe to be true for your future.

We're called to learn this new way of life. How do we do that? By becoming students of God's Word and His ways. It's through His Word and learning His precepts that we change from the beliefs we've had in the past to the truth of this new life.

Proverbs 4:7 captures a powerful instruction from the Lord: to get wisdom, which is the first and foremost thing. Where can we get wisdom? From God. He is all wise. He is all knowing. And because of who He is, we look to Him first for truth and wisdom.

The second part of this message emphasizes getting understanding. Why is that so important? Because as we gain understanding, we also grow in faith.

I like to think of God's wisdom as seeds that go into my heart. Once they're planted, I nurture those seeds by gaining understanding. The more I understand God's truth and wisdom, the deeper the roots of those seeds are implanted in my soul. As I gain understanding, God's wisdom becomes my wisdom. Because I understand, I am confident, strong, and stable.

God has designed us as thinking beings. He created us so that we think about different topics, subjects, and perspectives, and then we choose what to believe. Our beliefs inform our decisions, and the decisions we make fuel our actions. We move from thoughts to beliefs to decisions to actions—and the actions are like paintbrushes that create our future on the canvas of our lives.

I'm so thankful that as a young woman I set two significant goals for my life. The first was to be a lifelong learner. I have a passion for learning new things. I also value going deeper into my understanding of topics that I've been studying. The process of learning fills my heart with overflowing joy and thanksgiving.

My second goal was to be a seeker of truth. I made that decision even before I had given my life to Christ. While I don't know what led me to it, I'm so thankful for that choice. I praise God that I found the truth of Christ and that His truth set me free. The same has happened for you: The truth of Christ has set you free. That freedom comes in greater measure as we gain more wisdom, which comes from God, and more understanding, which is developed as we ponder, learn, and accept God's truth.

When we learn and gain understanding, we are feeding our souls. And when we base our lives on the wisdom of God, we're pointing our footsteps toward success. Jesus says, "Man shall not live by bread alone, but by every word that proceeds from the mouth of God" (Matthew 4:4). When we nourish our souls on the truth and the bread of life, we stay strong. We stay energized. And we stay in the safe ground of the truth, where we can stand and have assurance that we are in the best place.

We're accustomed to feeding our physical bodies when we're hungry. We spend money on food, we plan our meals, we schedule our days according to the times when we'll eat. Can we give the same attention to feeding our souls? As you carefully plan your physical meals during your fast, can you also plan the meals that you'll have for your soul? Can you plan your day around the times when you'll be eating the bread of life? Yes, you can. The question is, will you?

Take this opportunity to consider what your soul needs. Think of the topics that you want to study on your fast and afterward. Think of the areas of weakness that you would like to address so that you can become strong. And then plan your "meal," or the study that you'll undertake. Plan a time when you'll consume the teachings. And all along, keep in mind that wisdom from God is the principal thing. In all of your getting, get understanding. Set your feet on the course that will take you to the bright, successful future that God has for you.

Prayer: *Lord God, may I make getting wisdom and understanding a top priority. I want to be wise in the way I live, in my relationship with You, in my finances. Teach me Your ways.*

Fasting tip: Plan ahead if you dine in restaurants during your fast. Check out the restaurant's menu ahead of time (most are online for easy access). You might want to bring your own sugar-free salad dressing. And consider making a special request, as restaurants are becoming accustomed to meeting special dietary needs.

DAY SIXTEEN

Be Anxious for Nothing

Be anxious for nothing, but in everything by prayer and supplication, with thanksgiving, let your requests be made known to God; and the peace of God, which surpasses all understanding, will guard your hearts and minds through Christ Jesus.

PHILIPPIANS 4:6-7

My hope for you as you go through the Daniel Fast is that you're growing in faith, you're learning to trust in the Lord in a deeper and more profound away, and you're even beginning to receive insights, answers, and perhaps breakthroughs for the financial pressures or questions you've been experiencing. My sincere hope for you is that you're trading fear for trust and anxiety for prayers. God's ways and His Word are so powerful.

I spent much of my Christian life receiving Christ's words as suggestions rather than commands. Of course, I accepted the Ten Commandments as hard-and-fast rules to follow. They were the laws, and I was a law-abiding Christian citizen. *Thou shalt not kill. Thou shall not steal.* Those commandments were clear, concise, and easy to understand, and I knew that they should be followed. But Jesus' words didn't always hold the same authority for me.

Now, after many years of growing in faith and learning more about the ways of God, I understand that every instruction from Him and every precept in His Word is a command to be followed. The teachings of our Lord are not just suggestions about how to live effectively.

Before I get much deeper into this thought, please understand that I am not talking about legalism. Legalism is when you base your faith experience on following the rules. We don't want to be legalistic; we want to be followers of Jesus Christ. We want to love Him with all of our souls, with all of our hearts, and with all of our beings.

How do we show our love to Jesus? By following His commandments and practicing His ways. Here in Philippians 4, we're commanded to be anxious for nothing. Then we're given the alternative to anxiety—the instruction for what we are to do. Instead of being anxious, we're to have faith in God and believe that He will answer our needs. We're to make our requests known to Him with thanksgiving.

We're to be anxious for nothing because the answers to all of our troubles are available to us in the heavenly realms. So in this instruction, in this command from our Lord in His Word, we're to make our requests known to God, and then we're to have the assurance that He'll meet those needs. That's why we make our request with immediate thanksgiving. We're thankful because we are confident in the Lord and His promises. And this assurance opens our minds and hearts to receive His peace.

To the worldly way of thinking, this all seems crazy! And that's why our Lord says His peace "surpasses all understanding." His ways are not our ways. His way for us to live doesn't make worldly sense; it's a separate way of operating. We can live with our authority as citizens of heaven and be assured that God will meet our needs.

These words in Scripture are not suggestions; we're commanded to make our requests known to God. And Jesus speaks quite simply of following His every word in obedience to Him: "If you keep My commandments, you will abide in My love, just as I have kept My Father's commandments and abide in His love" (John 15:10).

We don't follow the commandments out of a legalistic way of thinking. We follow the commandments of our Lord because we love Him, because we trust Him, and because we want to follow Him. We have the assurance that He wants only the best for us. We develop our faith so that we can be anxious for nothing by putting our trust in God, by studying His Word, by meditating on His truth, and by renewing our minds with His wisdom.

Prayer: *Father, I admit that the asking is easier for me. It's the not-being-anxious part that I'm working on. I see that it's all about trust: trusting You and Your love for me, and trusting Your promises and that You will do what You say You will do. I am learning. I am growing. And I am so very thankful that I am maturing in trust as I bring my requests to You.*

Reflection: What specific requests are you bringing to God on your Daniel Fast, whether about finances or other matters? Set aside anxiety and ask with thanksgiving, knowing that He will do what is best for you.

DAY SEVENTEEN

Accept Your True Identity

You are a chosen generation, a royal priesthood, a holy nation, His own special people, that you may proclaim the praises of Him who called you out of darkness into His marvelous light.

1 PETER 2:9

My hope and prayer for you during your Daniel Fast is that you're learning more about who you are in Christ. You're brand new! You're not like the world. You're special. And not just a little special—you're out-of-this-world special.

Who are you? You're a member of a chosen generation, the royal priesthood, and a holy nation. You're God's own unique design and one of His consecrated people. You're above and not beneath. You're the head and not the tail. You're the blessed and not the cursed.

As you learn more about depending on God and living as His precious child, you'll start realizing how your life in the here and now can reflect being a member of the royal family, and you'll become more secure in your daily life. You can see that God wants prosperity for you so you can serve Him more fully.

Over the years I've worked with thousands of men and women throughout the world. And a common challenge so many people face has to do with their identity and how they feel about themselves. A confession I hear often is, "Susan, I feel so unworthy. I just can't seem to believe that God could love me."

I understand that way of thinking. I've been there. And even as a believer, this was an area that I wrestled with and worked on so my beliefs could become aligned with God's truth about me. I soon realized that unworthiness started knocking at the door of my soul when I was measuring my value, my worth, and my potential against the ways of the world, or when I was comparing myself with people of the world.

Can I tell you something? We will never succeed if we continue to measure our value against the world's system. We'll never find our true identity and our divine worth there.

I encourage you to wipe the slate clean. That's what your Father has done. Old things have passed away, and all things are new. Who are you now? You're His precious, beautiful child. He has set you up to be a vital member for His cause.

You're royalty. You're chosen. You're gifted. And you're separated and sanctified for the cause of Christ. Receive your new identity. Allow these truths to serve as the only mirror you use to see your reflection.

You were chosen not because of who you are but because of who Christ is. You're in the royal priesthood not because of who you are but because Christ is the High Priest and you're in Him. You're a member of the holy nation not because of who you are but because Jesus is the King of the Kingdom of God and has called you to be a resident in His land. You're a member of His special people not because of who you are but because of the deep, abiding love He has for you and the desire He has for you to be part of His royal family.

As long as you deny or feel unworthy of your God-given position, you'll be unable to fulfill the call that He has on your life. As long as you remain in bondage, you'll be unable to shine.

I know from my own experience that merely hearing words like these will not change your heart. What will change your heart is spending time with the Lord. Listen to Him and believe what He says about you. You're His treasure. You're one of His special people and His holy instrument. Jesus says, "I am the vine, you are the branches" (John 15:5). It's from those branches that fruit is produced. Accept your connection with Jesus the Vine. Accept your identity with Him, and then bear much fruit. Allow others to be blessed by who you are as a member of God's chosen people, a member of His holy nation.

Humble yourself before the Lord. Wear the robe of righteousness that Jesus gained for you through His sacrifice, and accept the identity that He has established for you. Believe in the Lord. He already believes in you. Be who He created you to be.

Prayer: *Lord Jesus, thank You for making me a part of Your Kingdom. Thank You that my identity is not dependent on who I am or what I've accomplished. I don't have to be worthy by my actions, because You have made me worthy by Your actions at Calvary.*

Reflection: Can you imagine Jesus walking up to you and placing a crown on your head? If the thought of Christ honoring you as highly favored royalty is hard to accept, then begin meditating on God's Word about who you are. You are a member of the household of God. You are above and not beneath. You are special because of who Christ has made you to be.

DAY EIGHTEEN

Blessed to be a Blessing

God is able to make all grace abound toward you, that you, always having all sufficiency in all things, may have an abundance for every good work.

2 CORINTHIANS 9:8

I can recall many times when I learned of a good work that I wanted to support financially. The desire to give was there, but I had to say under my breath, "I can't afford it." Now when I hear those words, I cringe. I hope they never enter my mind again. And I hope they never enter yours, either.

There's some reality to the phrase "I can't afford it," because when we're expecting the provision to come only from us, there will be many times when we can't afford to do countless good works. However, when we put our trust in God, His promise says that He will provide everything we need to help every time He calls us to action.

God declares that He is able to make all grace abound toward us, that we will have all sufficiency in all things. I've seen this truth work over and over again in my own life. God has provided me with all sufficiency in all things, allowing me to be involved in His good works. And frankly, if there are things that I still need, it's only because I haven't asked or because it hasn't been the perfect time for me to receive. As a child of God, I should never be in want. I should never be without. Not when my daily life is grounded on the promises of His Word.

I've come to believe that God is able to make all grace abound toward us, as 2 Corinthians 9:8 says. What is grace? It's the love-infused power of God working on our behalf. It's God in His wisdom working things out so that goodness will come to me and to you. He is able! Of that we can be assured. And His promise is that He's able to make all grace abound toward us. Think of that! The Greek word for "abound" in this verse actually means to superabound, be in excess, be superfluous.[1] So God is able to use His love-infused power to work on our behalf so that we will have everything we need. That's a huge promise.

I believe God fulfills His promise for us because of His great love for us. He is our Father. He wants the very best for us. He wants us to be joyful and fulfilled, and He wants us to be cared for. He will care for us. He will bless us.

Then we come to the next part of that 2 Corinthians passage. God will not only work things for good so that we have all that we need for life and godliness, but He will give us more than enough. All sufficiency in all things, and an abundance. And why does He want us to have more than enough? So that we will never again have to say, "I can't afford it" when it comes to supporting God's work.

Our Father calls us to be His hands and feet. He doesn't print money, yet good works need money to be funded. So when missionaries need funds so they can give of themselves to share the good news of Christ, we can be the blessing through the blessings we've already received. When children are hungry and need to have good, nutritious food to eat, we can be the blessing because of the blessing God has given to us. When a homeless shelter needs to expand, we can be the blessing because of the blessing God has been to us.

Our Father wants us to be a free-flowing stream of blessing to all the good works that He puts before us. He doesn't want anything to inhibit our ability to support what is needed. So He meets our needs, and then

He gives us more than enough so that we can meet the needs of others. That is the way of God. And that is the promise that He gives to you.

You and I need to stay close to God so that the fruits of the Spirit may flow through us and inform how we use our money. We are called to be kind, gentle, patient, and loving. We are called to be caring and joyful, and we are to shun any signs of greed, selfishness, jealousy, or pride.

We want to live a Kingdom lifestyle that impacts every part of our lives. It's how we think. It's what we believe. It's how we handle our finances. And it's how we support those in need.

Prayer: *Father, I want to be a free-flowing channel for Your love and care. I truly want to be an instrument of Your peace and a helping hand to those You call me to serve.*

Reflection: Where do you think God might be calling you to give more generously? How could you step out on faith to support a ministry He has put on your heart? Ask God for discernment as you move forward.

DAY NINETEEN

Speak the Truth

For assuredly, I say to you, whoever says to this mountain, "Be removed and be cast into the sea," and does not doubt in his heart, but believes that those things he says will be done, he will have whatever he says.
MARK 11:23

Are you ready to discover one of the most important achievements you could attain during your Daniel Fast? Do you want to know what it is?

Begin to believe and practice the profound Kingdom truth that Jesus taught His disciples about the power of their words and the potency of believing.

If we begin with the natural way of thinking, coming from the flesh and coming from our worldly ways, Jesus' teaching seems silly. That's why so many people, even Christians who believe in Jesus, don't explore this part of our Kingdom lifestyle.

The Lord, who is the Creator of all, proclaimed this truth: "'For My thoughts are not your thoughts, nor are your ways My ways,' says the LORD" (Isaiah 55:8). God's ways are different from our ways and the world's ways. So when we encounter an instruction from Jesus that seems odd, that doesn't make sense to us, we can choose whom we will believe. Will we believe the world? Will we believe ourselves and base our habits on our own practices? Or will we make the powerful and dynamic choice to believe the words of our Lord?

Jesus is instructing us to use our words. He's telling us that we're to command issues in this world to fall into alignment with God's promises. We're to speak to that mountain.

If you're struggling with a mountain of debt, then speak to that mountain. Call it paid. Call for income to come into your life. Call for insights and wisdom to enter your heart so you can make informed choices. Use your words.

However, using your words isn't enough. We're also called to believe. Can you say to that mountain of debt, "Be paid" and believe that it will come to pass? Do you trust in the Lord and His promises so that doubt shrivels and faith grows? Moving from doubt to faith is a significant part of our Christian journey. It's part of our transformation from living in the darkness of the world to living in the light as a citizen of heaven.

We have been raised in the world with the adage of "I'll believe it when I see it," but that's not the way of the Kingdom. Remember the Kingdom-of-God truth that Jesus taught in Mark 11:24, "Therefore I say to you, whatever things you ask when you pray, believe that you receive them, and you will have them."

Jesus is calling us to believe before the result is manifested in our lives. He's calling us to trust in God and believe in the ways of the Lord. Jesus is calling us to believe that we have received before our natural eyes see it.

Moving from operating in the world system to operating in Kingdom truth requires that we change. During your Daniel Fast, you can start seeding these truths into your heart, feeding them with the Word of God, and being transformed.

Yes, at first you may feel a little foolish. But again, look at the amazing truth that we find in God's Word: "The natural man does not receive the things of the Spirit of God, for they are foolishness to him; nor can he know them, because they are spiritually discerned" (1 Corinthians 2:14). You do have the Spirit of God, so ask Him to help you discern correctly and grow in His wisdom.

Operate from your spirit, believe in the Lord, and put your faith in God and His ways. Then begin to use your words. Speak to that mountain of debt—and to all the things in your life that are not aligned with the ways of God. Take the chaos and call it into order. Take that which is broken and call it to wholeness. Take that which is painful and call it to fall under the authority of God.

Use your words. Have faith in God. Only believe.

Prayer: *Lord Jesus, I admit that I'm not always comfortable praying this way. It's hard for me to believe what I don't yet see. Please increase my faith. Help me to trust that You will answer, and help me when I call to You.*

Fasting Tip: While biblical fasting is always about restricting food for a spiritual purpose, you can also use this time to abstain from certain practices, habits, or negative patterns. Your words are powerful. Use this time to abstain from negative self-talk. Use your words to declare the promises of God over your life. Speak truth into your life, and then make this new habit part of your everyday lifestyle.

DAY TWENTY

Ears to Hear

Then the righteous will shine forth as the sun in the kingdom of their Father. He who has ears to hear, let him hear!
MATTHEW 13:43

This powerful promise follows Jesus' teaching about the parable of the tares. The parable tells about a farmer who planted good seed in his field, but then an enemy came and planted weeds, or tares. The farmer told his workers to allow the weeds to grow alongside the wheat until harvesttime, when they would reap the wheat and burn the weeds. Later, Jesus explained the parable to his disciples this way:

> *He who sows the good seed is the Son of Man. The field is the world, the good seeds are the sons of the kingdom, but the tares are the sons of the wicked one. The enemy who sowed them is the devil, the harvest is the end of the age, and the reapers are the angels. Therefore as the tares are gathered and burned in the fire, so it will be at the end of this age. The Son of Man will send out His angels, and they will gather out of His kingdom all things that offend, and those who practice lawlessness, and will cast them into the furnace of fire. There will be wailing and gnashing of teeth. Then the righteous will shine forth as the sun in the kingdom of their Father. He who has ears to hear, let him hear!*
>
> MATTHEW 13:37-43

This addresses the last days when the final judgment comes and those who remain under the headship of the devil will forever be separated from God. I shudder to think about that day for those who don't enter into a saving relationship with Jesus Christ. I don't know when it will come, although I do know that each day is one day closer to the end of this age. However, for now let's focus on what this passage says about the Kingdom of God and what that means to you today.

We see that the good seeds are sown by the Son of Man, who is Jesus. When you believe in the Lord Jesus Christ and give Him your heart, you become His seed. You become a child of God. The Scripture says that the good seeds are the sons of the Kingdom. That means right now, today, you're a child of God and a citizen of the Kingdom.

Now I know you may be thinking that I've said this over and over and over again. And you're right. I have! But the reason is that I hope you'll see, through the Scriptures, the profound truth of your Kingdom reality. The Kingdom isn't something you have to wait for. The Kingdom of God is now.

The Scripture also teaches that those who follow the ways of the enemy will be plucked out of this world and sent off. The good seed will remain. The Scripture says that "the righteous will shine forth as the sun in the kingdom of their Father."

Then a very important message is spoken by Jesus. He says, "He who has ears to hear, let him hear." Are your spiritual ears hearing the words of our Lord? Do you understand that you're already a member of the Kingdom? Do you understand that you'll be separated and preserved? And do you understand that some don't yet know the love and saving grace of Jesus Christ? That they will be separated and removed? As we live as members of the Kingdom, our goal is to share the Kingdom with others. We want to be a part of spreading the gospel far and wide, that people may be saved and God's name may be honored.

In the book of Romans, the apostle Paul speaks of this same division. He notes that those of the flesh (the sons of the wicked one) are not children of God. However, you are! You're a child of God. You're a child of the promise and counted as the seed. "Those who are the children of the flesh, these are not the children of God; but the children of the promise are counted as the seed" (Romans 9:8).

Keep your identity in your heart. Let it infuse your being. Be who God made you to be. Shine in the darkness so others will be attracted to the light and can also be preserved.

Now thanks be to God who always leads us in triumph in Christ, and through us diffuses the fragrance of His knowledge in every place. For we are to God the fragrance of Christ among those who are being saved and among those who are perishing.
2 CORINTHIANS 2:14-15

Prayer: *Lord God, I want to shine brightly for You and be a part of sharing the good news of Your Kingdom with others. Teach me to live in such a way that Your light will shine through me.*

Reflection: Our spiritual hearing gets better and better as we spend time with God. Yet in today's culture there is so much noise that you may find it hard to quiet your mind and be present with your Lord. The solution? Practice. As your mind wanders, call it back to the center of your meditation. Learn to quiet yourself before the Lord. It's a learnable skill that requires repetition, but soon you'll be able to be quiet so you can hear His still small voice as He shares His thoughts with you.

DAY TWENTY-ONE
The Finish Line

Therefore we also, since we are surrounded by so great a cloud of witnesses, let us lay aside every weight, and the sin which so easily ensnares us, and let us run with endurance the race that is set before us.
HEBREWS 12:1

You've arrived! The finish line for your fast is in sight. You've run your race and you're completing this powerful spiritual experience. Congratulations on your diligence and endurance. Even if you stumbled a time or two, you've come a long way, and now you're ready to cross over into your typical everyday life.

I recall a finish line I crossed back in 2011. I had embarked on a spiritual pilgrimage called the Camino de Santiago, which is a five-hundred-mile walk across northern Spain that has been practiced by Christians since the Middle Ages. The pilgrimage was a formidable time of prayer and reflection as I walked about thirteen miles per day for thirty-seven consecutive days. In some ways, it was similar to your spiritual journey of fasting for twenty-one consecutive days on the Daniel Fast.

I'll never forget the joy I experienced when I completed the Camino at Compostela, the final destination. My heart was full of delight and I felt really good about my accomplishment. I had done well. My five-foot, four-inch body had walked the five hundred miles, and now I was finished.

After spending a couple of days in Compostela visiting with friends I had made along the way, I returned to my home in the United States.

The Camino was in my past. It was done. It was part of my life history. However, it didn't take me long to realize that while the walk was behind me, the multitude of lessons I had learned along the way were still in my soul. I received life-altering lessons on the walk that are forever mine. I also realized that the walking, sometimes on very sore and tired feet, actually served as a process that I entered into so I could receive the rich insights and experiences along the way.

The same will be true for you as you cross the finish line and complete your Daniel Fast. Yes, at first you may be eager to eat and drink some of the foods and beverages you've missed. But then, as you reflect on your journey and the lessons you've learned, you'll discover that changing the way you eat for twenty-one days is a necessary process that enables you to learn and experience God's truths in a unique and inimitable way.

On the Camino, I learned that quitting is a long-lasting response to a temporary problem. I kept going, even when my legs were tired and my body was weak. I discovered and embraced a question I still say to myself: "So what?" So what if I don't feel like walking today? Walk anyway. So what if I have a craving for potato chips? I don't have to give in. So what if I feel frustrated? I don't have to respond from that frame of mind. I uncovered a strength within me that I didn't realize was there, and I tap into that strength often whenever I need to push through a trying time or navigate a difficult situation.

And then there were the many spiritual lessons I received along the way. My love for God intensified as I walked the many hours in silence each day, praying and praising Him. I talked with Him freely and thanked Him for the surrounding creation and the many beautiful people I met. I began valuing people more fully, no matter what they look like, where they're from, or what they believe. We're all on a journey in this life, and God has called His children to love because He is love. So if any other pilgrim was in need along the way, I tried to help in whatever way I could. Some of my most cherished memories were cooking and sharing meals with others, even though we didn't share the same language. The common thread was our love for God and that we all were on our own yet together walking the Camino.

Insights about our experiences, ourselves, and our God come from reflecting on what has happened so we can carry forward the valuable gifts we've received along the way. I hope you'll take some time to think back on your spiritual journey during the fast. What have you learned about yourself? Did some weaknesses show up that you can work on? Did you discover some inner strengths that will serve you in other areas of life? Did God reveal Himself or His truths to you in a new way? Did you learn more about your identity and the measureless love your Father has for you? Did you grow to understand more fully that He is your Provider and that you can trust Him with your finances?

You're at the finish line. Celebrate your achievement. Be thankful. And then spend some time counting your blessings and realizing the many gifts you've received on this unique spiritual journey in faith.

Prayer: *Father, I am so very thankful for the lessons You've taught me during this twenty-one-day retreat with You. I have grown and learned during this time, and I don't want it to end. While the fast is coming to a close, my growth isn't. How wonderful it is to know that You are with me to teach me and help me as my faith matures each and every day. Thank You, Father.*

Fasting tip: Celebrate this last day of the fast! Reflect back on your experience, and take time to write down what you learned and what you think God is saying to you.

Endnotes

CHAPTER 1: A SPIRITUAL FAST TO DRAW YOU NEARER TO GOD

1. Sheryl Nance-Nash, "Is the Bible the Ultimate Financial Guide?," *Forbes*, May 24, 2012, https://www.forbes.com/sites/sherylnancenash/2012/05/24/is-the-bible-the-ultimate-financial-guide/.
2. Kari Paul, "The 'True State' of Americans' Financial Lives: Only 3 in 10 Are 'Financially Healthy,'" MarketWatch, November 16, 2018, https://www.marketwatch.com/story/only-3-in-10-americans-are-considered-financially-healthy-2018-11-01.
3. Paul, "The 'True State' of Americans' Financial Lives."
4. Paul, "The 'True State' of Americans' Financial Lives."

CHAPTER 2: PREPARING FOR YOUR DANIEL FAST

1. There are two primary theological views of the makeup of humankind. The view that a person is comprised of two parts (body and soul) is called *dichotomy*. The view that a person is comprised of three parts (body, soul, and spirit) is called *trichotomy*. There is also the philosophy of *monism*, which says there is no distinction between body and soul. Although I am not a theologian, I believe that Scripture teaches the trichotomy of humankind.

CHAPTER 3: YOUR PERSONAL FAST FOR FINANCIAL BREAKTHROUGH

1. Kari Paul and Jacob Passy, "A Decade after the Housing Crisis, Foreclosures Still Haunt Homeowners," MarketWatch, September 30, 2018, https://www.marketwatch.com/story/a-decade-after-the-housing-crisis-foreclosures-still-haunt-homeowners-2018-09-27.
2. Quoted in Allen Klein, *The Art of Living Joyfully: How to be Happier Every Day of the Year* (Berkeley, CA: Viva, 2012), n.p.

CHAPTER 4: FOLLOW GOD'S WORD ABOUT MONEY

1. James Strong, *The New Strong's Exhaustive Concordance of the Bible* (Nashville: Thomas Nelson, 2010), Greek word #3340.

CHAPTER 5: GOD'S BLESSING AND YOUR STEWARDSHIP

1. James Strong, *The New Strong's Exhaustive Concordance of the Bible* (Nashville: Thomas Nelson, 2010), Hebrew word #6743.
2. Strong, *New Strong's Exhaustive Concordance*, Hebrew word #7919.
3. Strong, *New Strong's Exhaustive Concordance*, Hebrew word #7951.
4. Strong, *New Strong's Exhaustive Concordance*, Hebrew word #2896.
5. Strong, *New Strong's Exhaustive Concordance*, Hebrew word #7965.
6. Strong, *New Strong's Exhaustive Concordance*, Greek word #2137.

CHAPTER 6: GOD IS YOUR PROVIDER

1. James Strong, *The New Strong's Exhaustive Concordance of the Bible* (Nashville: Thomas Nelson, 2010), Greek word #4559.
2. Strong, *New Strong's Exhaustive Concordance*, Greek word #4561.
3. Jeff A. Benner, "Covenants from a Hebrew Perspective," Ancient Hebrew Research Center, https://www.ancient-hebrew.org/studies-interpretation/covenants-from-a-hebrew-perspective.htm; "What Was a Blood Covenent (Genesis 15:9-21)?," Got Questions website, https://www.gotquestions.org/blood-covenant.html.
4. Benner, "Covenants from a Hebrew Perspective"; "What Was a Blood Covenent?"

CHAPTER 7: GIVING FROM A GRATEFUL HEART

1. *Inside Bill's Brain: Decoding Bill Gates*, directed by Davis Guggenheim, Concordia Studio and Netflix, 2019.

CHAPTER 10: MOVING FORWARD IN JOY

1. *Inside Bill's Brain: Decoding Bill Gates*, directed by Davis Guggenheim, Concordia Studio and Netflix, 2019.

TWENTY-ONE DAY DEVOTIONAL: DAY 13

1. Sylvester Stewart, "Stand," copyright © Warner Chappell Music Inc., Universal Music Publishing Group, 1996.

TWENTY-ONE DAY DEVOTIONAL: DAY 18

1. James Strong, *The New Strong's Exhaustive Concordance of the Bible*, (Nashville: Thomas Nelson, 2010), Greek word #4052.

Daniel Fast Recipe Index

About the Author

SUSAN GREGORY, "The Daniel Fast Blogger," launched *The Daniel Fast* blog and website in December 2007. Since then, her site has received millions of hits. Susan is passionate to see individuals experience a successful Daniel Fast as they seek God and endeavor to grow in the love and knowledge of Christ. Author of *Out of the Rat Race*, *The Daniel Fast*, *The Daniel Cure*, and *The Daniel Fast for Weight Loss*, Susan has written for nationally known ministries, and her work has taken her to more than thirty-five countries. A mother and grandmother, she lives in a small college town in Washington State. Visit her online at www.Daniel-Fast.com.

The Daniel Cure

The Daniel Fast Way to Vibrant Health

Susan Gregory, Author of Bestselling
The Daniel Fast, *and Richard J. Bloomer*

Though most people begin the Daniel Fast for a spiritual purpose, many are amazed by the physical transformation that takes place, such as a drop in cholesterol, healthy weight loss, a sense of well-being, and increased energy. Recently published scientific studies of the Daniel Fast documented many of the same findings, as well as a reduction in systemic inflammation and blood pressure, and improved antioxidant defenses. *The Daniel Cure* helps readers take the next step by focusing on the health benefits of the Daniel Fast. Following the advice in this book, readers will convert the Daniel Fast from a once-a-year spiritual discipline into a new way of life.

Includes a 21-Day Daniel Cure Devotional, frequently asked questions, ten chapters of recipes, a recipe index, and an appendix detailing "The Science behind the Daniel Fast."

ZONDERVAN®
.com